Design Literacy (continued)

Understanding Graphic Design

Steven Heller

ALLWORTH PRESS
NEW YORK

04 03 02 01 00 99   8 7 6 5 4 3

Published by Allworth Press
An imprint of Allworth Communications
10 East 23rd Street, New York, NY 10010

Cover and book design by James Victore, New York, NY

Page composition by Sharp Des!gns, Lansing, MI

Library of Congress Cataloging-in-Publication Data

Heller, Steven
    Design literacy (continued): understanding more graphic design / by Steven Heller.
        p. cm.
    Includes bibliographical references and index.
    ISBN 1-581-15035-0 (pbk.)
    1. Graphic arts—History. 2. Commercial art—History. I. Title.

NC998 .H45 1999
741.6—dc21
                                                        99-042995

Printed in Canada

Contents

OBJECTS

Propaganda

Media

Language

Commerce

ISSUES

PEOPLE

Acknowledgments

I would like to thank, first and foremost, Tad Crawford, the publisher of Allworth Press. I am grateful for his enthusiasm, confidence, and faith in me and, as well, for his major contribution to graphic design as the publisher of books of design criticism and analysis, which had no other champion in the publishing industry before him. Further thanks go to Nicole Potter, editor, for her devotion and expertise as well as to Bob Porter, Anne Hellman, Jamie Kijowski, and Nyier Abdou at Allworth Press. I am also indebted to James Victore for his excellent design of this and other books on the Allworth Press list.

Many of the essays herein were written especially for this volume, but others were previously published in magazines to which I regularly contribute. I wish to thank the following editors I work with for their invaluable input: Martin Fox, Julie Lasky, and Joyce Rutter Kaye at *Print;* Max Bruinsma and John Walters at *EYE;* Martin Neumeier and Nancy Bernard at *Critique;* Margaret Richardson and John Berry at *U&lc;* Chee Pearlman at *I.D.;* and Marie Finamore at the *AIGA Journal of Graphic Design.* I also tip my hat to Anne Knudson at the High Museum of Art, who commissioned the essay titled "Rebelling against Rockwell" for its Norman Rockwell exhibition catalog.

Finally, thanks to the following for their consultations and assistance in preparing this book and/or individual essays: Rick Poynor, Victor Margolin, Mirko Ilic, Rudy VanderLans, Zuzana Licko, Teal Triggs, Stefan Sagmeister, Mike Salisbury, Jeff Roth, April Greiman, Seymour Chwast, and Louise Fili.

—Steven Heller

Introduction

When he saw the cover sketch for *Design Literacy (continued)* taped to the wall next to my desk, the editor of the magazine that I have art directed for the past two decades declared, "Maybe if I read your book, I wouldn't have to talk to you anymore." He was referring to our regular tête-à-têtes, where I "pitch" cover ideas that either sail smoothly or sink under the weight of justifications. Taking the title of this book literally, my editor presumed that if he read *Design Literacy (continued),* he would indeed be sufficiently literate; he thought that it would no longer be necessary to ask: "What does this mean?"

I assured him that this was no magic pill. Neither *Design Literacy* (the book) nor design literacy (the concept) would alter his opinion about a particular cover image if he really disliked it for conceptual or aesthetic reasons. Possessing design literacy does not mean that a nondesigner will always see eye to eye with a designer (who presumably is already design literate). There are too many added factors that enter into the acceptance or rejection of a design solution, not the least of which is personal taste. In fact, good designer-client relationships are often based on the latter's willingness to overcome certain taste prejudices and accept the expertise of the designer. Which is not to suggest that my editor or any other client would not benefit from delving into the history and process of graphic design. But, even among literate designers, design literacy does not guarantee that everyone is on the same page at the same time. It means only that we share the same general body of knowledge.

Anyone reading this book with the expectation that it will provide a cure-all for ignorance about graphic design will be disappointed. True design literacy, which requires years of learning and experience, involves practical and theoretical understanding of how design is made in order to function as a marketplace tool and a cultural signpost. The book title *Design Literacy* refers to the sharing of knowledge—certain facts, impressions, and opinions—about graphic design and its broader cultural affiliations, but it is not a textbook about how or what to make. It will not walk the reader through conception, manufacture, and application. In fact, rather than a fulfillment of the reader's expectations of becoming more literate, the title more precisely reflects a personal journey. Although I hope that the book will be used to increase understanding and even debate within the field, the essays collected here and in the preceding volume, *Design Literacy*, are stepping-stones in my own education. In other words, they manifest how I became design literate, regarding not only the language(s) of design but, as well, the legacy of individuals and objects that comprise it.

I found that truly understanding and appreciating graphic design as both commercial art and cultural force requires one to examine the contexts for many objects and the raisons d'être of their makers. So, in a sense, this book is something of an analytical show-and-tell, in which I am reporting on objects and ideas that have relevance to my understanding of design. These subjects are, however, also components of a larger body of information about the design process as extrapolated from artifacts that, when taken as a whole, contribute to the definition of twentieth-century graphic design.

The first *Design Literacy* (co-authored with Karen Pomeroy) used various designed objects (some classic and others arcane) as touchstones for an examination of how graphic design and graphic designers function in respective contexts. The selection was based entirely on my own interest and fascination with diverse forms—including objects that I had previously researched over many years as part of larger histories or profiles. The selection of what to include was based either on what I believed to be an important work by a significant practitioner (an archetype of a particular genre) or simply on what sparked my curiosity (whether it loomed high in the design pantheon or not). The reason for writing the book was to share all available insight into the object (or genre of objects, as the case may be) through both interpretation and, when possible, the words of the creators themselves. Rather than merely comprising a linear narrative, the essays (or short stories, as I like to call them) ostensibly function as sidebars to a broader historical sequence as spelled out, for example, in Philip B. Meggs's *History of Graphic Design* or Richard Hollis's *Graphic Design: A Concise History*. However, in a comment to me, Milton Glaser critiqued the first *Design Literacy* as "all meat and no potatoes," suggesting that this sidebar approach lacked the intellectual glue necessary to bind the essays. According to Glaser and some other like-minded critics, the first book was flawed because it did not make cohesive links between one object (or essay) and another. Rather than accept these stories as self-contained units, as they were intended, my critics wanted a more definitive overview that used the selected objects and themes as support for grand conclusions.

My rationale for not doing that was simple: Conventional graphic design history has already been written as a linear narrative flowing from one movement, period, or style to another, and that form is just one approach of many. The problem for me is that not all design fits snugly into well-organized categorical berths. Moreover, I was not interested in repeating the narrative approach; Meggs and Hollis have already done this very well in their respective books. Instead, I opted to address individual works, genres, and ideas that appear to have exerted even a modicum of influence on overall practice. The fact that the story of one object does not link neatly to the next, like some complex jigsaw puzzle, is okay as long as the objects are formally or conceptually worthy of analysis—or provide the basis for good stories.

I realize, however, that some of the themes covered in both *Design Literacy* and *Design Literacy (continued)* are not recognized as part of the graphic design canon (past or present), and that it is a stretch on my part to inject them into serious design discourse. A designer whom I greatly admire said of the last volume that he strongly objected to seeing untutored or naïve design—such as anonymous shooting targets and raunchy 1960s underground newspapers— covered in the same venue and with the same reverence as highly professional work by, for example, Paul Rand, Will Burtin, or Saul Bass. Yet what better way to examine the comparative merits of design as visual communication than to look intently and respectfully at all forms on the design spectrum—high or low—if they reveal something important about the nature of what we do?

Since graphic designers draw inspiration from both professional and unprofessional sources—from known designers and anonymous craftspeople—there is no reason to limit our study to haute design. I believe that common "show cards," produced by job printers during the 1920s and 1930s, are as integral to the history of this field as the 1960s award-winning *West* magazine or the ultrahip contemporary magazine *Wallpaper** (all of which are discussed herein). Both recognized and forgotten objects are equally valid in the course of discovery. Incidentally, the selections in this book are not driven by any specific ideology (e.g., modern or postmodern), a fact that accounts for the eclecticism and diversity of the objects, ideas, and individuals presented here.

Design Literacy (continued) is not a second chance to correct what certain critics found lacking in the first volume. Although I respect their viewpoints and accept the notion that a less eclectic and more thematically unified book has distinct virtues, I have elected not to shift my perspective this time around. Rather, as the title indicates, this second volume is a continuation of my fascination for and inquiry into a variety of designed things and the ideas supporting them. *Design Literacy (continued)* is not a hellbox of what was cut from the first book, either. It is a collection of some previously published and new essays about subjects that have continued to capture my interest since the first volume was published in 1997.

And like the first volume, *Design Literacy (continued)* defines design literacy as a basic understanding of how design functions in the environment. This is addressed mostly in the section called "Objects" through analysis of artifacts that are organized into four categories: Propaganda (design that imparts political or social messages); Media (vehicles and environments, such as books and magazines, where design conveys messages or is the message); Language (typefaces, letters, symbols, codes, and stereotypes that serve as the lingua franca of visual communication); and Commerce (that which is used to sell ideas or things in the mass marketplace). Some of the objects in each category may well intersect with other categories—which is inevitable given the multipurpose nature of graphic design—but are included where they are because the stories are told from the vantage point of those particular categories. In addition, *Design Literacy (continued)* includes sections not present in the first volume: namely, Issues and People. The former consists of commentaries and histories about specific aspects of design, including censorship, plagiarism, and the Big Idea in advertising. The latter includes profiles of designers whose bodies of work, even though specialized (for example, type design, book design, and poster design), make better stories than excerpts of single objects. Together these sections serve as additional sidebars on the historical timeline of graphic design.

To borrow Milton Glaser's descriptive analogy, I can say that those readers who are looking for a full-course meal might indeed still be hungry after reading *Design Literacy (continued)*. This is fine, however, because there is no one book that will provide all the information or points of view required for complete design literacy. This sequel is a feast for those who are happy with large helpings of meat and who find these distinctive objects of design as mouthwatering as I do.

Objects

PROPAGANDA

A̲nticommunist print and film propaganda from the forties and fifties is as quaint as patent medicine ads from the last century. The stereotypes involved are so ludicrous, it's hard to give them any credence and even harder to accept their survival after several decades, almost into the present. Postwar rhetoric about godless communism so infused all media and invaded everyday life in America that just the word "communism" provoked irrational behavior. The power of anticommunist propaganda was so effective (and perhaps seductive) that Americans relinquished certain rights and liberties in order to allow the government to persecute its perceived opponents. While this is not an apology for real Soviet crimes, it is an analysis of why anticommunist propaganda was virulent and, therefore, unhealthy for Americans. The history of this propaganda, as for all propaganda, is rooted in the creation of recognizable stereotypes that oversimplify complex issues for the purpose of controlling mass opinion. The methods by which this government encouraged insidious red-baiting and witch-hunting through print and film—the longest continuous propaganda campaign of its kind—ultimately had a deleterious effect on all society.

During World War II, Americans referred to all Russians somewhat affectionately as Ivan, but, afterward, the name Boris was commonly used in American anti-Soviet propaganda, as in the aggressive battle cries so typical in vintage cold-war comic books: "Give Boris a taste of old glory" or "Teach Boris what it means to be American." This name, the equivalent of John or Jim in America, had a threatening ring to it. Neither Nikita, Alexi, nor Leonid conjured the same negative stereotype that Boris did, because it embodied all the evils of Russian Communism and Soviet expansionism. Therefore, when Boris (Yeltsin, that is) came to the United States in 1990 for his first whirlwind visit and was greeted by throngs of friendly Americans—some chanting "Boris, Boris"—it was symbolic that a terrible era, noted for its witch-hunts and vicious propaganda, had finally ended. Boris is now the leader of an independent, post-Communist Russia; on January 28, 1992, fifty-three years after the cold war began, he and President George Bush proclaimed its official end. This too was symbolic, since the cold war had actually ended over a year before when, under Mikhail Gorbachev, a punch-drunk Soviet empire went down for the count before the world's disbelieving eyes. After years of throwing wild punches, the West had finally scored a knockout.

"The Cold War was Stalin's war," writes William G. Hyland, the editor of *Foreign Affairs* and author of *The Cold War: Fifty Years of Conflict.* "He started it in 1939, when he struck a devil's bargain with Adolf Hitler to destroy Poland, partition the Baltic and Eastern Europe, and unleash World War II." Two years later, Hitler invaded the USSR, forcing Stalin into an alliance with America and England. The seeds of conflict over postwar Europe were planted before the Nazi invasion and sown during the Big Three summits, especially at the Yalta Conference, where Stalin was given free reign to carve up Eastern Europe into Soviet satellites and retain his much-disputed Nazi/Soviet spoils. However, the history of Stalin's empire-building, his brutality and perfidy, needn't be rehashed here. Suffice it to say that his cold war was not about ideology or winning hearts and minds; it was a straightforward power struggle that was confined, by Stalin's definition, to the range of the Red Army. If given the chance, the cold war might have turned hot, but Papa Joe died in 1953 before he could muster the resources to launch that critical offensive. Yet the cold war was certainly hot enough to raise American acrimony to a boil, causing this government to escalate the level of conflict on many fronts—including the home front, where vicious red-baiting of real and imagined foes became a spectator sport.

Years before our wartime alliance with Russia began, Americans were conditioned by politicians, businessmen, clergy, and the press to fear and loathe the Communist Party. Editorial cartoons portrayed them as bomb-throwing thugs. In fact, even the *New York Times* showed more respect for Mussolini than for Lenin or Stalin because, during the early years of the Italian fascist régime, Il Duce promised a social revolution that was more palatable to ruling-class Americans than the Soviet model. Indeed, to be anti-Mussolini in the mid-1920s or even anti-Hitler in the early 1930s was to be "prematurely antifascist" (an oxymoron coined after 1940 by red-baiters to describe early Communist sympathizers and fellow travelers). After the Russian Revolution, communism, like socialism and anarchism, was the dread of America's business and industrial leaders, who feared labor unrest because of their own exploitative practices. These same leaders forged secret alliances with racists, jingoists, and other America-first fanatics in spreading anticommunist propaganda throughout the nation; they thus succeeded in convincing masses of Americans that their lives and livelihoods were threatened by Communists and Bolsheviks—who not coincidentally were nestled among the throngs of foreign immigrants regularly entering the United States.

Huey Long, the populist, demagogue governor of Louisiana, once said that if fascism came to America, it would be on a program of Americanism. Years earlier, President Theodore Roosevelt trumpeted with typical bluster: "Keep up the fight for Americanism!" as he pointed his finger at all those who preferred systems other than our own. Hence, years before the American Communist Party was founded (in 1919), when Communists in America were virtually nonexistent, with only a few left-wing socialists like Eugene Debs carrying the banner, the word "communism" was synonymous with un-Americanism. Publications proffering bohemian or radical points of view, like *The Masses,* which published articles and cartoons representing a broader spectrum of opinion than just communist, were hounded by national and local authorities who stupidly believed that these relatively small-circulation journals could alter American policy. The diehard anti-Communists may well have been alarmed by the rapidity of social change. They may have given new meaning to the words of eighteenth-century thinker Edmund Burke, who in 1790 cautioned against complacency regarding the possible exportation of a French revolution to England in sentiments that reverberated in the twentieth century: "It's better to be despised for too anxious apprehensions than ruined by too confident security." The overanxious anti-Communists invented the threat of insurrection in America as a red herring to dupe people into believing that an escalation of labor problems was part of a foreign plot to foment a coup d'état. But America was rich and powerful, impervious to revolution, and, as Carl Marzani notes in *A Quarter Century of Unamericana,* "the opponents of organized labor saw Communism as a convenient smokescreen to obliterate trade unionism."

The chief government witch-hunter at this time was Attorney General A. Mitchell Palmer. He and his willing assistant, J. Edgar Hoover, organized the infamous Palmer raids on labor organizations suspected of radical tendencies, and they encouraged the creation of local red squads in municipalities across the country. A few years after retiring from his post, Palmer, in a bid for the senatorial seat of Georgia, accused the populist incumbent of harboring red sympathies in ostensibly the first use of red-baiting as a political weapon in an election campaign—a tactic that would reach virtuosic proportions when Richard Nixon ran against California Congressman Jerry Voorhis in the 1940s.

With America's entry into the First World War, many blatantly unconstitutional government prohibitions of radical organizations and publications were finally sanctioned by decree. Because of the Sedition and Espionage Acts (which temporarily abrogated First Amendment rights), the Trading with the Enemy Act, and the postmaster general's discretionary power to revoke mailing privileges, over thirty socialist, anarchist, and syndicalist publications were forced to shut down. Although the Supreme Court subsequently upheld the First Amendment, which allowed for an open, opposition press, the damage was already done.

After the 1917 Russian Revolution, the worst nightmare of American anti-Communists was realized when the Bolsheviks became totally entrenched in Russian life; adding to this fear was the fact that, in 1919, the American Communist Party was founded in Chicago. Refusing to recognize Lenin's government, President Woodrow Wilson committed arms and troops to the war against Bolshevism abroad and increased the level of anticommunist propaganda at home (or at least created a milieu in which it was encouraged). By 1923, Communism had indeed become a force to be reckoned with, but the myth that a monolithic communist vanguard was invading America was still unfounded. (In any event, dissension has always festered in and been the downfall of radical organizations in this country.) America's misperception was based on the fact that Marxist/Leninism promised the eventual demise of capitalism. In retaliation against American efforts, Soviet propaganda—including posters by Dimitri Moor and cartoons by other artists—overtly attacked capitalists by giving them the same sinister traits as those already given Communists by American cartoonists.

Suspicions were further exacerbated in America after World War I, when press freedoms were restored and socialist and communist groups in America were able to publish again with a mixed diet of homegrown and imported articles on the communist experiment. To counter this, books like the seemingly rational but factually inaccurate *Reds in America* (1924), an anticommunist exposé by R. M. Whitney, attempt to show that labor and political groups were taking orders directly from Moscow. Yet Whitney's assertion that "the World Revolutionary movement is exerting [influence] upon current political events" gravely overestimates the capability of post-revolutionary Soviets to have a marked effect on American opinion.

Books and pamphlets by Whitney are indicative of how anticommunist propaganda was mainstreamed. In *Reds in America*, Whitney attempts to prove through "documentary evidence" obtained after a red-squad raid of a Communist convention in Michigan that "Radicals, Progressives, and Pinks [from the term "Parlor Pink," indicating those who flirted with socialism]" were controlled by Moscow. Indeed, the Communist International (or Comintern), established by Leon Trotsky in 1919, would later send its operatives around the world, but they were rather ineffectual in the early 1920s and definitely incapable of the violent overthrow of the U.S. government. Nevertheless, Whitney's books, like *Back to Barbarism*, about the idea of "World Revolution" circulating among the "negroes" of the United States by the dissemination of Communist ideals, argue that Russian Communists planned to exploit the race problem. In it he comments: "A number of educated negroes, most of them from Harvard, were found sufficiently discontented and sufficiently unbalanced to make good Communists. They were enlisted in the work and from that time on have been preaching violence on every occasion." In *Peace at Any Old Price* (1925), a report on the Annual Conference of the Woman's International League for Peace and Freedom offering "full data concerning this pacifist organization; names, dates, places," Whitney takes aim at an early women's movement, suggesting that these poor, misguided folk are dupes of Moscow, too. He purports, as well, that his pamphlet "Youth Movement in America" (1928) is "brim full of information" on the "radical and communist connection of many given in full." Whitney's reports were effective in spreading the following gospel: "The ponderous machine which has been created and is dominated by a small Moscow group is . . . leading NOT to a *Dictatorship of the Proletariat* but a Dictatorship by an Alien Minority." Similar in effect to Whitney's work was a "history" by Mrs. Nesta Webster entitled *World Revolution: The Plot against Civilization* (1925), which argues that, like the French Revolution, the Bolshevik revolution is "threatening the free world's very existence." It was praised by one critic as "the most important contribution to history ever made by a woman."

During the Great Depression, Communism gained a foothold among American working and intellectual classes that opposed the policies of President Herbert Hoover (and Treasury Secretary Andrew W. Mellon), plunging the nation into economic disaster. "The world-wide ordeal of capitalism gave rise in two contrasting solutions," writes Carl Marzani, "fascism in Germany and the New Deal in America. The history of the thirties is basically the history of the struggle between these two solutions." Of course, the Nazis smashed labor unions and undermined democratic reforms, while the New Deal strengthened them. But because of the New Deal's nod to socialism, acrimony between diehard anti-Communists and New Dealers continued throughout Franklin Roosevelt's presidency. FDR's congressional opponents spent much of their time proposing bills that would limit immigration, free speech, and free assembly for suspected Communists—and deport foreign-born Communists as part of the bargain. Anticommunist rhetoric was typical on the floor of the U.S. House of Representatives. This is rather apparent in Kentucky Congressman R. Robison's statement: "Now why should we permit a lot of Communists from Russia or elsewhere—who hate religion, who hate this government, and desire to see it overthrown and a Communist dictatorship established—to organize on American soil, march under the red flag of Communism and engage in subversive propaganda and activities for the purpose of destroying our government?" Not surprisingly, Congress often flirted with the idea of legally prohibiting the Communist Party.

In the mid-1930s a special congressional committee was proposed to investigate subversion and subversives. Its most fervent advocate was New York Congressman Samuel Dickstein, the son of immigrants, who wanted to investigate (and, with luck, destroy) native Nazi and fascist groups in America. But in his zeal to protect this country from those radical fringes, he further proposed investigating any person, group, or institution purported to be un-American. Of course, liberals in Congress resisted the idea, wanting to know what exactly "un-American" meant. One of Dickstein's opponents is quoted in the *Congressional Record:* "Un-American is simply something that somebody else does not agree to." And John Steinbeck even more accurately defines "un-American" and "communist" in *The Grapes of Wrath* (1939): "A red is any son of a bitch that wants thirty cents when we're paying twenty-five."

In 1938, Congress established the House Un-American Activities Committee (HUAC) under chairman Martin Dies, a representative from Texas who, like his congressman father, was a fanatical anti-Communist. Before being appointed to the chairmanship he promised that he would not look for Communists under every bed, but upon getting the job he proceeded to ferret them out of every nook and cranny. By the end of its first year J. Parnell Thomas, a devout committee member and future HUAC chairman, called for sweeping investigation of the Federal Theatre and Writers Project of the Works Progress Administration (WPA), which he determined was a "New Deal propaganda machine" and, thus, a hotbed for Communists. Similar investigations were aimed at the AFL and the CIO, both of which were accused of harboring

Communists. Actually, such information that Communists were members of organized labor was rather aboveboard. Even the famed United Mine Workers leader John L. Lewis enlisted Communist support because, at the time, labor and Communism were logical bedfellows. However, this did not mean that he or his rank and file were members of the Party. Likewise, the WPA projects did include Communists who, as Walter Goodman writes in *The Committee* (1968), "tried turning the program into an agitprop machine." But this, too, was consistent with contemporary political tactics, since parties attempted to win converts through massive sloganeering. Liberals, who were by no means devout radicals, made alliances with Communists during the 1930s because of their mutual opposition to fascism, racism, and exploitative business practices. Often, however, they stayed curiously indifferent to known failures in the Soviet experiment, including Stalin's bloody purges. Anti-Communists may have found a reason to worry that the Communists were gaining support among liberals, but the paranoia was excessive. Actually, official Party membership was still minuscule; most liberals jettisoned their communist allies immediately once the Hitler-Stalin pact was signed in 1939, and all but the diehard Stalinists (like Earl Browder, chairman of the Party in America) resigned from the Party.

Nevertheless, despite other clear and present dangers, HUAC had only one real mission. "On the first day of hearings in Washington," reported *Life* magazine, "the Committee . . . heard testimony about the American Nazis. The next day it switched to Communism and stayed there. Opening its doors to anybody who cared to call anybody else a red . . ." The Dies committee became a bellwether of anti-radical sentiment in America—not just anticommunist, but anti-do-gooder, anti-big-city-type, anti-eastern-college-alumnus/a, anti-second-generation-American, anti-Jew, and anti-anyone holding "unsettling ideas about the condition of the negro." Even Shirley Temple was accused of endorsing a French communist newspaper. In 1939, a Gallup poll found that three out of five voters who had heard the committee were in favor of continuing the committee's investigations. According to Walter Goodman, support for HUAC ranged from wholehearted embrace from the far right to friendly acceptance from the center. Republicans and anti–New Deal Democrats (mostly from the South) realized that Dies's smearing of New Dealers had noticeably favorable results for their candidates.

In 1940, Dies published *The Trojan Horse in America,* in which he reviews the work of his committee—366 pages devoted to "Communist subversion." Among its half-truths and misperceptions, even Mrs. Eleanor Roosevelt is vilified as "one of the most valuable assets that the Trojan Horse Organization of the Communist Party have possessed." It is no wonder that Dies received favorable notices from the Nazi propaganda ministry in Berlin and Bunds in the United States. Though Dies's committee was so transparently foolish, it was never a joke to be called before it. "This committee has no desire to persecute anyone," Dies said with chilling irony, "certainly not those who see fit to cooperate."

The outbreak of war with the Axis and the alliance with the Soviet Union the following year put a temporary muzzle on HUAC. Somewhere between the fall of France and the attack on Pearl Harbor, the committee, as far as the public record indicates, disappeared. In fact, HUAC had become a one-person agency: The chairman became the committee. Dies still actively pursued Communists, waiting for the day he would again be in the limelight.

The war radically changed American sentiments. The majority preferred reds to Nazis, and almost overnight American propaganda was aimed at forging bonds of trust and friendship with the USSR. While official government posters and institutional advertising portrayed the Big Three Allies marching toward victory against the Axis foe, Hollywood films, like *Mission to Moscow, North Star,* and *Song of Russia* went overboard in sanitizing Stalin's brutal dictatorship. James Agee even characterized *Mission to Moscow* in the *Nation* as thus: "almost describable as the first Soviet production to come from a major American studio." After the war these films would be investigated by HUAC as evidence of communist infiltration in the film industry. One needn't dwell here on the reasons for maintaining an alliance with the USSR in order to defeat Germany on two fronts, but as early as 1942 Winston Churchill warned against trusting this odd bedfellow. And in April 1945, as Germany was collapsing, General George Patton, in a famous comment that cost him his job, urged that he be allowed to drive Soviet forces from Germany.

The war had been over only a few days when Stalin exercised his own expansionist plans. And peace was only months old when Congressman John Elliot Rankin of Mississippi, described by *Time* magazine as the number one Jew-baiter in America and the man who said the Ku Klux Klan was a 100 percent American institution, forced a vote that made HUAC a standing committee of the House (rather than a special committee, which must renew its existence at the start of each session). HUAC was given great latitude to investigate perhaps the only un-Americans worth investigating at the end of war, the Communists. Though he did not accept the chairmanship of the committee (Dies had retired), Rankin virtually ran its proceedings. One of his first attacks was on the artists of the *New Masses,* a leftist journal (which included contributions by Crockett Johnson, William Gropper, and Al Hirschfeld), whom he said produced 191 "loathsome paintings" that were owned by film stars. On the floor of Congress Rankin railed, "I am sure that some of them got into the home of Charles Chaplin, the perverted subject of Great Britain who has become notorious for his forcible seduction of little girls."

Rankin made countless idiotic statements, like his attack on Albert Einstein as a foreign infiltrator and this classic captured in the *Congressional Record:* "Communism . . . hounded and persecuted a Saviour during his earthly ministry, inspired his crucifixion, derided him in his dying agony, and then gambled for his garments at the foot of the Cross." This was the very man who initiated witch-hunts and propaganda campaigns that would soon be co-opted from the denizens of the pathological right by seemingly more moderate, albeit dangerous, conservatives. By 1953, when Joseph McCarthy had the presence of mind to red-bait for his own personal advantage, HUAC had already established a record of terror and had frightened, intimidated, and abrogated the civil rights of thousands of Americans. Aided by an acquiescent press, self-righteous church groups, and spineless film and comic-book industries, as well as other trash-culture entrepreneurs, a consistent barrage of red-baiting propaganda in print, on TV, and in the movies was being spewed into the public domain like toxic waste into the Great Lakes.

Every president from Franklin Roosevelt to John F. Kennedy condemned HUAC for its excesses but tolerated its existence. Harry Truman decried it as "the most un-American thing in America"; Dwight Eisenhower reminded us: "We are descended in blood and spirit from revolutionists and rebels—men and women who dared to dissent from accepted doctrines." Even the comic Jimmy Durante, who might have made a better president than all the rest, said, "Don't put no constrictions on da people. Leave 'em ta hell alone." But the committee was oblivious to pressure. It knew it had power, since even the Supreme Court had at one time refused to interfere with it, saying that the courts should "leave the responsibility for the behavior of its committees squarely on the shoulders of Congress." As Joseph C. Goulden notes in *The Best Years*, "with House support assured—even congressmen with qualms about HUAC didn't risk 'voting against anti-Communists.'" The committee was a wellspring for virulent anticommunist propaganda in the United States.

HUAC's first significant postwar probe of reds in Hollywood might be construed as an investigation into how communist ideas were propagated in America. During the 1930s and 1940s, Communists were indeed part of the film industry. Most of the actors involved were not ideological pigeons but rather idealists who sought to imbue films with messages of social import. (There have always been objections when members of the entertainment industry take political or social positions, and HUAC's investigation would prove to be the worst form of objection.) Even those in the trade unions with ideological motives were not totally in charge of the rank and file. Yet the slightest threat propelled the committee to act. While many anticommittee protestors—including some renowned actors, directors, and writers—refused to cooperate (even Frank Sinatra was an outspoken opponent), the level of fear was raised to such a pitch that the Motion Picture Alliance sent emissaries to Washington to make certain, in the spirit of conciliation, that the committee rooted out the right reds. The otherwise courtly Adolphe Menjou referred to himself as a red-baiter: "I make no bones about it," he chortled in a committee session. "I'd like to see them all in Russia." Naming names became the name of the game. Those that did were reviled by those that did not, and the animosities between these two groups continue even today.

Despite the committee's failure to unequivocally prove many of the cases of alleged communist subversion in the film industry, in the final analysis the committee prevailed in this and other matters. Among its successes was the imprisonment of the Hollywood Ten for contempt, even though it was later proven that none of the films worked on by the ten had favorably pitched the USSR in any way. More devastating, it called for a system of loyalty review boards (breaching basic civil liberties), which Truman instituted despite his personal misgivings. In addition, it laid the groundwork for blacklists that brought lily-livered Hollywood moguls and media executives to their knees. To appease HUAC, most film producers—believing that if they policed their own industry, the spotlight on them would dim—pledged not to employ Communists or anyone else belonging to groups supporting the overthrow of the government. It is no wonder, in this climate of hysteria and fear, that quite a few decidedly anti-red feature films, such as *I Married a Communist* and *I Was a Communist for the FBI,* were produced during the late 1940s and 1950s. Indeed, some of the most absurd examples of anticommunist cautionary films were made at the studios' expense as a kind of payoff for protection from the committee.

By 1948, anticommunist militancy had swept the country. Joseph C. Goulden notes: "the American Legion, such newspaper chains as Hearst and Scripps-Howard, and any number of ad hoc business and 'patriotic' organizations were providing investigators with information on the Communist conspiracy." They were also contributing to the volume of anticommunist literature. Sadly, the media failed to champion and uphold free expression, both on and off the page and screen. Many publishing houses gave ultimatums to their employees who were called to testify before the committee: Cooperate or be fired. Others would not publish or buy work by suspected reds. Media executives supported the blacklist by subscribing to publications like *Red Channels,* a regularly updated list of known or suspected Communists. They might also have engaged the services of American Business Consultants Inc., formed by three former FBI agents who offered, for a fee, background checks based on HUAC records and other inflammatory documents to any employer who questioned someone's loyalty. These services were not mandated by law, but those ignoring them risked harassment or blackmail.

In *The Best Years,* Goulden reprints a notice from the American Legion newsletter entitled "Summary of Trends and Developments Exposing the Communist Conspiracy," a primer on how to pressure the media or other businesses into taking the communist threat seriously: "Organize a letter writing group of six to ten relatives and friends to make the sentiments of Americans heard on the important issues of the day. Phone, telegraph, or write to radio and television sponsors employing entertainers with known front records. . . . DON'T LET THE SPONSORS PASS THE BUCK BACK TO YOU BY DEMANDING 'PROOF' OF COMMUNIST FRONTING BY SOME CHARACTER ABOUT WHOM YOU HAVE COMPLAINED. YOU DON'T HAVE TO PROVE ANYTHING. . . . YOU SIMPLY HAVE TO SAY YOU DO NOT LIKE SO-AND-SO ON THEIR PROGRAMS." This went hand in glove with other stratagems, like placing "pro-American" literature in doctors' and dentists' offices; announcing boycotts of corporations and businesses that aided Communists; and monitoring "Red newspaper reporters" so that they did not "slip in a neat hypodermic needle full of Moscow virus." The American Legion was also behind attacks on comic books during the mid-fifties. Typical of the mail in one Legionnaire newsletter is this: "We parents and the teachers and the principals do not like the horrors created by the comics. Are the Commies behind these books which appear in print by the thousands?" As a result of this hysteria, the self-regulating Comics Code was instituted by the comics industry, not only to prohibit horror and violence, but also to uphold American values. Nevertheless, violence was the prescribed cure for Communism in those comics sanctioned by the code.

The comic book was a popular medium for anticommunist groups. Typical of these was one published by the Houston-based Christian Anti-Communism Crusade titled *Two Faces of Communism,* which was mailed free of charge to anyone sending in a self-addressed stamped envelope. The premise was predictable: Youth of America are oblivious to the communist menace, but after thirty-six pages they are convinced by their elders to see things the way they really are and to help others see the light by starting a Teens for America group. "Everyone of us personally is needed in this battle, if we expect to survive," says an elder. "I received an excellent free pamphlet today. Entitled 'What Can I Do?' from the crusade. Let's look it over together and get into action." Another comic published by the Minneapolis-based Catechetical Guild Education Society titled *Is This Tomorrow?* offers a cautionary scenario of "this can happen here," very much like the last of the cold-war absurdities, the 1988 ABC miniseries *Amerika* and 1985 movie *Red Dawn,* both about an America overrun by the Russians. In the introduction to this 1947 comic the reason for vigilance is made crystal clear: "Today there are approximately 85,000 official members of the Communist Party in the United States. There are hundreds of additional members whose names are not carried on the Party roles because, acting as disciplined fifth columnists of the Kremlin, they have wormed their way into key positions in government offices, trade unions, and other positions of interest. . . . These people are working day and night—laying the groundwork to overthrow YOUR GOVERNMENT. The average American is prone to say, 'It can't happen here.' Millions of people in other countries used to say the same thing." Indeed, who can argue with a comic book, even though the number of American Communist Party members in 1947 was far lower that 85,000 and regardless that the fifth column was nothing more than a myth? With this barrage of misinformation, reality was turned into a joke.

The joke was also perpetrated through pulp magazines and newspapers, which offered a prurient mix of evil reds and sexy babes in danger. Or evil red sexy babes subverting democracy by duping handsome, all-American hunks into trading invaluable U.S. secrets for sex. Some pulps also offered "eyewitness" accounts of how Soviet secret police "taunted God" in one small Eastern European town or loaded "the blood wagon" with hostages. Actually, many of the stories in *Man's, All Male, Men's Stories* and *Siren* were originally about Nazis, only the uniforms have been changed.

If some Americans were still ignorant of the red menace, a plethora of pamphlets and books explaining Communism's evilest stratagems were distributed through mainstream publishers. One such is *The Red Plot Against America* (1949) by Robert E. Stripling and Bob Considine. Stripling was the chief investigator for HUAC for ten years, and Considine was a columnist for the International News Service and a television commentator; Considine reported on the electrocution of atom spy Ethel Rosenberg, commenting: "She's met her maker and will have a lot to answer for." In addition to half-truths about communist influences in the United States, the book includes five hundred questions that all Americans should be able to answer "about Communism in the U.S.A." Here are a few:

What is Communism?
   A system by which one small group seeks to rule the world.
Has any nation ever gone Communist in a free election?
   No.

How do the Communists try to get control?

Legally or illegally, any way they can. Communism's first big victory was through bloody revolution. Every one since has been by military conquest, or internal corruption. [. . .]

Why do people become Communists?

Basically, because they seek power and recognize the opportunities that Communism offers the unscrupulous. But no matter why a particular person becomes a Communist, every member of the Party must be regarded the same way, as one seeking to overthrow the Government of the United States.

What is the difference between a Communist and a Fascist?

None worth noting.

What would happen if Communism should come into power in this county?

Our capital would move from Washington to Moscow. Every man, woman, and child would come under Communist discipline.

Would I be better off than I am now?

No. And the next seventeen answers show why.

The following answers explain what would happen to labor unions, school, private ownership, religion, free elections, and so on, couched in typical anticommunist rhetoric. Indeed, most of the five hundred answers have a tone similar to these:

Where can a Communist be found in everyday American life?

Look for him in your school, your labor union, your church, or your civic club. Communists themselves say that they can be found "on almost any conceivable battlefront of the human mind."

Could I belong to the Elks, Rotary, or the American Legion?

No. William Z. Foster, the head of the Communists in the United States says: Under the dictatorship all the capitalist parties—Republican, Democratic, Progressive, Socialist, etc.—will be liquidated, the Communist Party functioning alone as the Party of the toiling masses. Likewise will be dissolved all other organizations that are political props of the bourgeois rule, including chambers of commerce, employers' associations, Rotary Clubs, American Legion, YMCA, and such fraternal orders as the Masons, Odd Fellows, Elks, Knights of Columbus, etc.

It's a pretty dreary outlook indeed—and, given the realities of Soviet policy in Eastern Europe, not far from the truth. But America was not the Soviet Union. And the number of actual members of the American Communist Party were so few that, even with financial aid from Moscow, they couldn't get a candidate elected, much less overturn the government. A former member of the American Communist Party once said that if only the Party been left alone, it would have destroyed itself from infighting in just a few years. But Communists were such a perfect scapegoat, they were too valuable to lose.

Indeed, Communism could be blamed for a multitude of sins, and reality fed into Americans' escalating fears. Spies *were* employed by Moscow to pilfer military and business secrets, but spies were also employed by the United States to gather its own intelligence. The Soviets *did* obtain A- and H-bomb secrets through this spy network, and so vigilance was necessary as a practical matter. The Soviets were indeed menacing, as evidenced by the blockade of Berlin and other cold-war maneuvers, but on the home front this aggressive behavior was exaggerated when related to American Communist activity. The American press, particularly *Time* magazine (which, in the early 1960s, coined the term "peacenik" to suggest that antinuclear and pro-peace advocates were somehow tied to Moscow) perpetuated the stereotype of the red tyrant on their covers (coincidentally, many of the covers were by Russian émigré Boris Artzybasheff). Other national magazines subvertly and covertly kept the fear of Russia percolating. A special issue of *Collier's* from 1955 vividly records the hypothetical "War We Did Not Want," in which American troops under the flag of the United Nations (Korea redux) fight and win a tactical nuclear war against the USSR. Unfortunately, Moscow, Washington, and Philadelphia were irradiated in the bargain, but it was a small price for victory. This very popular issue of one of America's highest-circulation magazines was not written by kooks, either, but by some of America's most respected journalists and writers. Even Bill Mauldin's popular World War II cartoon characters, Willy and Joe, were called up to fight in the nuclear war.

Fear of spies, threats of a communist takeover, and paranoia about nuclear war were exploited as reality and fantasy and presented in large dosages in print and on film, often as entertainment but with psychologically devastating results on the audience. If an older generation might have been skeptical, the barrage of nuclear metaphors definitely influenced the younger one for years to follow. TV offered another fearsome spectacle, which became regular home viewing for millions: Senator Joseph McCarthy's hearings challenging the loyalty of virtually everyone who once was or had ever thought of being a Communist. Since his record of constitutional heresy (with eventual defeat during the Army-McCarthy hearings) is legend, there is no need to review it here. Despite a modicum of media opposition (notably I. F. Stone, who courageously fought an unpopular battle against the red-baiters), McCarthy's reign of terror ruined the lives of many innocent people who were investigated by his staff.

Politicians had found that anti-Communism worked for them. But for some, the only thing better than anti-Communism was no communism at all. So the McCarran Act was passed to curtail the Communists. Based on findings from HUAC that the United States was in danger from an international conspiracy working through "force, violence, sabotage, deceit, etc.," the McCarran Act mandated that Communists and communist front groups register with the government. Originally proposed in 1948 as the Mundt-Nixon bill, it was passed in 1950 as Internal Security Act (over the veto of President Truman). According to Supreme Court Justice Hugo Black, it "marks a major break in the wall designed by the First Amendment to keep this country free by leaving the people free to talk about any kind of change in basic governmental policies they desire to talk about. I see no way to escape the fateful consequences of a return to the era of the Alien and Sedition Acts (1798–1801), in which all government critics had to face the probability of being sent to jail." The law states that, at the attorney general's request, the Subversive Activities Control Board would hold hearings and order an organization or individuals to register with it—not only one's own name but all other members' names and addresses. Under specific scrutiny were "communist action," groups directly controlled by Moscow; "communist front," those controlled by and supporting action groups; and "communist infiltrated," those controlled by an individual who is, or for three years past has been, a member of a communist action organization. The McCarran Act allowed for the building of internment (or concentration) camps for those determined dangerous to the security of the United States. And in addition to the American Communist Party, which the act effectively shut down, trade unions, free-speech movements, peace and antinuclear movements, and southern integration organizations were forced, and often refused, to register. McCarran undermined the First, Fifth, Sixth, and Eighth Amendments—those concerning free speech, self-incrimination, due process, and protection against cruel and unusual punishment, respectively.

How ironic that the very people who fought so fervently for Americanism were blind to the outcome of their beliefs. It would seem difficult for any right-minded person to read the following statement on this "Fight the Red Menace" card, one of a series published by the Children's Crusade against Communism, and not see that what anti-Communists said should never happen here was indeed happening under HUAC and the McCarran Act:

"A man is going about his business. A heavy hand falls on his shoulder. He is under arrest. Why? Perhaps he has criticized the political system that has taken over his country by force. And some stool pigeon has reported him. For this is happening in a police state, where no one is free to debate what is good for the country. One must accept, without protest, the ideas of the men in power. And we must never let the Reds turn our free America into that kind of fearful place."

Justice William O. Douglas warned in 1952: "Restriction of free thought and free speech is the most dangerous of all subversions. It is the one un-American act that could most easily defeat us." It almost did.

The legacy of red-baiting is unsavory at best. Joe McCarthy was defeated on television when he tried to take on the U.S. Army; later censured by Congress, he died of alcoholism in 1957. HUAC was disbanded in the early 1970s but not until after it investigated anti–Vietnam War activists. The McCarran Act is still on the books, and stories of the existence of anti-activist detention camps ran in alternative newspapers during the 1960s. Although the most vile period of red-baiting in the United States reached its zenith in the mid- to late 1950s, it remained a foolproof tactic for waging war at home and abroad until the Evil Empire hit the mat. Although the cold war is over, it sometimes seems that the propaganda gloves will be used once more for a bout with a new foreign enemy, the Japanese. But it can never happen here again—or can it?

There was probably no more galvanizing or polarizing emblem during the 1960s than the peace symbol—an upside-down, three-pronged, forklike mark in a circle, which symbolized the anxiety and anger of the Vietnam era. Although the basic form had roots in antiquity, it was popularized during the mid-1950s when H-bomb testing prevailed. The symbol was (re)designed in 1954 by an obscure English textile designer named Gerald Holtom for use by England's Campaign for Nuclear Disarmament (CND). Yet some sources claim that the sign, also known as the peace action symbol, was designed in 1958 for the British World Without War Council for use at the first annual Aldermaston Easter Peace Walk to promote world disarmament. It later debuted in the United States in 1962 in the cautionary science-fiction film about the tragic effects of nuclear testing, *The Day the Earth Caught Fire,* and within a few years was adopted for use as an antiwar insignia.

The symbol is supposed to be a composite semaphore signal for the letters *N* and *D* (nuclear disarmament), but its basic form also derives from an ancient runic symbol, a fact that casts some doubt on the *ND* theory. According to an article in a 1969 issue of *WIN (Workshop in Non-violence)* magazine, sponsored by the War Resisters League (one of the 1960s foremost anti–Vietnam War activist groups), the peace sign derives from an initial iteration of a white circle on a black square. This was followed by various versions of Christian crosses drawn within the white sphere, which in turn evolved into the ND form. Referring to the Aldermaston march, *WIN* asserts that for subsequent demonstrations an ND badge was "devised and made by Eric Austen," whose research into the origins of symbolism underscored that the basic forklike symbol, or what he called the "gesture of despair" motif, was associated throughout ancient history with the "death of man," and the circle with the "unborn child." The reason for calling the upside-down fork a "gesture of despair" derives from the story of Saint Peter, who was crucified upside down in Rome in A.D. 67 on a cross designed by Emperor Nero, known thereafter as the "Nero Cross" or the "sign of the broken Jew."

Few who wear the peace symbol as jewelry today are probably aware of its legacy as a once-controversial emblem. Rather, it seems like a quaint artifact of the sixties, not unlike psychedelic designs or bell-bottoms. Currently, it is used as a generic insignia for a variety of fashionable (if pseudo-) antiestablishment issues. In truth the symbol is anything but generic, and its origin is still controversial.

During the 1930s, decades prior to the nuclear disarmament and anti–Vietnam War movements but on the precipice of fascist dominance in Europe, the symbol was first devised by the English philosopher and socialist Bertrand Russell as an attempt "to depict the universal convergence of peoples in an upward movement of cooperation." During the late 1950s Russell was the chairman for the CND, present at numerous disarmament demonstrations and protests against English involvement in NATO at the very time the symbol was adopted as the CND emblem. It is therefore probable that Russell introduced to the organization the basic sign from which Holtom created his final design.

Russell was a former member of the Fabian Society (a fellowship of English socialists), which prompted the right-wing journal *American Opinion* to link the peace symbol, like the antiwar movement in general, to a broad communist conspiracy of world domination, "It is not at all surprising that the Communists would turn to Russell to design their 'peace sign,'" states a 1970 article in this journal, which continues: "A Marxist from his earliest youth, he greeted the Russian Revolution with the declaration: 'The world is damnable. Lenin and Trotsky are the only bright spots. . . .'" The journal further describes Russell as an active anti-Christian who was well aware that he had chosen an "anti-Christian design long associated with Satanism." In fact, the basic form, which appears both right-side up and upside down as a character in pre-Christian alphabets, was afforded mystical properties and is in evidence in some pagan rituals. Right-side up it represents "man," while upside down it is the fallen man. Referred to in Rudolf Koch's *Book of Signs* as "the Crow's foot" or "witch's foot," it was apparently adopted by satanists during the Middle Ages.

The Nazis routinely adopted runic forms for their official iconography, such as the SS runes (the insignia of Hitler's personal bodyguard). Indeed the Nazi iconography calls the crow's foot *Todersune,* or "death rune." Paradoxically, in a right-side-up position it was frequently used on death notices, gravestones of SS officers, and badges given to their widows. Not unlike the swastika itself, this runic symbol has positive and negative implications depending on its orientation. The downward version might be interpreted as death and infertility, while the upward version symbolizes growth and fertility.

Signs and symbols are easily transformed to mean good or evil depending on how they are sanctioned and applied over time—and who accepts said usage. Whatever satanic associations the crow's foot may have had (or still has), when Bertrand Russell "designed" this symbol he imbued it with more positive virtues of life and cooperation. Once adopted by the CND (and later by scores of other antiwar, ecology, civil rights, and peace and freedom groups), its meaning was forever changed to protest in the service of humanity.

End Bad Breath

DESIGNER: SEYMOUR CHWAST

End Bad Breath.

The Vietnam War polarized the American people like no other conflict since the Civil War. Domestic battles between hawk and dove, right and left, and young and old were passionately waged in the media and on the streets, through words, music, and pictures. The nightly news barrage of film and video directly from Vietnam battlefields impressed the horrific image of this war on America's consciousness and inspired the prodigious amount of protest posters aimed at leaders and policies. Not since after World War I, when pacifist organizations on both sides of the Atlantic launched what was called a "war against war," have artists and designers produced as many testaments of conscience.

The most ubiquitous icon of antiwar dissent, known simply as the peace symbol and designed by Gerald Holtom in 1954 as the logo of England's CND (Campaign for Nuclear Disarmament), appeared on countless Vietnam War–era flyers and posters and turned up in evening news footage emblazoned on some American soldiers' helmets. Other well-known poster images include the following: Lorraine Schneider's 1969 "War is Not Healthy for Children and Other Living Things," originally used as an announcement for the California-based organization Another Mother for Peace; Tomi Ungerer's series of satiric posters, especially "Eat," which showed a prostrate Vietnamese forced to lick the ass of an American soldier; "I Want Out," by Steve Horn and Larry Dunst, a parody of the famous James Montgomery Flagg "I Want You" poster showing Uncle Sam dressed in bandages with his outstretched hand begging for peace; Edward Sorel's caustic "Pass the Lord and Praise the Ammunition," showing New York's Cardinal

Spellman, vicar of the U.S. Army, charging into battle with rifle and bayonet; "And Babies? Yes Babies!" the poster with a color photograph of the My Lai massacre (an American platoon's savage attack on civilian villagers); and "End Bad Breath" by Seymour Chwast, a comic woodcut portrait of Uncle Sam with his mouth wide open, revealing airplanes bombing Vietnam.

"End Bad Breath," designed in 1968, was not as emotionally wrenching as "War Is Not Healthy . . ." or "And Babies?" But through comic surrealism—the juxtaposition of a typical mass-market advertising slogan, the familiar characterization of American patriotism, and the childlike rendering of an air raid—the poster spoke eloquently of the criminal and banal that was American Southeast Asia policy. It suggested that behind the façade of Americanism, this nation was keeping the peace by engaging in an unjust war in a distant land.

Furious that President Lyndon Baines Johnson ordered American B-52s to bomb Hanoi in order to pound the North Vietnamese leader, Ho Chi Minh, into a humiliating submission, Chwast, like others within the growing antiwar movement, believed that the immorality of such increased U.S. intervention would have disastrous effects on both nations. This also forced Chwast to explore ways in which a solitary citizen might somehow influence government policy. A poster, a mere one-sided sheet of printed paper, could not have the same destructive power as even an infinitesimal fraction of the napalm used to defoliate the Vietnamese countryside, but it could have a curative effect. Short of acts of civil disobedience, which were increasingly frequent during the late 1960s, a poster was the best means for Chwast to express his own growing frustration. And just maybe, through its visibility and recognition, the poster might reinforce the antiwar stance of others.

"End Bad Breath" was not the first antiwar visual commentary that Chwast, who cofounded Push Pin Studios in 1956, had created for public consumption. Nor was it the first time he was involved in antigovernment protests. In the early 1950s Chwast was a member of SANE, a group that advocated and demonstrated for nuclear disarmament and included the support of artists and designers. SANE was the first well-organized postwar effort in the United States to build grassroots support against testing of the atomic and hydrogen bombs. In 1957, a few years before American advisers were deployed in Vietnam, Chwast wrote, illustrated, and self-published *The Book of Battles,* a collection of woodcuts that ironically represented historic battle scenes not as heroic but banal events. The small, limited-edition book was in the tradition of artists' commentaries that dated back to the seventeenth century and included Jacques Callot's collection of prints *The Miseries and Disasters of War* (1633–1635), depicting the horrors of the Thirty Years' War; Francisco Goya's prints *Disasters of War* (1810–1820), about the Napoleonic occupation of Spain; and Pablo Picasso's 1937 painting *Guernica,* memorializing the bombardment of a defenseless Spanish town.

But Chwast's effort was even more consistent with a genre of antiwar fables, exemplified in *The Last Flower* (1939) by James Thurber, with its childlike drawings and terse text that served as a cautionary parable on the nature of armed conflict, and *War is No Damn Good* (1946) by Robert Osborn, the first antiwar book of the nuclear age, the first time that the mushroom cloud is transformed into a death's head. In this same spirit Chwast used a simple visual lexicon to show centuries of warfare's futile recurrence.

In the early 1960s American military advisers were sent to Vietnam, followed by a limited number of ground troops. In 1964, just prior to the launch of massive U.S. buildups, Chwast designed his first protest poster, "War is Good Business, Invest Your Son," the slogan based on a button that he had seen. During this early stage of the burgeoning "alternative youth culture," head shops as well as poster and button stores were popping up in so-called bohemian districts like the East and West Village of New York City and catered to a rebellious clientele. Wearing political and social statements on their clothing was fashionable, and buttons became one way of publicly expressing antiestablishment points of view. In addition to the ubiquitous peace sign and buttons with slogans like "I Am an Enemy of the People" and "Frodo Lives" (a reference to J. R. R. Tolkien's *The Hobbit*), "War is Good Business . . ." touched a very raw nerve among draft-age baby boomers.

Chwast borrowed the slogan for use on his darkly colored (blues, purples, and reds) poster, which included nineteenth-century decorative woodtypes and old engravings of a mother and a soldier. It looked akin to one of those vintage call-to-arms broadsheets that summoned civilians into battle in the days when war was a heroic exercise. Chwast sold the idea to Poster Prints, one of the leading commercial poster and button outlets, where it was retailed among an array of cheaply printed movie, rock-and-roll, and protest posters. Although it appeared decorative, "War is Good Business . . ." was by no means benign. Without employing such frightening images as dismembered bodies and napalmed children, the poster cautioned that war (and particularly the Vietnam conflict) exacted the most costly price.

By the time that the United States had committed total man- and firepower to the Vietnam quagmire, LBJ decided not to run for a second term as president (acknowledging public dissension). Nonetheless, he continued to aggressively pursue the war, which had gathered such momentum that it was not about to be concluded at that time. "End Bad Breath" acknowledged the frustration Chwast—and many Americans—felt over the inevitability of an out-of-control war.

"End Bad Breath" was distributed through Poster Prints, and—compared to the other inventory of celebrity and psychedelic posters—it was fairly strident. But Chwast admits it was by no means an innovation. "This was the kind of illustration method that was being done in those days," he explains. "Little people on shoulders, things in mouths—So I didn't break any new ground." The woodcut, which Chwast chose to use because of its sudden-death immediacy, was not new, either. It was the medium of choice for German expressionist artists, many of whom were members of left-wing political parties during the early twentieth century. Anyway, novelty was less important to Chwast than effectiveness, and the poster did have an impact "if only as an icon for those of us who had already made up our minds about the war," Chwast comments. "But it certainly didn't change any minds."

Chwast does not harbor any false illusion that his, or any, poster made a difference in the eventual outcome of the Vietnam War. But when taken as one piece of ordinance in a larger arsenal, its impact is very significant. It may not have had the same widespread exposure as the nightly network news broadcasts (which arguably changed Americans' perceptions more than anything else); it may not have been as influential as rock songs like Country Joe and the Fish's

"Fixin' to Die Rag." But it was a mnemonic representation of government folly that underscored deep-seated dissent and an effective component of the larger antiwar campaign. It was also ubiquitous in graphic design magazines and competition annuals, which presumably helped to raise the awareness, if not stimulate the activism, of those in the design profession.

Troilus and Cressida

DESIGNER: ANTHON BEEKE

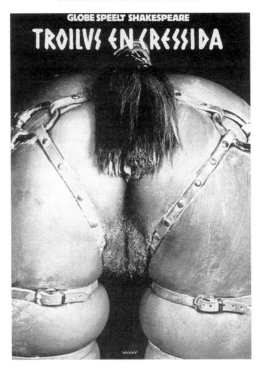

Anthon Beeke (b. 1940) is known in Holland for the design of theater posters that challenge convention. His work not only assails aesthetic norms but also involves subject matter with some quite explicit sexual imagery that society has deemed taboo. Still, he seems to hold a special place in Dutch culture, which allows him expressive license to create and display his work in public arenas ordinarily denied many of his colleagues. In 1995 his work was introduced to Americans in a small exhibition at the Herb Lubalin Study Center of Design and Typography in New York. The show and accompanying catalog, respectively curated and edited by Ellen Lupton, included many striking images created through the use of dramatic photography and photographic manipulation. Though all are unconventional by American standards, only one caused a row.

The poster for a Dutch production of Shakespeare's *Troilus and Cressida* showed a photograph of the rear of a nude woman bending over, buttocks tied up in a harness and short-cropped horse's tail hanging above the exposed genitalia. Beeke described this image as a representation of the Trojan horse, an evocation of Cressida in her role as a sexual go-between during the Greek siege of Troy, and a metaphor for the horrors inflicted on women during war in general. As further justification for the imagery, he argued that this adaptation of *Troilus and Cressida* was conceived as a metaphor for the Vietnam War, featuring phallic-inspired costumes and scenes rife with excessive debauchery and violence. On its own merits, however, the curator determined it was insulting to women and made the decision to remove it from the show, which already included many more posters than could fit in the small gallery.

Citing censorship, Beeke protested the exclusion and demanded the poster's reinstatement as a significant part of his oeuvre. Having defended her decision on "feminist grounds," Lupton listened to other arguments from students and colleagues and eventually reconsidered. After analyzing her reasons for excluding the poster she concluded: "I had in fact censored the work based on its content. I had no right to make that decision about what other people should see." She summarily reinstated the poster in the show.

As expected, however, it did become an object of attention. "The poster became a freak show with male students lining up to take a look," Lupton recalls. Yet despite the difficulty involved in making her decision, she believes that it was the right choice. "It was my decision alone," she adds, "and a test of my values regarding freedom of expression." School administrators did not protest, and Lupton believed that there would have been more acrimony among students if the offending work was censored.

The issue came to another boiling point when North Carolina State University School of Design agreed to mount the show in August 1990. Lupton had cautioned them about the *Troilus and Cressida* poster and stated emphatically that it must be included in any exhibition. However, upon seeing the posters, Dean J. Thomas Regan delayed the opening of the exhibition until the differences among faculty members concerning the inclusion of the poster could be ironed out. The show was suspended indefinitely. As reported in the Raleigh *News and Observer,* Regan indicated that it was premature at this stage to say this is an issue of censorship, since no decision has been made to cancel the show. Some faculty members reportedly accused Mr. Regan of stalling so that it would not become an issue in the campaign of Harvey B. Gantt against Senator Jesse Helms. (Mr. Gantt, a liberal, lost his bid to unseat the conservative Helms.) Mr. Regan, however, was reported as saying he was concerned about the school, not external politics. Nonetheless, the poster was not exhibited.

Beeke is not a stranger to this kind of controversy. Even in Holland and Belgium the *Troilus and Cressida* poster was attacked by the play's actors. "It's okay on stage," says a disgusted Beeke, "but not on the theatre wall." In fact, one member of the company placed red stickers on the genitals, which Beeke insists "made my communication into pornography." While he denies his images pander, he admits that he tries to create dialogue whenever possible. "This poster is not antifeminist, but rather a protest against male abuse of women throughout history," he says. "And an assertion on my part that women are forced to use their bodies to survive."

That Beeke argues the validity of his work on a moral plane makes it difficult to definitively judge this work as obscene in word or deed. "This and my other socially challenging posters must be judged in context," he says. That his work is shown in the Netherlands does not suggest the United States is more puritanical but that American standards for judging what is offensive are indeed vague. More important, the *Troilus and Cressida* episode proves that even graphic design can test the limits of freedom.

How to Commit Suicide in South Africa

ARTIST: SUE COE

As social conditions worsened in the eighties, the polemical art that Sue Coe (b. 1951) began in the seventies started to touch nerves among the middle class. Reaganism was not just a callous response to the needy, it had triggered the age of the greedy. Coe's images reflected, if not dramatically foretold, growing economic divisions. While social indifference had been a recurring theme in Coe's work before, it acquired more resonance when AIDS and homelessness entered the middle class's reality. It was at this time that Coe began to explore alternative means of getting the message out, specifically using the book as a medium for commentary.

Her first book, with Holly Metz, was an investigation into apartheid entitled *How to Commit Suicide in South Africa* (1983), published by Raw Books and Graphics. Inspired by the murder in prison of black South African activist Steven Biko, Coe decided to combine visual impressions with accounts from newspapers and to make a record of all the people who died in detention, supposedly from suicide. "I believe that if people know the facts, they'll change the system," Coe explains.

Torture was a government weapon used against the oppressed majority, and so Coe created the drawing *We Come Grinning into Your Paradise*, showing a male body representing the South African homeland on a torture table. Insects appear under translucent skin, denoting the social and moral decay; five sadistic monsters hovering around the table represent the power and greed of the slave. The viewer is forced to follow the details of the picture, much like a road map, before arriving at the destination—the central message. "The frightening surrealism of this dark portrait brings alive the physical substance of often-overlooked news headlines," wrote Frank Gettings in the catalog to Coe's 1995 retrospective at the Hirshhorn Museum in Washington, D.C.

The imposition of Coe's art as a kind of signpost in someone else's eyewitness account marked a strategic shift in the way Coe communicated ideas. The multipicture essay, comprised of related images in a more or less contiguous narrative and combined with text, addressed complex themes in greater depth. Furthermore, with this method she avoided the stereotypes that had hampered her earlier attempts at social commentary.

Coe received the most significant critique of *How to Commit Suicide in South Africa* from an African-American man who complained that it was not really examining his struggle in America. Taking this to heart, Coe's second book *X* (1986), also published by Raw Books and Graphics, was intended as a graphic complement to the *Autobiography of Malcolm X*. Coe visited places connected with the slain Muslim leader, including Harlem's Audubon Ballroom, where he was assassinated in February 1965, to commune with aspects of Malcolm's life and death. The resulting book contains images of Malcolm X in addition to grotesque representations of J. Edgar Hoover's witch-hunts and the Ku Klux Klan, and satirical caricatures of Ronald Reagan and the "sharks of Wall Street." A chronological text by journalist Judith Moore weaves Malcolm X's life throughout the history of American civil rights. It was a serious attempt, but in retrospect Coe is harshly critical: "No one told me, but this was a mistake," she admits. "It's too easy to say that I'm not black, and therefore do not understand the black struggle—that's like saying men can't be effected by sexism. But I made Malcolm into an icon, when I should have dealt with him as an individual."

Since then, Coe has attempted to imbue her essays with what she calls more humanist imagery—pictures showing optimistic, though not falsely optimistic, representations of the struggle. With *How to Commit Suicide in South Africa,* she recalls that *RAW* editors Art Spiegelman and Françoise Mouly convinced her that the humanist pictures were unnecessary. "That wouldn't happen now, because I am much more self-assured," she insists. However, Spiegelman describes Coe's humanistic drawings as "the Keane-eyes problem," referring to Walter Keane, the 1950s painter of schmaltzy, doe-eyed children. "Sue does not want to be admired only in her negativity," Spiegelman continues. "So she comes up with the soulful victim infused with all the warmth she can muster. The fact is, she's better fighting against sentimentality; when you deal with the angry stuff, the honest sentiment comes out." Spiegelman believes that Coe's need to make heroes out of revolutionaries is a superego desire to make a resoundingly positive statement and perhaps at the same time create an official art of the struggle. But Coe is best when her anger is directed toward change. "It is more useful to posit the negative," continues Spiegel-man, "rather than theoretically posit the positive, since there's nothing to attack. Even Milton found it was easier to have the devil do his bidding than Jehovah."

For years Coe has tried to find different means of expression that reveal the inherent content of a work. "I have resigned myself to recording deterioration," Coe demurs. "But I still keep records of any revolutionaries I meet in hopes that I can compose a history based on their faces." She often asks herself: "Is there a deeper way of looking or seeing?"

Why was there was such a paucity of effective antiwar dissent during the Gulf War? Every modern war has had critics, but some have been more vocal and/or visual than others for reasons owing to the context in which the wars are fought. America's first dedicated antiwar movement was triggered by the unpopular Spanish-American War in 1898; almost two decades later, a boisterous peace movement protested possible American involvement in the First World War, though it was ultimately suppressed by the government. A revived American peace movement was launched before World War II yet dissipated following the Japanese sneak attack on Pearl Harbor. In the wake of the "Good War," as Studs Terkel calls the fight against fascism, the Korean War—America's first official war against communism—generated little dissent back home. Well-organized antiwar activity was scarce throughout the 1950s and early 1960s, when the first group of military advisers were sent into Laos and American marines invaded the Dominican Republic.

As the world's policemen the American military had license to engage overt and covert operations wherever communists posed a threat. It wasn't until 1966, almost five years after John F. Kennedy committed advisers to Vietnam and when Lyndon Baines Johnson escalated the number of American combat troops there (making middle-class boys subject to the draft), that the most powerful antiwar movement in U.S. history began to take hold, and with it a massive, grassroots propaganda effort involving artists, cartoonists, designers—professional and amateur—creating posters, flyers, and buttons of all descriptions.

The generation born in the 1920s and 1930s accepted the Korean War as the paradigm of a

Good War, whereas, similarly, those born in the 1940s and 1950s saw the Vietnam War as the paradigm of imperialism and folly. The former were convinced that "Might Makes Right;" the latter contested "Make Love Not War." World War II and Vietnam were so influential in molding mass behavior regarding both blind acceptance, on one hand, and unremitting skepticism, on the other, of government leaders and policies, it should come as no shock that response to the Gulf War is a curious merging of these two behavioral models. The reaction by former antiwar advocates to the Gulf War was a kind of paralysis because the issues were confused between a just fight against an evil dictator, Saddam Hussein, and a misguided adventure to make the world safe for petrodollars. Many one-time antiwar activists, though skeptical of America's mission, were uncertain of their positions in the face of persuasive government assurances that this, like World War II, was a "just" war.

Before examining the reasons for a dearth of antiwar expression, it is important to briefly review the events: Saddam Hussein invaded and conquered Kuwait. President George Bush convinced the United Nations to impose sanctions as troops and matériel were sent to the Gulf. Everyone waited while sanctions failed. Hussein became further entrenched in Kuwait. An ultimatum was made and ignored. The air war began. The air war continued for a month with limited allied casualties. A ground war was threatened. Another ultimatum was ignored. The ground war began and ended in only a few days with minimum casualties. If the war had continued and the body bags had come home in numbers, an antiwar protest would certainly have grown more vocal; however, those possibilities never became realities, and so protest was minimal. Moreover, Deserts Shield, Storm, and Thunder were brilliantly coordinated PR coups, much like a desert tornado blinding observers and sucking the wind out of most dissenters.

The storm came and went so quickly that antiwar activists had little chance to formulate aggressive opposition. But more fundamental, since videotape and photographs of war's carnage were prohibited from the scene, the negative images so necessary in mounting a successful antiwar propaganda offensive did not materialize. Without the evidence of allied troops suffering more than sun blisters from the sweltering desert heat, the Gulf War, though serious, appeared like a beach maneuver. The most memorable image from the war showed the skies of Baghdad during a nighttime air raid aglow with fireflies: Desert Storm was not just clean, it was meticulously sanitized.

The opposition was mostly silent. A few voices could be faintly heard and some antiwar imagery seen. Among the earliest and most poignant of the protests was a march by a few thousand high school students in New York City, many of whom were arrested along the route on the charge of truancy. It is ironic that these kids, some of them children of children of the sixties, were less confused about America's war policy than their parents, who had once unquestioningly protested the Vietnam War. But this was not Vietnam, and the change in context made it harder for traditional "peaceniks" to target the enemy. During Vietnam, the president, congressmen, generals, and troops themselves were reviled as instruments of abusive power, not as pawns in a geopolitical game. Conversely, the troops of Desert Storm were universally praised as heroes from the outset for being heroes of a correct policy.

So what can an antiwar propagandist do when the politicians and generals are stars, the combatants are heroes, and the battles are sanitized? And what can one say when the despot under attack is guilty of torturing the vanquished in a land that he's invaded?

For most, the answer was nothing. "I wanted to see what sanctions would accomplish," said a former anti–Vietnam War activist who once made scores of posters for peace groups. "By the time CNN broadcast the air war, I was too confused to do much of anything, except voice my concern for the safety of our troops." For a stalwart minority, however, still very much conditioned by the memory of Vietnam, the only answer was to add their voices to what they hoped would grow, as it did in the sixties, into a boisterous chorus of dissent. But the early nineties were not the sixties, and the Gulf, as Bush said repeatedly, was not Vietnam. The voices of those who argued against Saddam Hussein were considerably louder than the few dissenters in the wilderness.

One of those faint choruses was organized by singers Lenny Kravitz and Sean Lennon (son of John) in a "We Are the World"–styled video in which a variety of musicians (M. C. Hammer, Peter Gabriel, Cindy Lauper, and others) sing reinterpreted lyrics to John Lennon's song "Give Peace a Chance." The images in both song and picture emphasize the virtue of peace while tiptoeing around the hot political issues over which the war was actually being fought. It was, however, a needed counterpoint to the "We Care" well-meaning music video organized and produced not in support of the war, per se, but to give succor to the troops in the Gulf (who, remember, were *not* the enemy). The Kravitz/Lennon collaboration (along with the documentary of the production of the video) was the only significant evidence of dissent in the mass media— and it was not aired as frequently as its popular counterpart.

Similarly, it was hard to find either publications or graphic materials voicing opposition to the war. Among the noteworthy, Steven Kroningner's readaptation of the famous James Montgomery Flagg "I Want You" poster stridently points out the other crises that "Bush's war" had so cleverly obfuscated: the economy, crime, drugs, and so on. Since it was one of the few acerbic commentaries on the war, copies could be found hanging in many of the art directors' offices to whom Kroninger mailed them at his own expense. However, despite the line on the poster that grants permission to nonprofit organizations to reproduce the poster "as they see fit," Kroninger's contribution barely opened an eyelid of those that one critic says were "sleepwalking through the war."

Having such tight management of news and image made antiwar sentiment seem knee-jerk and nostalgic. A commentator on national TV argued, "How can one be opposed to this war if one doesn't have the facts?" This statement might better be amended to "How can one wage an antiwar campaign without evidence of any real horror?" Though it can be argued that war of any kind goes against human values, it was nevertheless a problem for artists and graphic designers, who were forced to dredge up timeworn images such as skulls, gas masks, and bayonets to make their points.

While the brutality of war hasn't fundamentally changed in millennia, people have come to accept horror in larger doses, forcing up the necessary antidotal dosage. The brilliant graphic images created to fight the Vietnam War virus were not effective enough in this context because they seemed like clichés. As an example, David Lance Goines printed and self-distributed a silk-screened poster with the title "NO-WAR" emblazoned in blood-red type. The poster, showing a muscular torso with his hands holding a skull, printed in the muted dark and olive greens of army camouflage, is an aesthetic tour de force but nevertheless shows how frustrating it was for artists and designers to grapple with the specific issue of war in the Gulf. Likewise, Lanny Sommese produced two antiwar images, drawn in a loose linear style suggesting the immediacy of his response. One shows a globe with the Mideast speared by a bayonet and the word "NO" scrawled on the top; the other shows a soldier in a gas mask plaintively asking "WHY?" Both are poignant, but effective? Next to *Time* and *Newsweek*'s war maps and heroic coverage, Sommese's posters seem trivial.

During the Vietnam War, antiwar posters and publications were plentiful. During the short Desert Storm campaign, hardly anything appeared in national publications that could be construed as an emblem of dissent, save for a remarkable illustration by Sue Coe in, of all places, *Entertainment Weekly*. Like Sommese, Coe used the timeworn image of gas-masked troops marching en masse like cannon fodder to Armageddon, but, given the context in which her image appeared, it had more resonance than similar attempts. Coe also produced, at personal expense, anti-Gulf buttons to offset the plethora of yellow ribbon and flag badges being sold in great quantity, but few wore them. In the few issues of the *Village Voice* devoted to the war, illustrators with strong antiwar images were given outlet, but little else was done, other than an occasional editorial cartoon. One syndicated comic strip was, however, quite acerbic. Bill Griffith's *Zippy* has his pinhead protagonist questioning the necessity of war in sequences with titles like "Ziplomacy," "Blood and Quicksand," and "Is It Over Yet?" (a send-up of his own favorite line, "Are We Having Fun Yet?"). By including himself as a character in this series of strips, Griffith honestly questioned his own complex feelings. ("In this war there are no good guys," he says.) Matt Groening, creator of *The Simpsons,* also addresses the war in one panel of his syndicated strip "Life in Hell," in which he admits, "It's difficult to be funny about war."

Griffith and Groening had national distribution, but many comic-strip artists with antiwar passions did not have access to similar outlets or audiences. A few, however, were published in the two issues of *War News,* edited by Warren Hinckle. In the tradition of the 1960s underground press, *War News* was published as an alternative to what Hinckle, the former *San Francisco Examiner* columnist, perceived as dangerously distorted news coverage. However, since few Western news sources other than Peter Arnett in Baghdad were offering any alternative coverage, much of the *War News* content was, in fact, critique and comment. "Underground comix" artists, many of whom were veterans of the Vietnam protests, provided the visual satire, including *RAW* editor Art Spiegelman, who was its art consultant. Months after the war's end, the comics magazine *World War III* devoted almost its entire issue to an antiwar protest. These strips, motivated by real frustration, seemed like shrill cries in the wake of post–Desert Storm victory celebrations.

Desert Storm was admittedly a tough war to protest because the government mustered its might on two fronts, at home and abroad. The campaign was not just to free Kuwait but to expunge Vietnam from America's memory. Yellow ribbons outnumbered peace signs during this war, showing that the government learned one Vietnam-era lesson well: By not getting stuck in a quagmire, it could win a war and defeat an antiwar movement.

Stormfront

WHITE PRIDE WORLD WIDE

White Nationalist Resource Page

Stormfront is a resource for those courageous men and women fighting to preserve their White Western culture, ideals and freedom of speech and association – a forum for planning strategies and forming political and social groups to ensure victory.

Quote of the week:

Beauty is a manifestation of secret natural laws, which otherwise would have been hidden from us forever.

Hate literature was once cheaply printed and poorly designed. Pamphlets and flyers were sold by mail, sniped on hoardings, and deposited like bird droppings on car windshields. Today hate springs eternal on the World Wide Web, with white supremacist and neo-Nazi "cyber guerrillas" producing professionally designed home pages with remarkably sophisticated graphics and logos in addition to photographs of burning crosses, lynchings, and racial and ethnic caricatures. Adolf Hitler was the first demagogue to master the radio, and from all indications his great-grandchildren have carved out a niche in the new media, mastering the various authorship and design programs with skill and savvy.

Stormfront, a white nationalist organization, put up the first hate site on the Web, which offered a sheaf of electronic pages "to those courageous men and women fighting to preserve their White Western culture." Detailed reports on racial issues, militias, government violence as well as Waco and Ruby Ridge "massacres" are continually updated, as are links to cyberhate compatriots in Canada, Germany, England, France, and the Netherlands. So wide and insidious is this electronic Web that an acquaintance of mine, a scholar who was recently doing Web research on the Talmud, innocently found himself linked to Stormfront's "White Nationalist Resource Page," which contained a lengthy analysis of this sacred Hebrew text entitled "The Talmud: Judaism's Holiest Book Documented and Exposed" (© 1994 by the Old Order Brotherhood).

With its unregulated access (pages can easily be viewed using Netscape, which is offered for free on the Stormfront site) and simple programming software, the World Wide Web has become a virtual shopping mall for hate groups and fanatics of all persuasions, with new sites opening frequently. From the Stormfront site alone, a browser can link to an uncensored litany of home pages, including those of the Aryan Nation, the "official site" of the quasi-religious paramilitary group linked to various political assassinations; *The Watchman,* the publication of the Pennsylvania Christian Posse Comitatus; Freedom Site, which hosts the Canadian Heritage Front, Canadian Patriots Network, Digital Freedom BBS, and more; Resistance Records, featuring album covers, music, and video clips from the "premier pro-White record company"; *White Flame,* a racist cyberzine; Independent White Racialists, whose motto is "your skin is your uniform"; Skinheads U.S.A., the voice of the American youth wing; American Renaissance, "a literate, undeceived journal of race, immigration, and the decline of civility"; Be Wise As Serpents, a Hawaii-based Christian Identity movement that has a site featuring the anti-Semitic tract "The Protocols of the Learned Elders of Zion"; and the Institute for Historical Review, a source for World War II revisionist (i.e., denial of the Holocaust) publications. The Skinheads U.S.A. link page offers additional connections, including those of worldwide skinhead groups, the American National Alliance, Holland's Nationale Volkspartij, Christian and Euro-American Nationalism, the Underground Resistance, Aryan Crusaders' Library, Christian Identity Online, CNG (Cyber Nazi Group), the Knights of the Ku Klux Klan, and the Ku Klux Klan's home page. For those who seek interactivity, there are also a large number of newsgroups (or public forums) where white nationalists chat and "do battle with the anti-White bigots."

These groups would exist with or without the Internet, but access to such widespread communications has undeniably boosted their range and determination. Like the left-oriented underground press of the sixties, the ultraright hate wing has tapped into a medium (and has learned a language) that is potentially more influential than any propaganda method they used in the past. Only a few years ago, the cost of printing and distributing racist publications greatly proscribed distribution. The cheaply printed tabloid newspaper *WAR* of the White Aryan Resistance, for example, was published in a quantity of less than five thousand copies and had even fewer readers. Today, comparable cyberzines reach tens of thousands of readers without incurring any printing or distribution costs. The only expenses, in addition to the hard- and software, are modest server and access fees. Otherwise the end user is paying for the privilege of receiving the material. Since going online in March 1995, Stormfront lists its number of "hits" (the number of times a particular screen has been visited) as over half a million.

This interactive medium is dangerously seductive. The very presence of this material in such a public-access environment imbues it with a kind of authority. Just as, prior to 1933, the Nazis were able to infiltrate the hearts and minds of the German masses (particularly disaffected youth and the unemployed) through radio broadcasts that suggested legitimacy, cyber racists have staked out a medium that is quickly becoming an information wellspring. Sure, the ideas are not held by the overwhelming number of Internet users, but there is a huge potential for increasing the constituency. Moreover, interfaces have become easy to design (and more professional design tools are available than with traditional cut-and-paste layout).

There is no mistaking the Nazi-inspired graphics of spiky, black-letter type and a swastika-inspired logo (for Stormfront) or the skinheads' Großdeutchland eagle and SS runic logo (for the NS 88 Video Division). But the National Alliance home-page graphics are decidedly more benign and more deceptive. The three-dimensional forked-cross logo (reminiscent of an elongated peace symbol) framed by laurel leaves and set against a blue sky, looks like any mainstream television graphic. Considering the limitations of Web design, the uniform headline typeface and overall composition of the page is comparable to any professionally produced site. The Underground Resistance (the Resistance Records home page) is another strong mainstream-inspired design: Its full-color features include a mélange of computer-enhanced shining typefaces as well as hot buttons to access info screens and music selections (for such records as "Declaration of War" from groups like Rahowa, short for "racial holy war"). Photos of the record covers and group members are more stylishly professional than typical hate material. Even the typography for the Aryan Nation's home page, a derivative of Emigre's Mason typeface, eschews the otherwise pornographic aura of its printed matter.

The Southern Poverty Law Center and the Simon Wiesenthal Center, two groups that monitor cyberhate on the Net, warn that many of the browsers are college students who have free access to these systems. Various reasons account for their engagement, but one is certainly the appeal of "kewl" graphics, right-wing music, and the associated hype reminiscent of the appeal of sixties counterculture. Moreover, growing numbers of young and old hate-group supporters have gained access to the Net through privately or institutionally owned computers. This, in turn, has encouraged a new generation of cyberhate groups to emerge. CNG (whose founder, Jeff Vos, alternately calls his organization Cyber Nazi Group, Cyber Nationalist Group, or Computer Nationalist Group) is one online cell targeting cyberspace. CNG is anti-ethnic, anti-Jewish, and anti-homosexual and encourages followers to use tactics that manipulate the Internet. Since the Internet offers its users anonymity, CNG calls for widespread impersonation of the "enemy" as a way to embarrass liberals and the left, including sending messages to Congress pretending to be homosexuals supporting the legalization of pedophilia. CNG encourages flame wars (the relentless bombardment of angry messages between opposing groups), politically incorrect humor (with a "Kosher Net" that reports on Jewish activity to ban cyberhate), and conservative research to support organizational arguments. Most important, as Joseph Goebbels, Nazi minister of propaganda, might have advised them: Tell the big lie as often as possible. With the Internet, this is as easy as launching a special "bot," or automatic programming device.

Cyberhate mongers will never actually conquer the Net, but they have established a beachhead and an information delivery system that far exceeds the print efforts of even the best-organized, radical right-wing organizations. For the moment the Internet and USENET (the worldwide network of chat groups and bulletin boards) are safe havens for them because of a ruling by the U.S. District Court of Philadelphia in June 1996, which deemed unconstitutional that part of the 1996 Telecommunications Act governing appropriate speech on the Internet. None of the watchdog groups advocate censorship—the American Civil Liberties Union has vowed to defend the rights of these people should they come under further legislative attack—

but all would agree that there must be vigilance. "White supremacist organizations are doing a much better job on the Net than anti-hate groups," says Noah Chandler, a researcher at Democratic Renewal, an Atlanta-based organization that monitors hate-group crimes, in *Emerge* magazine (July/August 1996). Some Internet providers are clamping down, but there are others that refuse to tamper with access. To counter this trend, a few individuals are calling for boycotts or are launching their own opposition pages. But for now, cyberhate is a frightening reality. "USENET offers enormous opportunity for the Aryan Resistance to disseminate our message to the unaware and the ignorant," says Milton John Kleim Jr., a white-power activist, in an essay entitled "On Tactics and Strategy for USENET." "The state cannot yet stop us from advertising our ideas and organizations. . . . Now is the time to grasp the weapon which is the Net, and wield it skillfully and wisely while you may still do so freely."

Racism

DESIGNER: JAMES VICTORE

A New York street poster has got to grab viewers by the throats and knock them on their asses. Otherwise it's as useless as yesterday's newspaper and as forgettable as most theater, movie, fashion, and cabaret posters hung daily. In the competition for city scaffolds, longevity is measured by days, sometimes hours. A memorable poster must stand out in the crowd and also leave the viewer with a mental "cookie" that prompts Pavlovian recognition—a tough order, given the multitude of stylish bills posted these days. Yet one of the most startling posters in recent memory did leave a potent after-burn. This violently rendered scrawl of the word "racism" not only eclipses trendy designs but is a strident commentary on an onerous theme. The poster is the word itself with a menacing metamorphosed *C* shaped like a mouth with fangs, outlined in red and poised to consume the other letters in the word. Created by New York designer James Victore (b. 1962), it is a symbol of racial hatred that forces the viewer to feel the violence that the word conjures.

During the summer of 1993, Victore, like millions of other New Yorkers, was disquieted by race riots that erupted between Hasidic Jews and their African-American neighbors in Crown Heights, Brooklyn. The intensity of this atavistic behavior was alarming, but so was the voyeurism of television news viewers. Victore believed that nightly press coverage had caused people to misconstrue the essence of racism. The physical spectacle was the main attraction, not the deep-seated issues leading up to the hostility. Victore felt that the only upside of such a tragedy should be the public's heightened awareness of what causes racism in the first place, but this was not the case. "I was troubled that the word was so overused that it no longer meant anything," he explains. "In the press, everybody was talking about racism-racism-racism. But nobody really knew what it meant. So I had this idea to show [the word] eating its young, and created a poster as simply as I could."

Rarely is a poster more effective than live TV coverage, but Victore's "Racism" added a critical dimension to the event. If Victore never created another polemic after this, he should be satisfied that he made a contribution to contemporary visual iconography. But this was not the first nor would it be the last of his visual commentaries. Although it is a standard against which his future work will be fairly or unfairly judged, it is one of many memorable images that he has created in a little over a decade since becoming a graphic designer.

In 1992, Victore designed and produced his first polemical poster, "Celebrate Columbus"— or what he calls the "Dead Indian"—to commemorate the five-hundredth anniversary of the discovery of America by Christopher Columbus. "My reason for doing the poster," he explains, "was because, at the time, everybody in media was saying that from one man's accidental discovery we are such a great nation." Victore suspected that the hoopla around the celebration, which was being criticized by Native American and other human rights groups, demanded further scrutiny, and he wanted to add his voice to revelation of, in his own words, "what I like to call the 'pox-infested blanket story,' the genocide of indigenous peoples by the American government. I wasn't trying to throw a stone through anybody's window. I just wanted to inject the notion that there's always another side, which at that time was getting lost. The whole revisionist, nationalistic view was getting stronger and stronger. I wanted to offer a small counterpoint."

Using his rent money Victore printed three thousand two-color posters, which showed a vintage photograph of a Native American warrior, whose noble face he drew over graffiti-style in black marker to look like a skull. With a couple of volunteers, he illegally pasted about two thousand copies on walls and scaffolds around New York. He also obtained the addresses of Native American groups in the United States and Canada and mailed them tubes containing twenty posters each. For all his effort, Victore's first stab at advocacy went mostly unappreciated. A request for an appointment with a Native American organization in Washington, D.C., was ignored. "I left the posters on their porch with a note and got no response at all." Meanwhile, back in New York, the police tore down as many posters as they could so as not to mar the celebration, yet enough remained intact on Columbus Day to have something of an impact. "I witnessed few people actually looking and reading," he acknowledges. Although it was a small return, he was encouraged.

At the time, Victore veered somewhat from commercial work toward an indy sensibility. It is axiomatic that new ideas rarely emerge from tried-and-true venues, so Victore hooked up with kindred renegades. He had met two bartender/actors who founded the Shakespeare Project, dedicated to performing Shakespeare in public spaces presumably as the Bard had originally intended. The payment involved was negligible, but Victore was given carte blanche with the posters, which he rendered without a hint of Shakespearean pastiche. Instead, as for Henryk

Tomaszewski's theater posters, Victore rendered everything from image to type by hand to give a mood of immediacy and serendipity. At the same time that he did posters for *Macbeth, Twelfth Night, Taming of the Shrew,* and *Romeo and Juliet,* he produced "Racism" and had copies of them sniped around town together. "Racism" made an indelible impact on some, but Victore claims that the poster had much more recognition in professional competitions and design annuals (to which he submitted the work to give it added visibility) than on the street. Nevertheless, he was not deterred.

The first two posters were done on his own, but, accepting the adage about strength in numbers, Victore helped found a small alternative graphics collective along the lines of the Atelier Popular, the graphics arm of the 1968 French student uprising. Victore and five other young New York designers joined together to fund, conceive, and produce critical street graphics. "Traditional Family Values" was the first project done under the auspices of the group (although entirely his own concept) and his third poster. Designed to coincide with the 1994 Republican National Convention, it was an attack on right-wing U.S. Senator Jesse Helms's call for a return to so-called family values as a euphemism for his stands on antihomosexual and antiabortion rights. The image was an appropriated 1950s-era framed photograph of a real family of Ku Klux Klan members—Mom, Dad, the kids, and the Imperial Dragon—which, down South, when it was taken, was as natural as depriving "niggras" of their rights but in the 1990s served as a dark satiric commentary on these new objects of prejudice, not just in the South but all across America.

The second group project, "The Baby Bottle," showed a typical bottle with measuring markings down the side that read "Whitey," "Towel Head," "Kike," "Gook," and other bigoted aspersions about race and ethnicity; it was not done for a special occasion but, rather, as a reminder in the tradition of cautionary and instructive schoolroom posters. As Victore notes, the message was "not to hand down to our children prejudice and hatred through casual remarks." Using a baby bottle was an apt symbol to suggest the matter-of-fact feeding of healthy and unhealthy ideas to children who accept any and all nourishment. The poster, however, did not have the splash the group had hoped for. Nor did it grab proverbial hearts and minds.

Victore admits that although the group was able to get more posters onto the street, "the collaborative didn't work as well as I had hoped. It was too easy to work together because somebody had an idea, and everybody else said 'Yes.'" Without more of an internal dialectic, the group dynamic was less about pushing and shoving each other to better solutions than about consensus. So it was disbanded.

By this time Victore realized that producing his own posters at his own expense was also counterproductive. He mailed hundreds out (and many of them were hanging in offices all over town), but he decided that the most effective way to achieve saturation was to convince an appropriate group to sponsor the work. Of course, balancing the artist's want with the sponsor's needs is tricky, even when the work is done for free, and Victore quickly learned that pro bono arrangements do not always result in the holiest of marriages. He complains, "Groups of this kind don't (for lack of a better term) understand the tool of the poster and the power that it could potentially have." But after a few failed relationships he found the perfect client for one of his sharpest posters in the venerated NAACP (National Association for the Advancement of Colored People), which was trying to shed its moderate civil-rights image and regain its activist aura.

The NAACP had produced a documentary film called *Double Justice,* about the racism inherent in the death penalty, and asked Victore to design its promotional mailer. Instead of using film stills he decided to do a large rendering of a child's stick-figure hangman game, where players guess letters that comprise a word, and for every wrong guess a body part is hung from a scaffold—simultaneously presenting both an innocent children's pastime and a terrifying symbol (when presented in the context of racism). The word that Victore used was "nigger;" the poster shows three letters: *g, g,* and *r.* "I got the idea for the hangman game when I was in the elevator leaving the meeting," Victore recalls. "I ran to my bartender, who was the guy from the Shakespeare Project, and said, 'What do you think?' He said, 'James, it's brilliant; they'll never take it.' But they took it." The elegantly simple poster was mailed to a list of the NAACP Legal Defense and Education Fund, Inc., lawyers who help people on death row. It was also sent to school teachers along with the video. "The last thing that I had heard from them (which was a while ago now) was that they got a call from [former U.S. Supreme Court] Justice Blackmun's office to obtain copies," says Victore. "So it was in Justice Blackmun's office just before he reversed his opinion on the death penalty."

The hangman poster (titled "Racism and the Death Penalty") was the first of two posters for the NAACP that confront racially biased capital punishment. The second, "The Death Penalty Mocks Justice," is a white-on-black drawing of a skull with a stuck-out tongue in the form of an American flag. Here Victore resorted to known clichés (something that he has managed to avoid in his other work), but he argues that in this instance it is the most effective means for getting the point across. "I could have come up with something more intellectual or some offbeat imagery, but the problem was that, for the people I was speaking to, I think it would have been too coy or too design-y. This was also for the NAACP, and it was going to go to lobbyists and lawyers and teachers, and without being trite or belittling, I want to speak in really simple forms and get an idea across in a gestalt manner, whether it's through your heart or your intellect or whatever."

Victore has a litany of peeves, many of which revolve around living in New York. Over the past few years the city has become inundated with "official" signs (dos and don'ts) bolted on lampposts, addressing the basic etiquette of living with millions of other people. Consistent with this trend, he did one titled "Use Mass Transit," a bold gothic headline jammed together with childlike drawings of cars and trucks. Another poster, "Just Say No!" shows the severed head of Mickey Mouse with his eyes Xed out comic-style, which addresses Victore's assertion that New York is "being touristed to death. New Yorkers are becoming just like the great silverback gorillas who will now come down and will eat out of your hand." Victore believes that the Disneyfication of New York (the widespread colonization of Times Square and other city venues by Walt Disney Company hotels, theaters, and retail malls) is one of the city's root evils. In the vortex of New York's official celebration of Disney's civic improvements, this poster is a reminder that it is all a branding scheme.

Forever Free

ARTIST: MICHAEL RAY CHARLES

"What if the Jews never talked about the Holocaust?" writes Michael Ray Charles in the introduction to a catalog of his paintings, *Michael Ray Charles: An American Artist's Work* (the Art Museum of the University of Houston, 1997). This rhetorical question underscores an artistic exploration that delves deep into the history of commercial art stereotypes, which during the late nineteenth and early twentieth centuries relegated African Americans to graphic ghettos comprised of Sambos, mammies, minstrels, and coons. Charles argues that these once ubiquitous characters are now virtually unknown to blacks. He believes that graphic depictions of infantile, shiftless, and buffoonish black men and women are artifacts shedding needed light on the conflicts that black people experience in society even today. As both a reminder and a way to co-opt these negative portrayals, Charles (b. 1967), a painter and professor at the University of Texas at Austin, recasts ugly stereotypes in huge, satiric paintings that challenge the language of institutional racism.

The messages he conveys through his art, however, are not always welcome. "A lot of blacks don't want to see images like mine; perhaps they bring up too much pain," asserts Charles. A lot of whites are embarrassed and feel ashamed by them. But 'out of sight, out of mind' doesn't mean that it doesn't exist. It happened, and I feel it has not been dealt with."

Charles is a strictly representational painter whose early work addressed political and social issues with homage to such nineteenth-century commentators as Goya and Daumier, but without their rapier wit. However, with his most recent paintings of racial stereotypes found in vintage commercial art, he uses wit and irony to attack the racism of both the past and the present. His paintings are rendered in a primitive style and he quotes vintage circus banners, vernacular signs, and folk paintings, a pastiche that underscores the fact that these disturbing images were once America's most popular art.

Critics have attacked the artist for resurrecting images long hidden, ignored as a sad chapter in American history. Charles argues that the issues raised by these images continue to haunt society, albeit through different, contemporary stereotypes—"gangstas," rappers, and even characters on black-oriented TV sitcoms. Subjugation through imagery is something that is never totally expunged, and Charles wants to make certain that people understand the power that these images have over an audience's perceptions.

As a child, Charles may have seen the remnants of vintage imagery still around his native Louisiana, but he did not think much of them—then. "When I was in graduate school, however, a colleague of mine gave me a little Sambo figurine," he relates. "At the time I was doing paintings about the American flag, so I didn't use [these stereotypes] initially—I didn't think it was what I was searching for. However, since I began to use such images, I feel I will never view life in the same way."

Through reprises of these dubious icons of "Negro" America, Charles asserts that the roots of current stereotypes can be traced back to the history of disenfranchised blacks, but his art is also a form of self-exploration. "I want to know about these images—how they were used, why they were used, and when they are being used," he says. "But there's more to my work than just blackface image or the clown caricature. I am deeply motivated by various forms of communication." Common black stereotypes have changed—the poor, shiftless field hand has been replaced by the superman athlete earning a million-dollar contract—and Charles's visual archaeology has helped him see how these vintage images are reconciled. "I see images of the black basketball player everywhere. I know it's a hot fad, but I remember watching the Olympics when the first dream team was assembled. Oh boy, did Americans jump on the backs of those athletes. . . . But ultimately," he asks, "how does it affect the conditions of blacks?" That is the rhetorical question present in all his work.

The mammy, particularly in the images of Aunt Jemima (who continues to grace the package of her namesake product) is one of the characters that Charles singles out for scrutiny. In the history of stereotypes the desexualization of black people was deliberate, and the mammy—the caring house servant who often raised the white man's children—was the most desexualized. Charles portrays her in his work as a kind of heroine. In a stunning parody of Norman Rockwell's *Rosie the Riveter,* Aunt Jemima sits regally to suggest her unacknowledged contributions to white and black America (incidentally, the *Saturday Evening Post* never showed a black woman in an heroic light, if at all). At the same time, his ironic portrayals of mammy are harsh critiques of her diminution in mainstream popular art. Charles regards the way that mammies and other black types were portrayed in art as a wanton attempt to make them unthreatening to whites. "I think they had to remain childlike, overweight, lazy, and unintelligent," he explains, "for whites to remind themselves of who they were."

The minstrel show is another target. These popular late-nineteenth– and early-twentieth–century forms of musical entertainment, comprised of whites putting on a black face and cavorting about on stage, were as well attended as ethnic vaudeville shows. Minstrelry was the white's attempt to mimic and make fun of blacks as well as a way of experiencing otherness at a safe distance. Some historians have argued that the essence of black people was stolen. On the contrary, Charles insists that "it cannot be stolen. The essence of blackness, for me, is defined as being able to withstand, to evolve, to grow in spite of, to show one's wounds, to wear one's scars, and get right back up because there is nothing else left to do."

One wonders how African Americans viewed themselves as a result of the national ad campaigns and comics sections that routinely used these stereotypes. Did the bombardment of these stereotypes have an indelible impact on self-esteem? Charles believes that not only did the images influence blacks' interpretations of themselves, "they continue to influence white, Asian, European, African, and many other cultures' perceptions of [American] blacks. . . . These images are forever part of the vocabulary of what one should want and what one should not want."

Yet, given Charles's best intentions to educate blacks and whites through exposure to these images and his commentaries about them, he says that he has received mixed responses. "One woman once asked me, 'How does it feel to be the Clarence Thomas of the art world?'" he relates. "She believed that Clarence Thomas was a sellout, and by association, giving me the same title, she said that I was selling out, too. She had a very limited perspective. I am an individual who happens to be black. The fact that I am black does not mean that I represent, or support, every black cause." In fact, she is not alone in feeling that introducing these images, which took many generations to forget, does more harm than good. "Her comments initially bothered me," continues Charles. "But ultimately I found it more humorous than anything. I don't know, maybe she saw a part of herself in one of my paintings." Nevertheless, Charles is disturbed that people cannot see the symbolic intent of his work, fixating instead on the surface meaning. "I had a journalist walk up to me and say, 'So tell me about the black woman in this painting.' I responded by saying that it's not a black woman; it's an image that I use to refer to a black woman. I don't think she was able to separate the caricature image of a black person from the reality of knowing what a black person actually is."

Through these paintings, Charles is also attempting to understand when and if perceptions among whites toward blacks began to change for the better. "It's evident that some white people's perceptions about blacks have never changed," he says about his conclusions. "This process of change has been a gradual thing that is consistently gaining and losing ground."

One of the changes since the "Black Power" and "Black Is Beautiful" consciousness-raising days of the 1960s involves the perception of ugliness and beauty. After one of Charles's openings, a showing of paintings that included critiques of Little Black Sambo, the children's story (originally an East Indian folktale) of a little African boy's travails with a tiger, he tells of an elderly white woman who came up to him and said, "Please don't make the Sambo ugly; I love little Sambo. I grew up with the Sambo; it's so dear to me.'" As she started to cry, Charles was awestruck by how much she had invested in a fictional character. "She went on to say that she's not racist," Charles continues, "that her children grew up around black people, they had black people over all the time, and she worked in a school in which she taught black students. She began making a cradling gesture as if she was holding a little baby." But Charles concludes "she didn't get it." She did not see his painted interpretation of Sambo as anything but a black person rather than a representation of attitudes. "That instance is one of the things that really motivate me to continue my exploration into these images and how they affect us."

Michael Ray Charles's paintings are discomforting messages. He understands the difficult line he's toeing by reprising such charged images. Yet he insists that they deserve a certain respect that comes with scrutiny. "I think about so many people whose lives these images have affected. A lot of black people have died and many are dying under the weight of these images. That's motivation enough for me to explore and deal with these things."

Nineteenth Amendment Postage Stamp

DESIGNER: APRIL GREIMAN

The *Right of Citizens of the United States to vote shall not be denied or abridged by the United States or by any state on account of sex*. So says the Nineteenth Amendment to the U.S. Constitution as ratified in 1920, the first time since 1776 that suffrage was granted to women in this country. And to honor the seventy-fifth anniversary of this milestone of belated equality, the U.S. Postal Service issued a commemorative stamp in 1995 designed and illustrated by April Greiman (b. 1948).

The Citizens Advisory Committee to the Postmaster General, which recommended this stamp, is a body of unpaid "experts" from all professions (including graphic designers and illustrators as well as actors, academics, sports figures, and so on), who represent various cultural points of view. They are charged with selecting themes for stamps from a continually replenished suggestion box from all corners of American life. It is also the responsibility of the committee to advise the postmaster (who retains the final discretionary power) on a designer for a stamp, whose design is commissioned and supervised by a smaller team of art director/designers.

However, deciding on stamps is a more complex venture than who designs what. A commemorative stamp must convey a sufficiently weighty theme to represent America and a sufficiently distinct presence to appeal to consumer impulses. Since the U.S. Postal Service's operating budget depends in large part on the sales of stamps to the public, commemoratives are issued not only to honor certain people, ideas, inventions, and events but, equally important, to garner profit. In recent years, stamps have been issued on such popular themes as dinosaurs, comic strips, and cultural icons (for example, Elvis) to capture the hearts, minds, and imaginations of consumers. The Nineteenth Amendment stamp paid deserved tribute to one of this nation's most important legal decrees, and—like the earlier Susan B. Anthony stamp, minted in 1936 (and again in 1958), which celebrated the pioneer suffragette—this was to be the "women's stamp" of the year. It was hoped that it would be so popular as to generate substantial income.

Not all stamps are created equal, nor do they have the same intrinsic selling power. Hence, the Postal Service has become expert at marketing. Its print and television promotions appeal to average users as well as die-hard stamp collectors. A stamp is every bit as much a consumable as food or fashion. In fact, like logos on clothes, stamps confer status and prestige upon the user. Over the years, women's issues have faired well in the philatelic marketplace. Like the 1967 Henry David Thoreau stamp, known in its day as the "hippie stamp" for its wide use by members of the youth culture, the Susan B. Anthony stamp was the darling of feminist users. The Citizens Committee presumed that, if the design of the Nineteenth Amendment stamp was even more contemporary than its Susan B. Anthony predecessor, it would attract a new generation of women consumers.

The critical decision, therefore, was which designer or illustrator would succeed in transcending or transforming the timeworn images associated with women's rights to create a stamp that was fresh and immediate. Stamp imagery was once exclusively engraved, but today, all kinds of painting, drawing, and photography in various styles—from realism to abstraction—are accepted media. With this panoply the challenge was not how a contemporary image would be produced, but what form it would take.

The task was given to April Greiman, herself a pioneer woman designer in a male-dominated profession and a digital artist in an analog world. Prior to her being awarded the commission, the Nineteenth Amendment stamp had been assigned to two other designers who had failed. "It was my understanding that several passes had already transpired with various male illustrators," relates Greiman about the unsatisfactory iterations, "and that [Congresswoman] Pat Schroeder had thrown up her hands and said something like, Why do we always have to use a portrait of Susan B. Anthony to represent these current issues? And, moreover, why don't we have a woman design this? To my knowledge, I was the second woman in history to design a stamp."

Greiman was approached by Carl Hermann, one of the Postal Service's art director/ consultants, who had coincidentally taken an intensive Macintosh workshop with Greiman in the mid-1980s at the Maryland Institute College of Art. Although Hermann did not give her overarching parameters on what or how to design, she was told that no living individuals can be portrayed on a stamp. "I was also given a size 1½" × 1⅛" that a commemorative stamp has to be, and that's all!" she says about the apparently open-ended nature of what would become the most visible project of her career.

In the stamp business, size *is* everything, and mastering it is crucial. Visual ideas that may be effective on a book jacket or poster will not be effective when reduced down to Lilliputian proportions, and many designers are incapable of working in the designated space. An image must be stark, focused, and capable of withstanding the technical limitations endemic to printing millions of tiny stamps, and there are legitimate reasons for certain enforced taboos. Yet, even within the officialdom of stamp design, there has been room for taking risks.

Greiman may not appear the most obvious choice to design a U.S. stamp. Her work is usually larger than life and more detailed. Her layered, brightly colored approach is more consistent with progressive Dutch stamp designs, which afford considerable license to artists. American stamp design is extremely competent but not aggressively experimental. Nonetheless, Greiman was commissioned to apply her signature sensibility to the problem. After analyzing the conceptual and technical issues, she proposed a single concept that was put forward to the committee. "I did show some subtle variations on that idea," she says about her process, but she refused to create the typically mandatory three alternative designs.

Schooled in Basel and weaned on the grid-busting typography of Wolfgang Weingart, Greiman was among the earliest American graphic designers to introduce digitally manipulated imagery that combines layers of pictorial information with kinetic patterning. After the advent of Adobe Photoshop in the late 1980s, the approaches that she had pioneered became rather standard fare among so-called digital designers. Yet rather than fall prey to cliché, Greiman's work continues to push both technological and aesthetic boundaries in the realm of what she calls "hybrid imagery," a marriage of the traditional and nontraditional as well as the employ of representational and abstract images and concepts.

For this stamp Greiman did not design a conventional miniposter but, rather, combined four photographs into a conceptual collage—a historic suffragette march, a 1970s ERA demonstration, the U.S. Capitol building, and a blue/green cloud (a symbol of visionaries). Each individual piece is so detailed that Greiman was aware of possible resulting confusion; in addition to these pictures she also layered words. "Since the layering of the four images was going to render this very small space quite abstract," she explains, "I felt I should add words to give the literal-minded some sort of hook. I came up with the words 'progress,' 'freedom,' and 'equality.' I felt that these are key ideas regarding the Nineteenth Amendment and that they continue to be living issues."

The rationale was sound, but would the design and wording, in fact, be legible in this space? Would any of the experts on the design panel who have judged the success and failure of stamps pull the plug? "I understand that it was met with mostly enthusiasm," says Greiman about the initial response. "People felt they had not seen something like this before and that was good. At a later meeting with yet another committee (I think the Citizens Committee), a man said he had a hard time reading all the images . . . said it looked like MTV!" Apparently the graphic design expert on the committee countered that there was virtue to not having yet another portrait of a dead person on a stamp, and the idea passed muster.

Following acceptance of the basic design, Greiman continued refining the image, working on greater separation of color and contrast (which was necessary for such a dense composition to be readable) and also on the typography to make it "more spatial and elegant." A final comp with these refinements was sent to Hermann, who was concerned that presenting anything even modestly different from the artwork the committee had already approved might invite unwanted critique; he never showed this version to other parties involved. "I was very annoyed because I always perfect my work to the point of printing. But he did not want to rock the boat, as [my earlier version] had sailed through more smoothly than any other stamp," says Greiman. "Hence, my real final version never was used."

Once in the production pipeline, things did not go so smoothly. An outside (non-government) printer was chosen to do this job specifically because it required great care, which was a good decision. But prior to going on press, the printing representative who was responsible for oversight was tragically killed in an automobile accident, and the entire print run—all 150 million impressions—went unsupervised. The final printed stamp was not how Greiman had envisioned the result. The separation between image and type was not as clear as she wanted, and the color appeared smudged. But she does not entirely blame the unsupervised press run for the less than satisfactory result; Greiman's was a breakthrough stamp in part because it was the first digital file ever used as artwork by the Postal Service, and in 1995 digital output was in its infancy. "The print technology was not up to the level of the technology that produced the art," she moans. "Actually it may still not be yet."

One aspect of the printing was a success. The printing representative had suggested that the price wording—"32 cents"—be printed in intaglio after the four-color offset process. "If you run your finger across the surface of the stamp, it has this wonderful raised surface, which I like a lot," says Greiman.

Feedback was not entirely positive: Greiman explains that she received some criticism of the stamp, which "was really not in my control and was not reproduced as high a quality as my other work is." In *Print* (July/August 1996) Martin Fox critiqued the stamp, not as an aesthetic failure, but as a lapse of forethought: "What everyone, including Greiman, seems to have forgotten is that the stamp would be canceled, a routine procedure that renders her design more or less indecipherable." It was further voted the worst stamp of 1995 by one of the philatelic magazines. Greiman observes: "When called by the writer to comment . . . I first asked what was voted the best stamp of '95. 'Civil War,' he responded. Then I will take it as a compliment that 'progress, freedom, equality' are at the bottom when 'war' is at the top! They seem to have things upside down! I asked what the average age of one of their readers was: 'Sixty-nine to seventy-two' was his answer. I also asked if the readers were mostly men, and the answer was yes." The final result proved the stamp to be not quite as popular among collectors as had been anticipated. After a year, as is the policy of the Postal Service for all commemoratives, the stamp was removed from circulation.

The Nineteenth Amendment was a great leap forward in American social and political equality. Similarly, this stamp was an audacious attempt to represent a significant issue and, through the same instrument, redefine the nature of U.S. stamp design. Although it did not meet expectations, the stamp is the nexus for a distinct visual signature and a significant idea.

41 Shots, 10 Cents

ARTIST: ART SPIEGELMAN

On a cold January night in 1999 four plainclothes New York City police officers, members of the special Street Crime Unit assigned to patrol the Bronx's Forty-third Precinct, fired a fusillade of forty-one bullets into twenty-two-year-old Amadou Diallo, a West African immigrant and street peddler. Police say he reached into his pocket, presumably for a weapon. A search of the body found that Diallo was unarmed.

Immediately, protests were instigated, investigations were launched, newspaper stories appeared, magazine columns were written, and public opinion was marshaled. Yet with all the media attention given to this tragedy, one form of redress was curiously absent: strong graphic commentary. With the notable exception of Art Spiegelman's cover for the *New Yorker* (March 8, 1999), not a single image was published that condemned this event of excessive police force. Why?

Decades earlier, graphic commentary was a common means of venting public concern, but in an age of tabloid electronic media it seems to have become an anachronism. With the exception of "editorial cartoons" found in most daily newspapers, which are fairly benign, or the more acerbic comics by Jules Feiffer syndicated to a limited number of newspapers, graphic commentators with distinct points of view have few mass venues to express themselves in ways that stir popular debate. At one time, artists such as Thomas Nast, the great nineteenth-century American cartoonist, or the acerbic twentieth-century graphic critic Robert Osborn created indelible visual commentaries that condemned corruption and lampooned moral bankruptcy;

today few of their heirs jiggle, much less rattle, cages. During the 1990s, even the master commentators, such as Ed Sorel and David Levine—who savagely skewered Richard Nixon during Watergate and Ronald Reagan during Irangate, seem to have mellowed somewhat.

The insufficient diet of strident visual commentary may account for why the cover of the *New Yorker* magazine by Spiegelman (b. 1948) got New York Mayor Giuliani, Police Commissioner Howard Safir, and the rank and file of the NYPD angry enough to publicly voice their ire. These days public officials are not easily incensed by cartoons. But this cover, by the *New Yorker*'s resident artist-provocateur and Pulitzer Prize–winning author of *Maus: A Survivor's Tale*, was an unexpected graphic barb at a pattern of excessive police force.

Rendered in a somewhat goofy, Depression-era comic-book style, the rather ironic illustration shows a police officer at a carnival shooting gallery with his pistol aimed at the silhouettes of a man on a cell phone, an old woman, and a child. The title "41 Shots, 10 Cents" left no question as to the real target. Proof that the artist hit his mark included an immediate rebuke by city and law enforcement officials, a demonstration by 250 off-duty police officers in front of the *New Yorker* offices, and a finger-wagging editorial in the *New York Post*. (It reads: "If you're burglarized, or your family is menaced by thugs, you should be consistent. Call Al Sharpton instead of 911. See where that gets you, Spiegelman, you creep.")

On the day of the publication, Spiegelman was flooded with interview requests ranging from National Public Radio to the *New York Times*. When was the last time that artwork, no less a cartoon illustration for even a top-notch magazine, garnered such intense heat? Not even the most scabrous political satires by the best cartoonists of our age—Sorel, Levine, Feiffer—have sparked this much media coverage.

Spiegelman acted upon a journalistic instinct once apparent in most social/political cartoonists but now atrophied, given the paucity of current venues for such critical work. Once local and national issues were fair game for jugular-squeezing cartoonists, a situation Spiegelman wants to revive as a *New Yorker* contributing editor and cartoon editor for *Details* magazine (where he assigns other cartoonists to do comic-strip essays on news events). In this case, identifying an important news story that had fallen off the front pages and was summarily fading from consciousness, he decided to create an image that would rekindle the issue. He called the *New Yorker* editor David Remnick, waking him from sleep, and convinced him to turn over this most valuable piece of magazine real estate to a provocative editorial statement. That is rare indeed.

Graphic journalism is a term that gets bandied about these days by artists, illustrators, and cartoonists who believe they are as credible as reporters and columnists. However, few editors trust artists to knowingly lead a publication into controversy. Editors invariably find practical excuses for why drawings or paintings are "too strong," or why it's okay to say something in words but not in pictures. So Remnick's decision to green-light Spiegelman's idea and put the month-old Diallo shooting on the cover was a courageous move for more than the obvious reasons. "Here is a magazine read by whites dealing with an issue that affects blacks," says Brent Staples, an editorial writer for the *New York Times*, "suggesting to me that conditions common to the black community are finally seeping out."

How Spiegelman used this opportunity raises a question of the effectiveness of graphic commentary in addressing such a charged topic. A cartoon usually has limited appeal and impact. Spiegelman's cover, however, combined the weight of the Diallo shooting with a drawing of a stereotypically comic cop in such a disturbing image that for a moment attention was drawn toward the artist, not the issue. Some critics contend that Spiegelman may have given the mayor and the police department an opportunity to sidestep the real issue of police excess while pretending to be victims of an irresponsible commentary that paints *all* cops as killers. In another artist's hands, an editorial cartoon on this theme may have been more restrained (which is to say it would not condemn the entire police force for the actions of a misguided few). But Spiegelman's brand of satire is neither polite nor compromising. At worse, Spiegelman is heavy-handed; at best, his cynicism ignites fierce debate.

Brent Staples asserts that the cover's positive upshot was the attention it drew to "how black and white lives are not valued equally." But not everyone applauded the artwork's efficacy. An editor of another publication, who declined to use his name, argues that Spiegelman did not go far enough in terms of linking the cartoon to reality. The targeted silhouettes, for example, are decidedly white; Spiegelman's decision in this regard generalizes the victim and, thus, unfairly suggests that picking off civilians is, indeed, a common police practice. If the intended message is that police abuse occurs more against minorities than whites, a precise representation is imperative for the argument to make sense. On the contrary, Staples insists, "if the characters were black, it wouldn't have the humor and would be read in a much different way. This was a black comedy that had to be humorous to succeed." Spiegelman says that silhouettes are neither black nor white. Nevertheless, others argue that the cover was something of a cheap shot, that to achieve attention Spiegelman reduced complex circumstances to absurd simplicity. "A successful political cartoon leaves one with something to think about and act upon," says Michael Valenti, a newspaper art director, "like George Grosz's great antiwar image 'Fit for Active Duty,' which shows a doctor saying those words while examining a skeleton. This makes you ponder how gruesome warfare is and prompts one into action against it. Spiegelman's cover, on the other hand, is a kind of unsubstantiated sensationalism that indicts all police and leaves the viewer unable to act."

Spiegelman is no stranger to criticism and no neophyte in the art of provocation. His first significant *New Yorker* cover showed a Hasidic Jew kissing an African-American woman, which was conceived in the wake of racial violence between two Brooklyn neighborhoods. The image argued that some kind of reconciliation was necessary to end hostilities. But Orthodox Jewish leaders loudly condemned it as an insult to their faith. Some of his other controversial covers have featured armed schoolchildren (to reflect a back-to-school autumnal theme), a crucified rabbit on a tax form (to mark the coincidence of Easter and the deadline for filing annual U.S. income tax returns), and a construction worker breast-feeding her baby on a girder high above the city (to celebrate Mother's Day).

Taken as a body of work, Spiegelman's *New Yorker* covers are not always drawn or painted in the most stunning manner, but they consistently evidence his intent to use the magazine as a soapbox. He does such in a fashion very similar to how Thomas Nast, Honoré Daumier, and George Grosz, in the nineteenth and early twentieth centuries, used their newspapers—*Harper's Weekly, Le Charivari*, and *De Pliete,* respectively—as outlets to express demands for social change. Or the way George Lois used to use the cover of *Esquire* magazine in the 1960s to make social/political commentary. Today there are only a handful of these outlets, and only the *New York Observer* publishes a weekly front-page color cartoon—often a caricature—that lampoons local and national events.

Spiegelman's "41 Shots, 10 Cents" may not be as polished as other *New Yorker* covers, but it is significant as an object lesson: Artists have the ability to stir emotion, and mass publications have the responsibility to influence policy—even at the risk of offending someone. At a time when constant Internet and TV exposure leads to information overload and makes people blasé about a presidential sex scandal and impeachment hearing, it is important to capture attention—particularly with a magazine cover, since it is not a fleeting image, and especially about an issue as significant as police violence. Spiegelman asserts that he was just doing his job as a graphic commentator, which, these days, is not done properly by most. Ultimately, he provides a model of graphic commentary for emulation by others.

MEDIA

If only American advertising agents had been exposed to German design at the turn of the century, posters and billboards might have made an aesthetic quantum leap into the twentieth century. Although the art poster was born in Paris prior to 1900—with works by Jules Chéret, Henri de Toulouse-Lautrec, and Alphonse Mucha—by the mid-teens, Berlin was the acknowledged capital of *Plakatstil* (poster style), a witty, colorful, and sophisticated graphic method. The clarion of German poster exuberance was a magazine called *Das Plakat*, which not only reproduced the finest posters from Germany and other European countries, but offered the highest editorial standards—underscored by estimable black-and-white and color printing—establishing high qualitative criteria that helped define graphic design between 1910 and 1920.

Das Plakat was launched in 1910 as the official journal of the Verein der Plakat Freunde (the Society for Friends of the Poster), founded in 1905 to champion art-poster collecting and increase scholarship. The society was one of a few collectors' groups throughout industrialized Europe, but *Das Plakat* was unique. During its comparatively short span it incomparably covered the poster scene and raised aesthetic, cultural, and legal issues about graphic design hitherto unexplored. In addition to surveying the most significant German—and, ultimately, international—work, the magazine addressed such themes as plagiarism and originality, art in the service of commerce, and the art of politics and propaganda. Through the years, its influence on design increased as did its circulation, from an initial print run of a mere two hundred copies to over ten thousand at its peak.

Das Plakat was the invention of Hans Josef Sachs, a chemist by training and dentist by profession, who as a teenager was obsessed with collecting French posters (he owned a renowned Sarah Bernhardt *affiche* signed by the artist Alphonse Mucha). In his twenties, Sachs became the leading private collector in Germany, with thousands of acquisitions. In 1905, at age twenty-four, he cofounded the Verein der Plakat Freunde with Hans Meyer and, after a few fits and starts, built it into a formidable national dues-supported organization with regional chapters throughout Germany. In 1909 he proposed to his board of directors the idea of publishing a journal that would represent the organization yet under his auspices become a much broader chronicle of poster art. Without Sachs's dedication, German commercial art would have developed apace, but as editor of *Das Plakat* he almost single-handedly promoted German *Gebrauchsgraphik* (commercial art) into an internationally respected applied art form.

Sachs's family had moved to Berlin in 1899. A few years later he was inspired when a group of advertising artists known as the Berliner Plakat enlivened that city's grand boulevards with posters that transformed the dominant commercial graphic style from painterly and decorative to graphic and stark. In the early 1900s a Berlin printing firm cum advertising agency, Hollerbaum and Schmidt, introduced a new wave of posters that wed the fluidity of French art nouveau and the bold linearity of German Jugendstil in a hybrid form that was comparatively economical. In 1906 a novice graphic artist named Lucian Bernhard won a competition that further changed the nature of poster design. Officiated by Hollerbaum and Schmidt's advertising manager, Ernest Growald, and sponsored by the Priester Match Company, which needed a fresh advertising image, the competition was open to all comers, with the ultimate prize of fifty marks and a printed poster. Bernhard submitted what at the time was an unprecedented, reductive composition that introduced a style called *Sachplakat* (object poster), characterized by the rejection of all ornament in favor of an unambiguous image of the product (in this case twin red- and yellow-tipped wooden matches), with the only text being the brand name in block letters.

The *Sachplakat* monumentalized the mundane—a typewriter, shoes, matches—and in this sense was the proto-manifestation of pop art in the twentieth century. Compared to the more ornate posters on Berlin hoardings, the Priester composition was an eye-stopper that showcased its creator as Berlin's foremost poster-maker. Sachs quickly befriended young Bernhard. (In fact, their relationship continued throughout the run of the magazine and even after their emigration to the United States.)

Bernhard was invited by Sachs to design the society's logo and stationery; the society's mascot that he developed was a witty drawing of the back of a slightly hunched woman clad in nineteenth-century garb looking through pince-nez at the black-letter logotype, as if it were a poster. He also became one of its board members. The magazine devoted an entire issue in 1916 to Bernhard's prolific oeuvre and frequently showcased his new individual works. Bernhard also helped Sachs and Meyer identify worthy artists and new trends. That *Das Plakat* favored the *Sachplakat* sensibilities was no accident; Bernhard had strong ties to Hollerbaum and Schmidt, and they, in turn, took out many advertising pages in the magazine.

Sachs had only minimal interest in the actual business of advertising. He simply loved the poster. And as a connoisseur rather than a professional he had the freedom to study the poster more for its formal than functional attributes. He once wrote, "Words like type area, nonpareil, scrum, offset, and coated paper were all Greek to me." But he was not a dilettante. In fact, before he launched *Das Plakat* he took a leave of absence from his dental practice to apprentice with a "typographically sophisticated" printer who gave him a crash course in publishing. *Das Plakat* was not, therefore, an arcane journal for aesthetes laden with academic art-historical jargon. Given the stiff conventions of German writing and typography (black letter was commonly used) at the time, the magazine's text was fairly accessible and very informative. From a visual standpoint, generous use of expensive color plates and tip-ins made *Das Plakat* the most ambitious magazine published at that time—not only among periodicals about art and design but of those about any subject.

In the tradition of German (and European) art/culture magazines that preceded it (e.g., *Jugend*), each issue of the bimonthly *Das Plakat* had a different cover and masthead; the covers were designed as miniposters, with emphasis on a central, often abstracted image. Most covers were printed on a bulky, uncoated stock that allowed for concentrated color saturation, and occasionally a special paper or ink was used for aesthetic effect. The interior layout was more or less consistent—mostly black-letter type (Antiqua designed by Bernhard) set in justified columns. The illustrations were frequently mortised out of the columns and framed inside black borders. The magazine's format preceded the era of white space and cinematic pacing of images so common today; nevertheless, *Das Plakat* was profusely illustrated and lively.

The popularity of the poster and other forms of *Gebrauchsgraphik* during the early teens was similar to the boom in television in the 1950s. More than merely a selling tool, the poster was street art that addressed the public in both utilitarian and aesthetic ways—as message and form. This fascination with the object accounted for the increase in the society's membership and the concomitant rise in *Das Plakat*'s readership. Although Sachs continued to maintain his dental practice, he was nevertheless an indefatigable poster impresario, constantly mounting regional poster exhibitions and competitions for businesses in the market for fresh poster art.

In 1914, at the outbreak of the Great War, Sachs was drafted into the army and left editorial duties to Hans Meyer and another director, Rudi Bleistein. But in 1915 Sachs's collaborators were drafted, and he was released from service to assume sole editorship and authorship (using different pen names). Without Sachs's force of will the magazine would surely have succumbed to wartime privations, but he maintained operation by attending to the wartime propaganda needs of the imperial government. Articles in *Das Plakat* reported on war bond campaigns and exhibited posters of both Allied and belligerent nations. After the war the new Weimar Republic sought out the services of the society to develop new postage stamps; Sachs helped organize a competition and jury. He also published a supplement that exclusively covered the evolution of political posters in an attempt to influence contemporary practice. Moreover, *Das Plakat* turned its attention to media other than posters, including articles on trademarks, typefaces, and the art of *Notgeld*, ersatz currency or scrip regionally produced to offset rampant postwar German inflation. Sachs was increasingly concerned with international copyright protection, and in 1913 he dedicated an entire supplement to the theme of plagiarism, in which he discussed the subtle distinctions between influence and theft.

The magazine continued to publish until 1921, when internal disagreements among the society's members and its board of directors began to have deleterious effect on operating decisions. Problems developed between new and older chapters; indeed, the society's expansion outside Berlin led to a breakdown of central control. Sachs ultimately left under a cloud of acrimony. Embittered by the experience he folded the magazine and shelved his own poster collection in the attic of his Berlin house, left unseen by him for three years. When afterward he decided to establish a poster museum in a brand-new building, a fire erupted there and destroyed a portion of the collection. In 1926 another space was built to house, display, and protect posters, and he made plans to start a museum for *Gebrauchsgraphik*. The Nazis, however, had other plans.

In 1937 Sachs mounted his last exhibit at the Jewish Museum in Berlin. That year he was detained for twenty-four hours by the Gestapo and forbidden from owning any politically related materials. His entire collection was confiscated by order of the minister of propaganda, Joseph Goebbels, and earmarked to be the basis for a new museum dedicated to the art of commerce. Sachs was sent to Sachsenhausen concentration camp in 1939 but after a few weeks was released; he emigrated with his family to London and then New York with only a few of his posters. He sold thirty by Toulouse-Lautrec for $500 to make ends meet before earning his dental license in New York. He spent the rest of his life as a dentist and in 1965 received reparations for his stolen collection, which he thought had been completely destroyed. In fact, many were miraculously preserved. Some were sold at auction, others retained by the Berlin Museum of German History.

Das Plakat is a tribute to Sachs's diverse artistic interests, but it is even more important as a document of the early period of European commercialization and industrialization as seen through the lens of graphic art and design. While Sachs was concerned less with the function than with the end product of design and, therefore, promoted the poster as transcendent art form, *Das Plakat* is a chronicle of how business patronage and graphic virtuosity gave birth to modern graphic design.

In an article titled "Art as a Means to an End," advertising pioneer Earnest Elmo Calkins argued that unlike anything else in the realm of aesthetics, art is subject to such constant scrutiny that each innovation "adopted by the radicals" is in turn resisted by the conservatives, then tolerated, and finally copied until it too becomes "old stuff and the vanguard are already in full cry after something newer." Although this has a familiar and current ring, Calkins's statement appeared in the first article in the premier issue of *Advertising Arts* on January 8, 1930, marking a new and sophisticated way of addressing graphic and advertising art.

This unique trade magazine sought to integrate modern art into stodgy mainstream commercial culture. While other American trade journals promoted the status quo, *Advertising Arts,* a perfect-bound monthly supplement of the weekly trade magazine *Advertising and Selling,* professed ways to integrate new design fashions and progressive ideas "adopted by radicals" into conventional practice. Although it could only report on rather than actually originate these advancements, it nonetheless presented them with such practical fervor that the magazine became the vortex of progressive American graphic and industrial design of the era.

Advertising Arts is not to be confused, however, with the radical European design manifestos issued by constructivists, futurists, or the Bauhaus, which introduced the New Typography and changed visual practice and perception. In the 1920s, the United States did not have design or advertising avant-garde rooted in utopian principles. The United States was resolutely and unapologetically capitalist, and advertising was the foremost means of influencing the consumer. Commercialism was far more advanced here than in Europe, yet our marketing strategies were much more conventional and word-based. In Europe, quotidian "publicity" was more image-oriented, and modern avant-garde design was an alternative to antiquated aesthetics born of bourgeois culture and politics. In the United States, modernistic design was a product of the commercial concept known as forced (or style) obsolescence, devised by Calkins as a somewhat devious way to encourage consumers to "move the goods" despite the ravages of a worldwide economic depression.

When *Advertising Arts* made its debut during the Great Depression, the economy was at its nadir and desperation was at its zenith. Unless advertising and public relations men like Calkins could help resuscitate the economy, the nation would plummet further into the abyss—and with it the advertising industry. *Advertising Arts,* edited by Frederick C. Kendall and Ruth Fleischer, was developed as a vehicle to encourage innovative work and celebrate the determination of advertising designers to manipulate popular perception using pseudo-science. It was indeed a magazine with a mission. So rather than publishing the usual diet of gossip, trade talk, and technical notices, Kendall and Fleischer tapped the movers and shakers of what was then called "art for industry" to flag the new progressivism. Touting their own achievements as "artists" and imbuing art with commercial value involved a massive public relations effort that required the most articulate practitioners. Granted, the readers of *Advertising Arts* were primarily other advertising artists and designers, but nonetheless the magazine gained authority within the offices and boardrooms of industry. The articles validated contemporary design in ways that businessmen could understand.

The magazine served as a blueprint for how to market modernity as both an ethos and a style—in print, on packages, and as industrial wares. For their part, the writers, including influential graphic and industrial artists such as Lucian Bernhard, Rene Clark, Clarence P. Hornung, Paul Hollister, Norman Bel Geddes, and Rockwell Kent, passionately advocated the new. In "Modern Layouts Must Sell Rather Than Startle," for example, design pundit Frank H. Young writes: "Daring originality in the use of new forms, new patterns, new methods of organization and bizarre color effects is the keynote of modern layout and is achieving the startling results we see today." At the same time, however, *Advertising Arts* cautioned against excess, as is indicated in this observation by Young: "In some instances enthusiasm for modernism has overshadowed good judgement and the all-important selling message is completely destroyed."

Selling was the real credo of *Advertising Arts,* despite some grand pronouncements on the sanctity of art, such as Rockwell Kent's statement in the first issue: "[Art] is the concept of the visual mind. It is concerned with images and not ideas. Art is imagination." Art was used in various forms to help create environments that enticed consumers to purchase products, whether they needed them or not. This is not to say that all consumer products were celebrated by the magazine; to the contrary, not all products were packaged in the manner supported by

Advertising Arts. Its bias was toward approaches that were decorative or modernistic rather than toward nonornamental modern; everything else was ignored.

Advertising Arts promulgated a design fashion unique to the United States during the early 1930s, called the streamline style. Unlike the elegant austerity of the Bauhaus and kindred European movements, where the right angle and reductive form was paramount, this was a futuristic mannerism based on sleek and smooth aerodynamic design. Planes, trains, and cars were given the swooped-back appearance (not unlike design styles applied today) that symbolizes speed and motion. Consequently, type and image were designed to echo that sensibility. As a result, the airbrush became the medium of choice, and all futuristic mannerisms, be they practical or symbolic, were encouraged. There was a clarion call to "make it modern"—and "it" was anything that could be designed.

Clarence P. Hornung, a package and logo designer who later published influential books on antique design resources, argued somewhat prosaically in *Advertising Arts*, "The average American trade-mark is born of late Victorian ancestry. It is colorless in dress, overwrought in detail, sedate and somber in mien. Thrown into modern advertising society, it evinces the propriety of gingham and 'yellow tans' at a formal function." His solution was to make trademarks modern by streamlining and geometrizing. In *Advertising Arts,* his words were law. Lucian Bernhard, the master German poster artist who in the United States designed the era's most emblematic typefaces, announced in his equally authoritative *Advertising Arts* article, "Putting Beauty into Industry," that the new desire for "beauty in industrial products, only recently started in this country, has not come from the side of manufacturers," suggesting that the modernistic designer must be responsible for recasting American products. And these are but two of the many examples of the magazine's obsession with modernization as the panacea for the world's ills (and if Calkins was to be believed, it was the cure for all the United States' economic woes). Therefore, it is fascinating that in the first issue the *Advertising Arts* editors featured "The Bolshevik Billboard" as a possible direction that should be taken by capitalist advertising agencies.

Advertising Arts continued publishing until the late 1930s but ceased, when *Advertising and Selling* folded, prior to the 1939 New York World's Fair; the World of Tomorrow, where so many of the modern graphic, package, and industrial design concepts championed by the magazine were realized. By that time it also had a viable competitor, *PM* (later *AD*) magazine, a graphic design journal launched in 1934 by the Composing Room type shop, which went further in its investigation of the Bauhaus and the New Typography while being more balanced in its coverage of traditional forms. But *Advertising Arts* maintained a niche and succeeded in raising the level of design sophistication through advocacy of the "modernistic." And today, over sixty years later, it remains an important historical document in defining the evolution from workaday commercial art to sophisticated graphic design.

Photography records the gamut of feelings written on the human face, the beauty of the earth and skies that man has inherited, and the wealth and confusion man has created.

—Edward Steichen, *Time* magazine (1961)

Photography changed how the world was recorded. Likewise the "picture magazine" changed how the world was seen. The photojournalist Edward Steichen referred to this genre as a "major force in explaining man to man." But just as the invention of the photograph in the early nineteenth century made representational painting obsolete, during the past thirty years the spontaneity and immediacy of that other revolutionary medium, television, has made the picture magazine an anachronism.

Yet before television, picture magazines with rotogravure pages awash with halftones, printed with luminescent inks on velvety paper, were veritable eyes on the world. Photography may have been static, but, when edited like a motion picture and narratively paced to tell a story, the images of never-before-recorded sights offered audiences the same drama—and more detail—than any newsreel. Innovative editors at the leading magazines advanced revolutionary story-telling ideas that altered the way photography was used and perceived. With the advent of faster films and lightweight cameras, photography was freed from the confines of the studio; photographers were encouraged to capture realities that had been previously hidden in the shadows.

As photography evolved from single documentary images into visual essays, the forms and formats of presentation changed as well. From the mid-nineteenth to the early–twentieth century, the picture magazine evolved from a repository of drawn and engraved facsimiles of daguerreotypes into albums of real photographs. With new technology in place, innovation was inevitable. Soon sequences of integrated texts and images, designed to capture and guide the eye, were common methods of presenting current events of social, cultural, and political import.

While photojournalism (though not officially referred to as such) had been practiced since 1855, when Roger Fenton made history photographing the Crimean War, the ability to reproduce photographs was really possible only after 1880, when Stephen H. Horgan's invention of the halftone was tested at the *New York Daily Graphic* and ultimately improved upon by the *New York Times*. Moreover, prior to 1880, cameras were so large and heavy that they impeded candid or spot news coverage. That is, until the Eastman Kodak Company reduced the camera to a little box, which launched a huge amateur photography fad in Europe and America (and encouraged publication of amateur photography magazines). These pictures were often informal; they were the turn-of-the-century equivalent of Polaroid's instant pictures in the 1960s and of digital snaps today—immediate photographic gratification.

Professionally speaking, the most important technological advance occurred in Germany after World War I. In 1925, two compact cameras, the Ermanox and the Leica, were marketed to professional shooters. These cameras made unobtrusive photography possible while providing an excellent negative for crisp reproduction. The Leica was the first small camera to use a "roll" of film (actually, standard motion-picture film) and was fitted with interchangeable lenses and a range finder. The Ermanox was equally efficient, although it used small glass plates, which were soon superseded by film. The small camera became merely an extra appendage, freeing the shooter to make quick judgments.

One of the chief beneficiaries of this new technology was the weekly *Berliner Illustrierte Zeitung,* then the most progressive of the early picture magazines, whose photographers elevated candid photography to high art and viable journalism. *BIZ* captured the artistic tumult and political turmoil of the 1920s and bore witness to extraordinary global events in a way unlike any other picture magazine. Its photographers—precursors of the now-pesky paparazzi—reveled in shooting candid poses of the famous and infamous. And in concert with a new breed of "photo" editor they set standards for the picture magazine built on what photographer Erich Salomon called *Bildjournalismus,* or photojournalism. In the decades that followed, *BIZ* was a model for imitators and a point of departure for innovators.

Erich Salomon fathered the candid news picture for *BIZ* and dubbed himself "photo-journalist." Although a lawyer by profession, once he was bitten by the camera bug, he devoted his life to photography. By force of will, tempered by an acute understanding of the social graces, he secured entrance to the halls of government, homes of the powerful, and hideaways of the well-to-do. He devised intricate ways to capture the rich and famous unawares on film, and he published these photographs with impunity. He busted the formal traditions that the high-and-mighty found acceptable and brought mythic figures down to size. Today these images, collected in books, are vivid documents of his times.

When Salomon began shooting in the late 1920s, Kurt Szafranski was appointed editor-in-chief of *BIZ* and its sister publication, the monthly *Die Dame*. Both magazines were part of the House of Ullstein, Germany's largest periodical publisher. Salomon was already working in Ullstein's promotion department when photography became his obsession. He showed Szafranski his now-famous candid pictures of exhausted delegates to the League of Nations and was immediately awarded a contract to work for *BIZ*. Szafranski also employed other pioneers of photojournalism—Martin Munkacsi, the action photographer, and André Kertész, then a travel photographer.

Szafranski and his colleague, Kurt Korff (both of whom eventually moved to *Life* magazine in New York), were early experimenters with the essay approach—a form that required a variety of pictures and concise captions linked together to build impact and drama. According to the principle of the "Third Effect," when two pictures are brought together and positioned side by side, each picture's individual effect is enhanced by the reader's interpretive powers. This juxtaposition was sometimes possible with disparate images but usually required thematic pictures reproduced in radically different scales. Sometimes, it would be accomplished with serious conceptual photographs; at other times, novelty pictures—such as a stark close-up of a horse's head next to, say, a close crop of a similarly featured human's head—made a comic statement. Yet for all their innovation, *BIZ*'s photographic essays were usually strained juxtapositions of pictures, not stories in the truest sense. The key to success—the integration of image, idea, and words—was frequently lost amid poor and ineffectual layouts.

Münchener Illustrierte Presse, a popular Bavarian picture magazine, however, took the photograph and ran with it. Its editor and art director was a young Hungarian émigré named Stefan Lorant, who, before leaving his native Budapest in his early twenties, was already an accomplished photographer and film director. He decided to settle in Munich rather than America or England because he was fluent in German. Fortuitously, he fell into the job as assistant to the editor of *MIP* and, owing to his remarkable energy and ambition, was very soon afterward named its photo editor. Lorant was inspired by *Berliner Illustrierte Zeitung,* yet he also understood that it had failed to use photographs as effective narrative components.

Over the course of a few years, he guided *MIP* into a realm of unique photographic endeavor. Partly through intuition, partly through basic inquisitiveness, he discerned exactly what was wanted of a picture journal and directed photographers to follow his vision. Lorant convinced Erich Salomon to contribute to *MIP* and also sought out new talents who, as he said, "not only took beautiful pictures but who had similar curiosity and journalistic savvy." An elite corps was assembled, including Felix H. Man, Georg and Tim Gidal, Umbo, Kurt Hubschmann, and Alfred Eisenstaedt (who was later hired by Henry Luce to shoot for *Life* magazine).

Lorant said that he encouraged photographers "to travel and shoot as many pictures as possible" so that he could mold an essay. Editorial space was no object; a good feature story would run for as many pages as warranted. Lorant, who was an admitted autocrat, designed the layouts himself. Although the basic layout conventions already existed, Lorant introduced certain design tropes, including what might be criticized today as excessive use of geometric borders, overlapping photographs, and silhouettes. But despite a tendency to fiddle, he acknowledged that his most successful layouts were those where he left pictures alone. He believed that when astutely edited and dramatically cropped, one striking picture reinforced the next and so furthered the narrative. He was partial to photographs that emphasized pure human expression. And one of his most famous assignments was sending Felix H. Man to spend a day with Mussolini in Rome. The photos—an exclusive—were extraordinary exposés of a day in the life of the duce in the course of his mundane acts of power. Lorant's layout focused on two key, though contrasting, features: Mussolini's rarely seen, relaxed body in the context of his charged imperial surroundings.

Although *MIP* was not devotedly partisan, total objectivity in a Weimar Germany fraught with dissonant ideologies and political violence was difficult. *MIP*'s picture exposés often focused on the darker side of Nazi rallies and leaders. It wasn't surprising, therefore, that Lorant was summarily imprisoned when Adolf Hitler assumed power in 1933. Had it not been for the persistence of his wife, a well-known German actress at the time, in obtaining his release (and the fact that he was still a Hungarian citizen), Lorant's future would have been bleak. After being released, he emigrated to England, wrote best-selling book entitled *I Was Hitler's Prisoner,* and launched two new picture magazines: the *Weekly Illustrated* in 1934 and *Picture Post* in 1938. Between these two publishing milestones, Lorant also founded *Lilliput,* a humor magazine to rival the venerable *Punch.* After the war he emigrated to the United States, where he edited documentary picture books.

During the late 1920s and 1930s, the impact of German *Bildjournalismus* had spread to many of the world's capitals, but none more so than Paris. *Paris Match* was arguably the most popular picture magazine, but the newsweekly *VU,* founded in 1928 and edited by Lucien Vogel, a photographer and publisher of *La Gazette du Bon Ton* and *Jardin des Modes,* was the most innovative in terms of the picture essay. Vogel had always been interested more in politics than in fashion and was fascinated by the power of photography to document (indeed, comment upon) current events. The early issues of the magazine had an erratic mix of politics, sports, culture, and spot news as well as carrying book excerpts about the adventures of Babar the Elephant by Vogel's brother-in-law, Jean de Brunhoff. But in later years photographers like André Kertész, Robert Capa, and Brassaï provided memorable reportage. Capa's most famous photograph, which depicted a Spanish loyalist soldier in midfall who had been hit by a fascist's bullet, was originally published in *VU.*

Vogel believed that graphic design was critical to the success of his magazine. *VU*'s logo was designed by French poster artist A. M. Cassandre while Charles Peignot, proprietor of the Deberny and Peignot Foundry, consulted on interior typography. A Russian émigré, Irene Lidova, was the first art director; beginning in 1933, her layout assistant was another Russian, Alexander Liberman. He assumed her position a few years later (and subsequently became the art director of *Vogue* and the creative director of all Condé Nast publications until his retirement in 1995).

Vogel knew the trick of how to make pictures tell a story. One of his pioneering efforts was the double-truck spread, for which a strong photograph was greatly enlarged to mammoth proportions. Pacing photos from large to small to huge to small again provided impact and surprise. Vogel had a profound influence on Liberman, who later finely tuned the journalistic photo essays in *VU*. He ascribed his ability to freely manipulate pictures to the fact that "there was no cult of photography at that time." He could edit photographs and design layouts without the kind of interference from egotistic photographers that is often tolerated today. He further spent long periods ensconced in the darkroom, projecting photos onto layout sheets, cropping and juxtaposing images. He also played with photomontage. Eventually, he took responsibility for *VU*'s covers. Vogel would often make rough sketches that Liberman would execute via photomontage (signing them "Alexandre").

By 1936, Vogel's left-wing leanings had a profound effect on *VU*'s overall content (essays excoriating the fascists became more frequent), and the magazine's bias was alienating advertisers as France was turning more vociferously toward the right. Owing to diminishing capital, Vogel was forced to sell the magazine to a right-wing businessman who kept Liberman on as managing editor for a year. Ultimately Liberman could not tolerate *VU*'s new political orientation. After his departure, the quality of *VU*'s photographic essays declined.

Photography as both information and propaganda medium did not go unnoticed by manipulators of thought and mind. Throughout Europe, and especially in Germany, the picture magazine was used to win the hearts and minds of certain constituencies. Among the most influential of these was the socialist/communist-inspired *Arbeiter-Illustrierte Zeitung* (Worker's Illustrated News), which began in 1921 as an offshoot of *Sowjet Russland im Bild* (Soviet Russia in Pictures), designed to propagate a positive image of the Bolshevik workers' paradise. *AIZ* was edited by Willi Münzenberg, who was a fervent supporter of the Russian Revolution and saw the picture magazine as a vehicle for aiding German workers in their struggle against capitalism.

When *AIZ* began, obtaining photographs that addressed workers' concerns from the leading picture agencies was difficult. Münzenberg developed a strategy to encourage societies of amateur photographers who would, in turn, become photo correspondents. In Hamburg, in 1926, he established the first Worker Photographer group, which grew into a network of viable shooters throughout Germany and the Soviet Union. He further founded a magazine called *Der Arbeiter Fotograf* (The Worker Photographer), which offered technical and ideological assistance.

Bertolt Brecht once wrote Münzenberg that "the camera can lie just like the typesetting machine. The task of *AIZ* to serve truth and reproduce real facts is of immense importance, and, it seems to me, has been achieved splendidly." Actually, while the photographs in *AIZ* were objective accounts of workers' triumphs, the layouts often served to heroicize (and therefore politicize) the activities covered. Except for its ideological orientation, *AIZ* was really no different than the Nazi counterpart, the *Illustrierte Beobachter* (founded in 1926), which employed similar photojournalistic conventions. But when the Nazis assumed power in 1933, *AIZ* was deemed contraband.

Three years earlier (1930), John Heartfield, who was then art director and copublisher of the *Malik Verlag*, had begun doing satiric photomontages (a marriage of dada and caricature) that graphically ripped the facade off Nazi leaders and functionaries. Montage was key to *AIZ* in the years of the Nazi ascendancy because, with the Worker Photographer Movement in Germany officially crushed, obtaining usable (socialist) imagery was impossible. Only through photomontage—the ironic juxtapositions of realities in the service of polemics—could the magazine continue to convey strong messages.

The last issue of *AIZ* to be published in Berlin was dated March 5, 1933; Münzenberg then moved the operation to Prague. But *AIZ* went from a circulation of 500,000 copies in Germany to around 12,000 in Prague. Attempts to circulate a smuggled miniature version into Germany were unsuccessful. In 1936 *AIZ* was renamed *Volks Illustriete;* two years later, when German occupation of Czechoslovakia was imminent, the magazine was moved to France, where it published only one issue. Until *AIZ* ceased publication in 1938, it was a satiric thorn in the side of the Nazi régime. Most of the picture stories are now forgotten, but Heartfield's photomontages are celebrated today as prime documents of agitation and protest.

AIZ influenced *USSR in Construction,* which published monthly between 1930 and 1940. Founded by Maxim Gorky, its declared editorial mission was to "reflect in photography the whole scope and variety of the construction work now going on in the USSR." Toward this aim *USSR in Construction* was published in editions of five different languages—German, English, French, Spanish, and Russian. As rotogravure magazines go, with its multiple die-cuts, inserts, and gatefolds, it was exceedingly more lush and inventive than others of its genre. The magazine employed the leading Soviet documentary photographers, including Max Alpert and Georgy Petrusive, and the most prominent graphic designers, notably Lazar El Lissitzky and Alexander Rodchenko (with Varvara Stepanova). Constructivist typographer Solomon Telingater was also brought in on occasion to design the type.

Early issues contained unremarkable pictorial sequences with expanded captions. But by 1931, when John Heartfield arrived in Moscow for an extended visit, he was invited to design an issue on the Soviet petroleum industry. His photographic cover showing oil derricks cropped on a dynamic incline was a stunning departure from the previous, somewhat bland, typographic treatments. The magazine's nameplate (or title) was composed in a dynamic manner using sans serif letters thrusting, like a gusher of oil itself, toward the sky. Heartfield showed that a graphic designer was capable of transforming the most common photographs into dramatic tableaux. Nevertheless, another two years passed before the editors allowed Lissitzky the freedom to make radical changes in layout and typography.

Both Heartfield and Lissitzky contributed something that had been missing: a sense of narrative. Lissitzky, who had been practicing book design, seamlessly integrated pictures and text and allowed generous space for mammoth blowups of documentary photos and heroic photomontages across spreads and gatefolds. Juxtaposing unaltered and manipulated images told the story of Stalin's "glorious" régime and the progress that technology and industry brought to the post-revolutionary Soviet Union. Gradually, *USSR in Construction* evolved a style of visual rhetoric characteristic of socialist realism. Maxim Gorky introduced *USSR in Construction,* pushed the boundaries of this genre, and became a paradigm of pictorial propaganda later used in magazines published in fascist Italy and Nazi Germany. Indeed many of tropes—overlapping pictures, multiple duotones on a spread, mortised inserts—have ultimately been used in commercial catalogs and corporate annual reports. Maxim Gorky introduced the concept of "romantic realism," which addressed the idyllic future of the state. But the magazine folded during the war years and returned afterward in a smaller size and with more mundane layouts.

Photography is a uniquely viable medium (and inexhaustible art form); as practiced in these pioneer picture magazines, the journalistic photo essay is all but extinct (except in coffee-table art books). Despite the attempts of such contemporary magazines as *Double Take* and *Blind Spot,* the photography magazine, that weekly window of news and views, is an anomaly today.

West

DESIGNER: MIKE SALISBURY

Rarely is a magazine's cover as well designed as its interior (presuming that the interior is well designed). The cover is such a charged piece of editorial real estate that few publishers and editors are willing to relinquish control over its appearance to a designer (or art director) alone. Instead, most magazine covers are determined by marketing and editorial requisites and, therefore, laden with teaser cover lines surrounding a fairly obvious image (a photograph of a celebrity, often the flavor of the moment). Too many magazine covers look the same month after month after month.

Of course, there have been some notable exceptions, and one of the most extraordinary of these was *West* magazine, the Sunday supplement of the *Los Angeles Times,* art directed and designed by Mike Salisbury (b. 1946) from 1967 to 1972. Each cover was an uncommon visual experience smartly conceived to pique and engage the reader—from the issue with a trompe l'oeil of house flies crawling over the masthead to one of a human skull with red wax lips over the headline "SMACK." *West's* covers were not false advertising either. The inside was just as sharp as the front.

A Sunday supplement is not governed by the same marketing regulations that constrict the design of a newsstand magazine. Since the supplement has a decidedly captive audience, it need only compete with other sections of the same newspaper. In the days before color was common throughout American newspapers, the supplement was a colorful treat sandwiched between black and white pulp. But not all Sunday supplements were or are created equal. The chemistry between publisher, editor, and art director determines whether the publishing opportunity is taken or missed. In its day, *West* was far superior to most Sunday magazines produced by other major newspapers, and the model against which all other supplements (and many newsstand magazines) were measured.

Before Salisbury, a native Los Angeleno, joined *West* in 1967 he was a surfer with a fairly checkered early career. He began in Chicago, at *Playboy*, where under art director Art Paul he learned about the finer aspects of magazine design ("I still don't think that there's a better body face for a magazine than *Playboy's* Baskerville 9/10," he says). After a year, he returned to Los Angeles to an advertising agency job, where he worked along with the following notables: Terry Gilliam, later of Monty Python; Ed Ruscha, who became known for his paintings and photographs of vernacular architecture; and Joel Siegel, who moved on to become an ABC television commentator. "Joel introduced me to Yiddish, liberal Democratic politics, and the importance of vintage advertising design. But most important, he told me that the *Los Angeles Times* had a year-old magazine in need of an art director," recalls Salisbury, who also says that his friends warned him not to take the job because the *Times* was "very square." The late 1960s was a conservative period for newspapers, before they were forced to compete with the growing electronic media. But the period also nourished a counterculture, and even the most conservative Los Angeles media could not afford to ignore the zeitgeist.

Salisbury leapt at the opportunity to art direct and design his own magazine and "have some fun" in the bargain. At the same time, a new publisher/editor, Jim Bellows (who later created the television show *Entertainment Tonight*), was hired to revitalize the magazine. He, in turn, guaranteed Salisbury freedom to make a radical transformation. In the original *West*, articles started on single pages on the left and ran through the book on partial pages, a format that, Salisbury notes, "felt wrong to me. So, using what I learned at *Playboy*, I first reformatted the magazine to emphasize feature spreads, then went to work on the covers."

West's early covers were bland stock shots of Southern California, which was the exact trope employed by another *Times* Sunday supplement for home interiors. Influenced by the "Big Idea" method that prevailed in New York advertising and editorial at the time, Salisbury decided to focus on ideas in conceptual art and photography. Although this was not his invention—he admits being influenced by George Lois's conceptually acute *Esquire* covers—his approach was somewhat different in its variegated use of symbolic objects, metaphorical ideas, and comic illustration. He further cites the influences of the demonstratively art directed *Twen* of Germany and *Nova* of England (which he later worked for as a freelance photographer) in his decision to integrate expressive typography and narrative illustration and photography. Salisbury encouraged creativity in others. "When I assigned art or photography, I asked [the artists] to contribute their impressions, just as the writers did." He admired film titles by Saul Bass and Steve Frankfurt, which had an impact on his own kinetic pacing and storytelling. He did not use art or pictures gratuitously but rather as components of cinematic layouts. "I tried to deal with the value of negative space and then I tried to undesign," he says of this process.

Salisbury did not simply create a frame for *West's* content. He also molded that content according to his own interests, authoring articles on pop culture, such as Coca-Cola art, Levi's advertising, Los Angeles dwellings, orange-crate labels, custom cars, and more. *West* was the first mass-audience publication to use these highly visual features, designed in a totally novel "catalog style," where radical scale changes gave breadth and motion to the images; such artifacts had never been seriously employed (or ephemerally employed, for that matter) by other periodicals aimed at a wide readership.

Salisbury was a compulsive experimenter; since *West* was a weekly magazine, he had many opportunities to play. "I could learn and grow and be depressed when an idea didn't work," he says about the emotional highs and lows. But not all of *West* was a creative Shangri-La. There were various endemic business hurdles to overcome, and the most challenging was to design the dread advertorials—hybrid features that attempted to look like editorial content while hawking a product. "Rather than roll over and do it lame or with stock," Salisbury explains, "I tried to put a concept into these themes. Like dressing showgirls in custom outfits to match the new cars we were advertising or ripping off the look of *National Geographic* for a travel feature."

West was a total creative package, but it will be best remembered for covers that enticed the reader while influencing publication design. Among the most exciting, and perhaps the most imitated, was an extreme close-up of Charlie Chaplin—just his emblematic eyes and mustache— on a white field with only a line of headline type and the logo on the page. Like a stop sign, the Chaplin image forced the reader to look twice before deciphering the image, but the result was unique. "How many people had portrayed Chaplin graphically before me?" asks Salisbury about the challenge involved in portraying the iconic comic. "I tried to use the medium as part of the message—the cover of the magazine became his face." Chaplin was also an attempt, he says, "at that classic Rand-era style of minimalism." The previously mentioned housefly cover, which was basically an empty page with only the masthead on top and some pesky flies casting small shadows on the page, was, says Salisbury, influenced by Ed Ruscha, who painted flies spelling out words. "I tried to use the flatness of print as an element to create the illusion of real flies on the paper." Incidentally, this was one of many cases when Salisbury had the accompanying article—a story about bugs—written to fit the art. "Both of these covers are not visual puns, but they are examples of what is for me almost pure design," he adds.

The five-year ride with *West* ended when Salisbury admittedly "got too big for my britches." *West* became the most-read part of the newspaper and he liked to think "it was all because of the content and ideas I added. I was trying to stimulate and educate. Design was the vehicle to do that." But despite assurances to the contrary, the editor was really "not the most challenging or receptive, and the subeditors were jealous of my influence, except for one, Nino Tossi, who went to *City* [film director Francis Ford Coppola's magazine] with me. So I bitched to Bellows. I was spoiled and arrogant, like a minor rock star." In response Bellows hired a new editor. "He had to," adds Salisbury, ". . . because he was also getting heat from the *Times* about our liberal attitudes. Anyhow, my first encounter with the new editor was over some art that I had commissioned by [underground cartoonist] Robert Williams to illustrate the California funeral business. Williams was a cross between George Harris, the car customizer, and Hieronymous

Bosch, and his art was spiritually akin to Jessica Mitford's *American Way of Death* [an exposé of funeral homes]. The new editor was like an actor playing an editor—he looked like a male model for *Esquire* of the 1940s and had no sense of humor, no sense of irony, and no appreciation for design, art, or journalism. He was no fun, so I quit." Salisbury says he was begged to stay on, which he did, but one year later the *Times* killed *West*.

Salisbury moved to San Francisco ("I was a carpetbagger") to become art director of *Rolling Stone*, which by then (1973–1974) was strictly a newsstand magazine, a fact that limited his ability to do "high concept" covers. Afterward, from 1975 to 1976, he went to work for the short-lived magazine *City*, where he once again tried to rekindle the spirit of *West*. Although *City* seemed to allow more opportunities for innovation, the "design purity" that Salisbury had attained with *West's* covers was somehow more difficult to recapture.

Back in 1968, underground comix attacked the peremptory values of a conservative society that less than a decade earlier had imposed strict rules of conduct on its youth. During the early to mid-1950s, at the height of the social and political purges known as McCarthyism, Congress was engaged in an investigative frenzy to root out Communists in government and adverse influences on the culture at large. They believed that American kids—the offspring of a victorious postwar nation—were susceptible to forces of evil filtered into the collective unconscious through such inflammatory media as comic books. Threatened with government regulations and fearing diminished profits, the comics industry agreed to police itself through the Comics Code Authority, which, like the film industry's Hays Office, applied strict watchdog standards to any and all content prior to bestowing its seal of approval. Any deviation from its list of standards (which prohibited gratuitous violence, sex, and disrespect toward authority) was met with swift punitive measures, notably banning distribution to all stores in which the majority of comic books were sold.

Pressure on the creators, manufacturers, distributors, and retailers of comic books resulted in products that upheld prescribed American values. Neutering comics did not hinder sales; instead, restrictions fomented rebellion over time. After almost a decade of a predictable *Superman,* puerile *Archie,* and tiresome *Sgt. Rock,* a generation of American kids became teenagers, with pent-up inhibitions that demanded venting. During the late 1960s, the busting of strictures emerged in youth movements that were expressed through political radicalism, civil disobedience, hallucinogenic experimentation, free love, and raucous rock and roll. Virtually overnight (after fermenting for a decade), American culture was transformed by a youth culture that reclaimed art, writing, music, and, ultimately, comic books from the guardians of propriety.

Thirty years ago, *Zap #1* was the spearhead of the comic book revolution. The 1998 release of *Zap #15* marked the comic's extraordinary longevity; it is still published, once every two years. Before *Zap,* early underground comics appeared in such underground newspapers as New York's *East Village Other* and its sister publication*, The Gothic Blimp Works,* where R. Crumb, Kim Deitch, Gilbert Shelton, S. Clay Wilson, and Spain Rodrigues launched assaults on convention. To describe the effect of this work as inspirational would understate the incredible power of such fervent taboo busting on a generation weary of trite comic superheroes and superboobs. While these undergrounds looked like comics and read like comics, in fact they were "com-mix," a combination of a conventional visual language (that is, the panel and balloon motif that dates back to the late nineteenth century) and scabrous story- and gag-lines heretofore banned from mainstream comic books.

Zap began as a co-mix of artists bound together by their collective contempt for conventional mores, yet their various individual perspectives allowed them to showcase a number of themes through different forms and distinct characters. Among *Zap's* earliest contributors, founder R. Crumb was known in the counterculture for his string of bizarre, ribald, and racy characters, including Fritz the Cat, Mr. Natural, Angelfood McSpade, Dirty Dog, and Schuman the Human; Victor Moscoso and Rick Griffin were progenitors of the vibrating, psychedelic rock-concert posters that took San Francisco and the world by storm; and S. Clay Wilson was known for living out his perverse fantasies through dark comic figures.

Zap #1 featured Crumb's work exclusively as a vehicle for the artist to pay homage to pre-code comics and to communicate his admittedly deranged view of conventional life. Under the caustic advisory "Fair Warning: For Adult Intellectuals Only," Crumb introduced a selection of tales that had spiritual roots in *MAD* magazine's irreverent satire. But while *MAD* eschewed sex and politics, Crumb reveled in it. Among his earliest stories, we find "Whiteman," a tale of "civilization in crisis;" "Mr. Natural Encounters Flakey Foont," a jab at spirituality; "Ultra Super Modernistic Comics," a tweak at high art; and his now classic "Keep on Truckin'," an absurdly funny slapstick. In retrospect, these comics seem tame when compared to later underground raunchiness. But, at the time, even comical gibes at frontal nudity, recreational drug use, and racial stereotyping (for example, Angelfood McSpade, a bug-eyed African cannibal, sold a product called "Pure Nigger Hearts") tested the tolerance of accepted standards.

When *Zap #1* premiered, Victor Moscoso and Rick Griffin were among the most prominent graphic artists of the San Francisco rock-and-roll ballroom scene. A year earlier, Wes Wilson, Stanley Mouse, Griffin, and Moscoso launched a graphic style that undermined prevailing modernist notions of formal rightness by introducing vibrating color, illegible lettering, and vintage graphics to posters that were complex assemblies of type and image, designed to be read while high. Always the experimenter, Moscoso, who had been interested in serial imagery when he was a painter studying at Yale in the early 1960s, was beginning to play with skewed sequential photographs for use as a Christmas card for an old high school friend, the animator and film title designer Pablo Ferro. Also in an experimental mode, Griffin had done a poster send-up on the *San Francisco Chronicle*'s comics section. After seeing this poster, which was "like Disney on LSD," Moscoso recalls, "it turned me in the direction of cartoons as opposed to photos."

At first, Moscoso was hesitant to devote himself to comic strips. He was already spending the better part of a week designing two and sometimes three rock posters, which were printed on good paper and therefore more tangible than the underground tabloids printed on cheap newsprint and destined for landfill. "Why should I do something that's going to be thrown away?" he asks rhetorically. Instead Moscoso and Griffin together created a series of posters for Pinnacle Productions in LA, promoting Janis Joplin and Big Brother, B. B. King, and PG&E.

"At the bottom [of the strip] were three comic panels, which Rick drew," Moscoso says about the inspiration that gave them the idea to do a comic magazine combining their talents through alternating panels. "I did a template for each of us on eight-by-five-inch cards," he says about the format. "We were using a Rapidograph at the time, and, since we each had the same template, we'd start drawing anything that came into our mind in a box and alternately put one next to the other in a nonlinear fashion so that the development would be purely visual."

Originally, the comic was just going to include Moscoso and Griffin's collaborative artwork. "We were already doing our respective drawings when we saw *Zap #1* [after] Crumb had started selling it on Haight Street," Moscoso recalls. "Crumb asked us to join because he admired Griffin's cartoon poster. In fact, Crumb did a comic strip in *Zap #1,* which was a direct bounce off that poster. So he asked Rick, and Rick said, 'Moscoso and I are already working on this stuff.' So he invited both of us to join in." Crumb also asked S. Clay Wilson, who offered up a ribald comic-strip drug fantasy titled "Checkered Demon." With this, Moscoso and Griffin decided to shelve their collaboration, and each did their own strips.

Given the quartet's respective popularity on the two coasts (Moscoso and Griffin on the West, and Crumb and Wilson on the East), *Zap #2* was an immediate success. However, despite their hippie ("mine is yours") roots, Moscoso wanted to ensure equitable distribution of profits and copyright. "After having been burned so much in the poster business," he says about his intellectual property travails, wherein he was denied the rights to many of his images, "I set up a publishing deal with Print Mint, which was a distributor of my and Rick's posters already. When *Zap #2* came out, here's Moscoso and Griffin and these two new guys, Crumb and Wilson, in the same stores where Rick and I were selling very well." The poster and head shops that had sprung up in hippie strongholds of big cities and college towns allowed independent distributors a network that bypassed the Marvels, DCs, and all the other Comics Code Authority publishers. By the time *Zap #3* and *#4* were published, sales were as high as 50,000 copies each for the first printing. (Subsequent printings increased that number into the six figure range.) Originally, half of the profits after expenses were earmarked for the distributor, and half for the artists. In the meantime, however, the Print Mint changed ownership; after some unfair dealings on their part, Moscoso renegotiated with Last Gasp (the distributor of *Zap* today).

The first two issues of *Zap* were fairly innocuous compared to *Zap #3,* the special 69 issue ("because it was 1969," explains Moscoso). Rocking the boat with its risqué content that lived up to its "Adults Only" advisory, *#3* was spiritually akin to Tijuana bibles (the cheaply produced, sexually explicit eight-page comics imported to the United States from Mexico during the 1930s and 1940s). This issue was sandwiched between two separate front covers designed by Wilson and Griffin, respectively; it could be read front to back and back to front. The hinge was in the middle, a Moscoso-designed turnaround center spread that featured drawings of Daisy and Donald Duck engaged in comic-book hanky-panky.

At the same time that *Zap #3* was in the works, Crumb revealed a set of photocopied pages that he had originally prepared for what was to be the first *Zap.* Unfortunately, he had given the artwork to a publisher who disappeared with the originals before publication. "Fortunately, Crumb had xeroxed the pages, including the covers," recalls Moscoso. He continues: "In those days, the xeroxes picked up the line, but not the solid black. So Crumb had to fill in all the solids." Moscoso and Griffin agreed that, since Crumb had this entire comic book together, he should publish it just as it was, without the other contributors, and they would call it *Zap #0.* The only thing he changed from the original was the cover. "We didn't very often ask each other for advice," says Moscoso about the time that Crumb asked for him for his thoughts about a drawing showing a man floating in a fetal position with an electric wall cord plugged into his derriere. "I looked at it and I said, 'It don't look right, Robert. The guy is in a fetal position with electricity surrounding him, so to have the cord go into his ass doesn't make as much sense as if it went into his umbilical cord.' And he actually took my advice."

Not to diminish Crumb's major contributions to *Zap* or underground comix in general, Moscoso credits S. Clay Wilson with inspiring the contributors to feistily bust taboos. "First Wilson comes out with the 'Checkered Demon,' then 'Captain Piss Gums and his Perverted Pirates,' in which he is drawing my worst fantasies! Frankly, we didn't really understand what we were doing until Wilson started publishing in *Zap.* I mean, he's not a homosexual, yet he's drawing all these homosexual things. He's not a murderer, yet he was murdering all these people. All the things that he wasn't, he was putting down in his strips. So that showed us that we were, without being aware of it, censoring ourselves."

Once the self-imposed constraints were lifted, the *Zap* artists, who now included Spain Rodrigues and Robert Williams, began to explore their own addled fantasies. "Each one of us started looking at our own work asking, 'How far out can we go along the model that Wilson had set up?' The only thing was it had to be our individual stories. I, for one, was not going to do 'Captain Piss Gums.' Instead, I had Donald and Daisy eating each other in the '69 issue because I was getting back at Walt Disney! I mean, I love Walt Disney. But here Mickey and Minnie have nephews, but nobody fucked. So this was my chance."

In this sense, *Zap* quickly became an arena to test the Supreme Court's "community standards" doctrine, which allowed each community to define pornography in relation to the local consensus. As on the edge as it was, *Zap #3* was unscathed. *Zap #4,* on the other hand, stretched those standards beyond the limit and was, therefore, enjoined by the San Francisco police. The seeds of discontent were born in features including the explicitly titled "A Ball in the Bung Hole," by Wilson, "Wonder Wart-Hog Breaks Up the Muthalode Smut Ring" by Shelton, and "Sparky Sperm" by Crumb, which was placed between front and back covers of a dancing penis. But the strip that forced the police's hand was Crumb's "Joe Blow," featuring Dad, Mom, Junior, and Sis in a satire of the incestuous all-American family. Or, as Moscoso explains: "You can cut off a guy's penis and devour it (as in 'Heads-Up' by Wilson), you can even chop people up into little pieces, but you can't have sex with your children." The *Zap* artists thought they "could knock down every taboo that there was." Instead, the police busted City Lights bookstore in San Francisco, and, in New York, *Zap #4* was prohibited from being sold over the counter.

Nevertheless, after paying a fine, City Lights proprietor and poet Lawrence Ferlinghetti continued to sell the contraband and subsequent issues without incident. Predictably, the attention caused *Zap*'s reputation and sales to rise. As for the artists, "I never did an incest story," says Moscoso, "and Crumb never did an incest story again, as far as I know . . . not for *Zap*. However, we did not self-censor. . . . It was just after a while we got it out of our systems."

Although subsequent issues were spared legal harassment, they were no less explicit than the offending issue. By the seventies the raunch factor in underground comics was commonplace, and, with the liberal court's First Amendment rulings, it was fruitless to expend legal energy in cracking down on them. Moreover, *Zap* seemed to serve a purpose in venting the urges of a generation that needed to push boundaries. In fact, *Zap* is today a textbook study of how fringe ideas are no longer mysterious or threatening when they are unleashed. In *Zap #7*, for example, Spain introduced "Sangrella," which serves as a paean to sadomasochistic lesbian eroticism with a sci-fi twist, addressing the extremes of such weird fetishism. In retrospect it is little more than a ribald jab at the sexlessness of superheroes. In *Zap #8* Robert Williams's "Innocence Squandered" is less prurient than it is a satiric commentary on how pornography is adjudicated in the courts. Actually, by *Zap #11*, although sexual references proliferate, the strips became more experimental in terms of form and content. In this issue Crumb's "Patton," about the great blues performer Charley Patton, is a masterpiece of comic strip as documentary. In the same issue Spain's "Lily Litvak: The Rose of Stalingrad" transforms a little-known historical fact into a comic strip that is kindred to the heroic comic books of the World War II era. And in *Zap #13* even Gilbert Shelton turned his attention from fantasy to real life in "Graveyard Ghosts," a brief tour of Père Lachaise Cemetery in Paris.

Thirty years, fifteen issues, and (according to distribution figures) millions of copies later, *Zap* has not changed all that much. The same contributors, minus Griffin (who died in 1995), are still pumping out an issue every two years. During a period in American history when political ultraconservatives are blaming the sixties for all social ills, it is interesting to note that even in maintaining its consistency, *Zap* is not the wellspring of radical raunch that it once was. American tolerance for the abhorrent was long ago stretched beyond *Zap*'s boundaries. "The fact that we're even still selling these things actually is remarkable," Moscoso admits. "These things should have gone by the wayside a long time ago, by all logical standards. But there are people who still read this crap! Not bad for a piece of trash. Really."

Story

DESIGNER: R. O. BLECHMAN

It is hard enough these days for an illustrator to get a regular gig at any magazine, no less draw or paint every cover. In the entire history of twentieth-century magazine publishing, only a few artists have been so able: In the early 1900s, Coles Phillips did them for *Good Housekeeping;* from the 1930s to the 1950s, Norman Rockwell painted hundreds for the *Saturday Evening Post;* in the 1970s, Richard Bernstein did all of *Interview*'s cover portraits; and for the better part of the 1960s and early 1970s, George Lois conceived every *Esquire* cover. Today, only R. O. Blechman (b. 1930) has such sinecure. And knowing how rare this is, he has invested considerable energy and imagination into making the covers for *Story,* a quarterly literary journal devoted to new fiction, among the most extraordinary of any magazine currently published.

Granted, *Story* is not the typical newsstand magazine trapped by stifling cover-design conventions, such as excessive cover lines and restrictive color palette. But, like most literary magazines and scholarly journals, its covers could easily have been undistinguished had not Blechman, the veteran animator, cartoonist, and illustrator, offered to create every cover. In order to get original artwork on a meager budget, *Story* publisher Richard Rosenthal decided to have various illustrators contribute preexisting work. The first *Story* cover was a previously done piece by *New Yorker* cartoonist Ed Koren. However, when Blechman was asked to contribute artwork for the second cover, with so few opportunities to do illustrated covers, he decided to make something original. Afterward he couldn't wait to do more. "I was chafing at the bit to do something like this," Blechman explains about his offer, "and they jumped at the opportunity." Although David Goldin did the third cover, Blechman has designed and illustrated the rest of them, including the hand-drawn *Story* logo, for over six years now.

His covers appear as fresh as the first time his innovative nervous line was seen as the talking stomach in an animated commercial for Alka-Selzer in the early 1960s. After all this time his line has not withered nor have his ideas gone limp. There is nothing outdated or nostalgic about these cover images. His resilience is underscored by the variety of approaches he employs while maintaining his distinctive wit. Individually, each *Story* cover is a single comic vignette on a literary theme. Collected, they are a critical mass of sophistication, intelligence, and, most important, play.

Blechman has never stopped playing. He obsesses over every minute detail and is known to paste teeny-weeny squiggles onto drawings when his eye fixates on an incongruity that is otherwise invisible to the naked eye. But he is not afraid to push the boundaries of his own style. For example, his cover for spring 1991, of a bunny in the Thinker pose contemplating an egg, is a subtle wash drawing printed in pale green against pure white, a tricky method that most illustrators would probably be reluctant to attempt. Likewise, his cover for spring 1992, a comic contrast showing a Hamlet-like character holding a skull sitting back-to-back with a court jester likewise marveling at a bubble, is a study in subtle watercolor values; the cover for autumn 1992, of two jousting characters each galloping respectively atop a huge quotation mark and a period, is a rough, though energetic, sketch. For winter 1993, on the off chance that viewers were becoming too familiar with his concepts, he created a beautiful cover out of a scrivener's nightmare—a drawing of a character being engulfed by a collage of illuminated script. And for winter 1995, he combined ink drawing and computer-generated graphics to make a moody, though comic, seasonal scene in which the snowflakes are futuristic icons.

Blechman's covers are, perhaps appropriately, more like book covers than magazine fronts. Moreover, they are nothing like the original *Story*, which was founded in the 1920s by Whit Burnett and Martha Foley to showcase the fiction of young new authors, including Carson McCullers, William Saroyan, J. D. Salinger, Truman Capote, Norman Mailer, and Joseph Heller. In its earlier incarnation the cover was all type; the *Story* nameplate, set in a variant of Kabel, and the price of "25¢," set huge in a circle above the logo, demanded the most attention, followed by the date and the table of contents. The magazine had been out of print for twenty years at the time Richard Rosenthal bought it in 1989. But he and the editor-in-chief, Lois Rosenthal, wanted to continue the tradition by publishing original short stories. As one of the few viable outlets for new writing, what Lois Rosenthal calls the "welcome back" issue garnered good response. Today the magazine receives between fifteen and twenty thousand submissions a year.

While aware of the original *Story*'s history, Blechman has nonetheless added a comic visual personality that those early covers did not possess. In addition, his art transcends the stereotypes of conventional literary magazines that are either stodgy or ethereal. *Story*, therefore, is not the typically exclusive literary journal aimed at a few cognoscenti. Although it is specialized, Blechman's covers are signs that anyone who enjoys good fiction is welcome inside.

DESIGN DIRECTOR: MICHAEL GROSSMAN

Lingerie and gardens are easily the two most popular fetishes of the 1990s, accounting for the tremendous success of the mail-order catalogs for Victoria's Secret as well as Smith and Hawkins, respectively representing body and earth. After one reaches a certain age, gardening is possibly just as satisfying as sex—perhaps even more so—which is why the rest of this essay will forgo an analysis of publications devoted to undergarments and focus on the most sensual of all garden magazines, *Garden Design.*

One needn't be a practicing gardener to appreciate the beauty of this bimonthly, which is the responsibility of creative director Michael Grossman (b. 1958) and art directors Paul Roeloff, Christin Gangi, and Toby Fox. The type is impeccable, the photographs stunning, the layout classic yet contemporary. If one indeed is a garden aficionado, this is the next best thing to rolling in the mulch.

Garden Design is to magazines what the Brooklyn Botanical Garden is to flowers: a tasteful and tasty, though now and then daring, display of the most common and unusual treats born of nature and domesticated by man. This is not just gratuitous flowery language; *Garden Design* has truly set a standard for the look and feel of so-called lifestyle and shelter magazines—a hybrid of both yet distinctly different.

Even the most rustic garden must be carefully planned and continuously pruned to ensure the integrity of its basic design while exploiting the serendipity of its natural behavior. Similarly, a garden magazine must be meticulously maintained so that its format doesn't overpower the natural beauty of its contents.

It is a fine line to hoe, and *Garden Design* does it quite well, especially compared to *Horticulture,* the granddaddy of garden magazines. With its transparent format and nondescript typography, *Horticulture* is as manicured as the White House rose garden and just as predictable. Conversely, *Garden Design's* format is not strangled by uniformity. Each feature spread, which is unified by a basic grid and three type families, beautifully frames the featured subjects. Like an English garden, variations in scale underscore the graphic impact. Broad panoramas and tight close-ups of plants, bushes, foliage, beds, and environments are key, but graphic details help further the narratives and underscore the magazine's distinct personality. In a typical feature titled "The Voluptuous Fig," photographer Kathryn Kleiman focuses on the fruit's supple form in one spread, pulls back to show its elegant grace on a tree in the next, and then reveals its moist juicy interior in a stunning close-up. Avoiding dew-soaked clichés, these particular images, like most others in *Garden Design,* make for a truly original portfolio.

But photographs are not the only visual focal points. While *Horticulture's* graphic elements are reduced to pure essentials, *Garden Design* has a complex, but unobtrusive, design vocabulary. All page numbers are dropped out white in black squares—somewhat horsy conceit in other contexts that works very well here. Most front-of-the-book pages are framed by gradated color bars on the outside edges, intersecting in the corner at the page number. These also contain short quotes or factoids to add a further level of information. The reason that this complex treatment does not interfere with the overall design is the generous margin of white space framing each of these pages. In addition, color tints, which have become clichés of magazine design, are used judiciously (and with pleasing colors) on some pages to set apart sidebars and special items, while the occasional black boxes with drop-out type are always accented by color rules or images so as not to overpower the page. "Leaves," an unslick, colored-paper insert toward the back of the book, introduces a handsome section devoted to garden literature that is usually illustrated by either landscape or humorous watercolors and gouaches.

Most magazine covers, even in the house and garden genre, are ruined by excess cover lines and intrusive mastheads. *Garden Design's* cover is so smart and tasteful that it could teach all magazines a lesson in restraint—from its elegant logo (with a little graphic accent of a trowel in the corner), to the discreet main headline and tasteful secondary over lines, to the painterly cover photograph.

Inside, throughout the feature well, color evokes the season when the magazine is published. In summer, sunlight drenches many pages while forest greens and terra-cotta browns are also interspersed. In fall, russets, siennas, and oranges fill the editorial well. In spring, newborn colors sparkle on the pages. In winter, the most deadly period for a garden magazine, a triumphant sun hitting the icy glitter of gardens offers a warm glow. And, as with nature itself, after a complete cycle is over, one doesn't get tired of seeing it repeated. Here is where *Garden Design* really triumphs. Even after almost four years of publishing, the stories are not routine, the pictures are still enticing, the gardens are always sensual. This just might be the best-designed fetish magazine on the market today.

Past generations have each produced magazines that define their respective periods. A "lifestyle book" called *Wallpaper** (**the stuff that surrounds you*) has found a snug berth as the magazine of the late nineties. Like other popular-culture magazines that preceded it, *Wallpaper** projects an au courant attitude and proffers a distinctive air, much of which comes through the magazine's stylish typography and photography. From the moment the British-based *Wallpaper** (now published by Time Warner, Inc.) was introduced to the United States in late 1996, there was a discernible buzz in periodical circles. *Wallpaper** would capture the demographic of an ostensibly white, upwardly mobile twentyish to thirtyish post–Gen X audience whose primary interests are "interiors, entertaining, and travel." And, true to this promise, it has delivered the goods through a plethora of catalog-style flacktoids (editorial advertisements for products) and easily scannable features about hip habitats and daring destinations. Likewise, as a touchstone of contemporary editorial design—indeed, the next stylistic wave—*Wallpaper** has earned plaudits from design juries and proudly announces on its covers the receipt of SPD's Gold Medal for Overall Design 1997.

"The format is very lively and original," said a juror of the 1997 Society of Publication Design competition, who, explaining why she voted to bestow the gold, added: "I'm just so pleased that it's not another *Ray Gun* clone." Given the excessive number of magazines mimicking David Carson's designs, it is refreshing to find a magazine that is a tad reactionary— where type is used as type, not as an abstract pattern. While many magazines slavishly follow youth culture's codes, whereby illegibility reigns and distorted layouts prevail, *Wallpaper** has turned the corner on this early nineties style, offering a kind of late modernist sensibility with bold, crisp gothic type framed by generous white space and skillfully styled photographs with a certain tongue-in-cheek irreverence. In addition, there is a maximum of only one piece of overlapping type found per issue. Just think of the implications of that!

In contrast to various contemporary monkey-see-monkey-do magazines, Herbert Winkler, the art director, has not downloaded a template off the Internet in a vain attempt to make *Wallpaper** magazine simulate multimedia, and he has assiduously avoided the "end of print" aesthetics of chaotic design. Instead, this format follows the traditional form of magazine pacing, where highs and lows are modulated to keep the reader moving sequentially through the feature well(s). Since editorial wells are ever more frequently interrupted by advertisements, maintaining the semblance of one is an achievement in itself.

But for all these virtues, the format has limitations too. First is a seemingly unavoidable one: Although it has a few editorial wells for each thematic section (the magazine is divided into three or four of them), also included as components of these sections are many single editorial pages that face advertisements. In some cases, when text and images are balanced, these pages are easily distinguished from the ads. But in most cases the pages are so colorfully visual that the editorial and advertisements blur the line of church and state, save for the identifying kicker (or over line) in the corner (e.g., "In House," "The Space," or "The Event"). Although tied together by its close-fit sans serif typography, *Wallpaper** is dominated more so by choppy than by cohesive pagination. The second flaw, a seemingly avoidable one, is the catalog nature of many single pages—with as many as six boxes per page, each including a picture of merchandise. This practice is so accepted in magazines today that one almost forgets how it encourages bad design. The variously colored, overlapping one-point rule boxes, with different-colored, tight-fitting type, make *Wallpaper** a cluttered mosaic. Don't get me wrong, each is perfectly readable, but as a whole it is little more than Penny-Saver quality. Finally, each thematic section is introduced by a single page "billboard" announcing the stories therein. Although this concept is designed to aid navigation and prevent an abrupt switch from ad to editorial, in fact, they give the appearance of ads. In a magazine so fraught with them, this solution does not have the desired impact.

For all its departures from accepted youth codes, *Wallpaper** is not so truly innovative as it is a backlash against and a synthesis of certain sixties/seventies magazine ideas (including revivification of Hearst's late-sixties lifestyle book, *Eye,* which was a hybrid of psychedelia and modernism). Compared to a new shelter book called *Nest* (subtitled: *a quarterly magazine of interiors*), *Wallpaper** is fairly conventional. *Nest,* however, is radical without being absurd. In fact, *Nest,* which is art directed by its founding editor-in-chief, Joseph Holtzman (with assistance from "design technician" Tom Beckham and typographer Michael Zöllner), is a perfectly readable, yet remarkably unconventional, portfolio of features. Granted, it has neither the circulation nor advertising of *Wallpaper*,* but it is nonetheless a slick, glossy, full-color newsstand magazine, which attracts some of the same advertisers. Yet, from a design point of view, it is so much freer and more imaginative than any similar magazine in its class.

Nest avoids the pitfalls of the editorial blurring with ads by simply not having a "front of the book." After a number of pages of classy ads, the second issue, for example, begins with a classically designed black-and-white page of text introducing a portfolio of photographs printed on translucent rice paper. The rest of the features are on glossy paper printed mostly in color, modulated by some black-and-white imagery. Each feature is so uniquely designed, there is no standard format. While this variety may be disconcerting to some, the spreads nevertheless fit perfectly together in the overall editorial flow. Of course, *Nest* does not have any advertising in its expansive editorial well; if it did, these feature spreads might not hold up as a well-constructed whole. Nevertheless, it requires a certain amount of risk to design a spread of full-color posed photographs of how women inmates decorate their prison cells (with minimal accompanying text), followed by a strange feature focusing on the full-page color advertisements of upholstery designer Hasi Hester, which looks like it came out of a trade magazine. Individually, not every feature works, but there is magic in the juxtapositions. To top off the uniqueness of *Nest,* its covers are trimmed with a curved corner at the top right, like a notebook.

Wallpaper* and *Nest* are two models within a fascinating spectrum of contemporary magazine design. In their respective ways, they provide a rejection of the early 1990s obsession with "deconstructed" typography. One is a return to tradition through a synthesis of older ideas; the other is simply an attempt to have fun by matching interesting content to unfettered design.

Until 1997, I never looked at a sports magazine. For that matter, I had not watched a spectator sport since I was fifteen. But now, with my ten-year-old son, I go to basketball, soccer, and baseball games (and even attended David Wells's perfect game at Yankee Stadium in May 1998), read the daily *New York Times* and *New York Post* sports pages, watch ESPN SportsCenter, CNNSI, FOX Sports, and MSG on television, play Nintendo 64 and Sony Playstation sports games, regularly scan Yankees and Knicks Web sites, and subscribe to three sports magazines: *Sports Illustrated, Sports Illustrated for Kids,* and *ESPN* magazine. I've become as much of an authority on the subject as Rose the waitress at the Times Square Deli, a fifty-five-year-old Brooklyn-born grandmother and longtime Mets fan. Of course, she's got me beat when it comes to statistics dating back to the seventies, but I've got a leg up on her when it comes to judging the design quality of sports magazines—as if she cares.

In fact, why should anyone care whether a sports magazine has good typography or not? The reason that Rose reads sports pages and magazine articles is to get facts and insights into her favorite teams and players. When asked which she thinks is the best-looking sports magazine, Rose replied: "Are you kiddin'? It doesn't matter what this stuff looks like. I just want to know who's doin' what and when. I like a good picture now and then, but that's not why I buy these things." Therefore, it is logical that Rose is not the demographic of choice for the two major sports magazines: *Sports Illustrated (SI),* which has been around since 1956 and targets a middle- to upper-middle-class male audience (somewhere between eighteen and aging baby boomer), and

ESPN, which is geared to a younger pre– and post–Gen X group. For both readerships, graphic design may not be the first or fifteenth thing on their minds, but it is an incredibly important hook in attracting them to consume the product.

When I asked if she reads either magazine, Rose answered, "Nah, not regularly. The *Daily News* and the *Post* are good enough for me. But I bought my son a subscription to *ESPN* magazine for Christmas, and he loves it." So why not *Sports Illustrated*? "I don't know," Rose replied. "*ESPN* looks a bit more lively to me. . . . Why don't you ask him?"

Actually, Rose's analysis is fairly good. *Sports Illustrated*'s design is excellent. The content is well paced, the photography is striking, and the typography is contemporary yet not slavishly fashionable. But there is something that makes it feel, well, stodgy. Perhaps it's the standard *Time* magazine size. Perhaps it's the fact that, while typographically handsome, it doesn't plow any new ground. Even the famous annual swimsuit issue, of which the release is an American cultural event (hey, that reminds me—I didn't receive my copy this year!), does not have as much vitality as *ESPN,* despite the fact that it *is* well designed. So I asked Rose's thirty-year-old son, Carl, a drugstore manager, why he prefers *ESPN* to *SI.* "Well, aside from the lively shorter articles and all the bits and pieces of information"—factoids, in magazinese—"I really like the size of the magazine. It reminds me of *Rolling Stone.* And I like the way the stories look; I mean, the text parts are not as tightly packed in as *Sports Illustrated,* and the photos go over the pages a lot more."

Carl took the words right out of my mouth. Speaking in terms that are relevant to most nondesigner readers, Carl has accurately defined *ESPN* as more accessible, less demanding, and also comfortable to the touch.

I would add that *ESPN* magazine, like its older brother ESPN the cable TV network, expertly presents bite-sized nuggets culled from untold masses of sports trivia, cut with some insight, and underscored with lots of interesting pictures. *Sports Illustrated* is largely concerned with serious disquisition by veteran writers aimed at those devout sports buffs who cannot get enough replay analysis. But *ESPN* is not so much sports lite as it is sports highlight; it's perfect for the casual sports fan, like myself.

ESPN also exhibits a very smart approach to magazine design at a time when virtually every sports magazine—and there are scores of genre-specific publications for basketball, baseball, football, women's sports, and so on—resembles its competitors. Like it or not, *ESPN* has carved out its own design niche, consistent with other components of the brand.

ESPN forged a track record of innovation when it initially defined itself as a credible TV network. Although it was not the first all-sports cable channel, it was launched with the most novel and hip sports-related advertising graphics to date. ESPN's design aesthetic was arguably influenced by the innovative apparel designs of Nike and Reebok, which redefined the sports shoe (or sneaker) through radical redesigning and perpetual restyling—and which, I believe, had a great impact on how sports and related industries have packaged themselves in the nineties. ESPN's print advertising in the mid-1990s used many current graphic-design tropes—blurred and overlapping type, surreal and color-saturated images, and enigmatic visual concepts. The magazine, while not a carbon copy of the network's ad campaigns, employs equally contemporary visual cues to underscore the idea that this is a new generation of sports magazine, designed for a younger generation of fans.

In competitive sports, size may not be everything, but for *ESPN,* its expansive *Rolling Stone* size (as well as the unslick, calendered paper inside) allows design director F. Darrin Perry to make striking spreads that account for one of *ESPN*'s signature conceits. Like *Sports Illustrated,* which starts each issue cinematically with four or five double-truck photos of the week's greatest moments, *ESPN* leads off with a portfolio, not always of great plays but of alluring current and historical pictures.

That's where size does matter. It's the difference between watching the big game on a thirteen-inch or thirty-six-inch TV screen. Sure, there is a slight problem in flashy spreads competing with flashy advertisements, but the distinction is usually maintained. An editorial "opener" in a February 1999 issue, titled "We'll Miss You, Mike" (about guess who?), with its extreme close crop of His Airness's eyes, is designed in such a way as to prevent confusion with the ads. And such distinction is generally accomplished throughout the magazine. Indeed, sports photography for editorial and advertising tends to fall into two frequently used categories, heroic action and repose. *ESPN* has always managed to find alternative forms, including some innovative sports illustration, without resorting to artsy esoterica in the bargain.

Another key *ESPN* design signature is its use of variegated and cluttered factoid columns and featurettes, which comprise a large percentage of the magazine. Making these elements unique and inviting—especially in the statistic-obsessed arena of competitive sports—is a real challenge, but *ESPN* succeeds through changing color palettes, typographic variation within consistent families, and intelligent pictorial and icon applications that keep these items lively and readable.

The third and stylistically most demonstrative signature element is a relentless use of hairlines, as boxes, borders, frames, way-finders; there's even a feature called "In the Crosshairs," in which a sports figure is deconstructed, with gun-sight crosshairs locating the body parts analyzed. *ESPN* has more rules running every which way than a road map of the United States. And while this may sound like a predictably tiresome ornamental indulgence, it provides identity and enhances navigation. *ESPN*'s designers further seem to revel in the excessive appliqué of tchotchkes—a surfeit of small special-feature logos, subheads within subheads, odd running feet, and often as many as two ESPN logos on a single page (just in case the reader forgets the brand).

The overall design is undoubtedly beholden to QuarkXPress and Photoshop for its special effects, and in this sense it could easily have embodied the rampant clichés of desktop publishing. In fact, however, there are only a few mediocre Photoshop tricks. One involves the back-of-the-book column heads for NHL, Basketball, College Basketball, Baseball, and so on, which use overlapping blurred and fading photo-illustration and colorforms. These are sore points when compared to the design originality of the front of the magazine. But *ESPN* works very well to establish its personality and convey its message. Its designers seem to understand when to increase and decrease the visual volume to make a very entertaining publication. As Rose's son Carl aptly puts it, "I know where everything is in this magazine, but I'm also always surprised."

Dr. Strangelove

DESIGNER: PABLO FERRO

As an attack on cold-war hysteria, there was no more biting comedy than Stanley Kubrick's 1964 doomsday film, *Dr. Strangelove: Or How I Learned to Stop Worrying and Love the Bomb,* in which an overzealous U.S. general, Jack D. Ripper, launches an A-bomb attack against the USSR. This send-up of nightmare scenarios depicted in the nuclear dramas *Fail Safe* and *On the Beach* fiercely lampooned the era's hawkish fanaticism, suggesting that the world was close to the brink of the unthinkable.

The film's frightening absurdity is established in the very first frame of the main title sequence designed by Pablo Ferro. As the ballad "Try a Little Tenderness" plays in the background, a montage of B-52 bombers engage in midair coitus with their refueling ships, underscoring the subplot that sexuality is endemic to all human endeavor, especially the arms buildup. Surprinted on these frames, the film's title and credits are full-screen graffiti-like scrawls comprised of thick and thin hand-drawn letters, unlike any previous movie title. The sequence brilliantly satirizes the naïve pretense that America was protected from nuclear attack by oversexed flying sentries. It also contrasts beautifully with the film's concluding montage, edited by Ferro, which shows atomic bombs rhythmically detonated to the accompanying lyric, "We'll meet again, don't know where, don't know when. . . ."

This was not the first time that a movie title sequence added narrative dimension to a film. During the brief history of modern film titles, which began with Saul Bass's 1954 *Carmen Jones,* a handful of designers (among them, Maurice Binder, Steven Frankfurt, and Robert Brownjohn) established film identities by compressing complex details into signs, symbols, and metaphors. By the time that Ferro made his 1964 debut, the stage (or rather the screen) had already been set for ambitious artistry. Although the *Dr. Strangelove* titles were a distinct departure from Bass's animated, geometric forms in the German expressionist manner, they were consistent with the experimental film-within-a-film concept that gave title sequences momentary independence while serving the practical needs of a motion picture. Moreover, this film launched the long career of Pablo Ferro as title designer, trailer director, and feature filmmaker.

Yet, before he started designing film titles, the Cuban-born Ferro (b. 1935), who had emigrated to New York City when he was twelve years old—quickly becoming a huge film fan and aficionado of UPA cartoons—had earned a reputation for directing and editing scores of television commercials.

After graduating from Manhattan's High School of Industrial Art, Ferro began working at Atlas Comics in 1951 as an inker and artist in the EC-horror tradition. A year later he began learning the ropes as an animator of UPA-styled cartoons and worked for top commercial studios, including Academy Pictures, Elektra Films, and Bill Stern Studios (where, among other things, he animated Paul Rand's drawings for El Producto cigars). In 1961 he founded the creative production studio Ferro Mogubgub Schwartz (later changed to Ferro Mohammed Schwartz, Mohammed being a mythical partner invented only to retain the cadence of the studio name). As a consummate experimenter, Ferro introduced the kinetic quick-cut method of editing, whereby static images (including engravings, photographs, and pen and ink drawings) were infused with speed, motion, and sound.

In the late 1950s most live-action commercials were shot with one or two stationary cameras. Conversely, Ferro took full advantage of stop-motion technology as well as shooting his own jerky footage with a handheld Bolex. Unlike most TV commercial directors, Ferro maintained a strong appreciation and understanding for typography such that in the late 1950s he pioneered the use of moving type on the TV screen. He had a preference for using vintage woodtypes and Victorian gothics not only because they were popular at the time but because they were vivid on television. In 1961 he created an eclectic typographic film sequence for Jerome Robbins's stage play *Oh Dad, Poor Dad, Mamma's Hung You in the Closet and I'm Feeling So Sad,* an innovative approach that, similar to a film title sequence, preceded the opening curtain and announced the different acts within the performance.

After seeing Ferro's commercials, Kubrick hired him to direct the advertising trailers and teasers for *Dr. Strangelove* and convinced him to resettle in London (Kubrick's base of operations until he died there in March 1999). Ferro was inclined to be peripatetic anyway; ever anxious to bypass already-completed challenges, he agreed to pull up stakes on the chance that he would get to direct a few British TV commercials, which he did.

The black-and-white spot that Ferro designed for *Dr. Strangelove* employed his quick-cut technique—using as many as 125 separate images in a minute—to convey both the dark humor and the political immediacy of the film. At something akin to stroboscopic speed, words and images flew across the screen to the accompaniment of loud sound effects and snippets of ironic dialogue. At a time when the bomb loomed large in the fears of the American public (remember, Barry Goldwater ran for president promising to nuke China) and the polarization of left and right—East and West—was at its zenith, Ferro's commercial was not only the boldest and most hypnotic graphic on TV but also a sly, subversive statement.

Dr. Strangelove was key to Ferro's eventual shift from TV to film. And working with Kubrick was the best possible introduction to the movie industry, since this relationship allowed Ferro to bypass the stultifying Hollywood bureaucracy. Ferro was free to generate ideas, and Kubrick was sufficiently self-confident to accept (and sometimes refine) them. For example, once the sexual theme of the opening title sequence was decided upon, Kubrick wanted to film it all using small airplane models (doubtless prefiguring his classic spaceship ballet in *2001: A Space Odyssey*). Ferro dissuaded him and located the official stock footage that they used instead. Ferro further conceived the idea to fill the entire screen with lettering (which, incidentally, had never been done before), requiring the setting of credits at different sizes and weights, which potentially ran counter to legal contractual obligations. Kubrick supported it regardless. On the other hand, Ferro was prepared to have the titles refined by a lettering artist, but Kubrick correctly felt that the rough-hewn quality of the hand-drawn comp was more effective. So Ferro carefully lettered the entire thing himself with a thin pen. Yet only after the film was released did he notice that one term was misspelled: "base on" instead of "base*d* on." Oops! Incidentally, Kubrick insisted that Ferro take "front credit" rather than "back credit," a rare and significant movie industry protocol.

Ferro's work is not always immediately identifiable, although he has reprised his signature style from *Dr. Strangelove* a few times since 1964. *Stop Making Sense,* the Talking Heads concert film (1984), *The Addams Family: Family Values* (1993), and *Men in Black* (1997) all employ his distinctive hand lettering. But Ferro is less concerned with establishing a personal identity than he is with creating titles that support the movie they frame. Ferro defines each problem according to the ethos of the specific film; hence, titles for *The Thomas Crown Affair* (1968), with its quick cuts and innovative multiple-screen technique, or *Midnight Cowboy* (1969), with its lyrical narrative sequencing, are individual works born of the same vision and purpose—to introduce another artist's work.

The World According to Garp

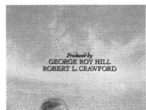

In 1982, a baby flew onto movie screens across America, and Richard Greenberg landed in the annals of design history. The airborne infant was the centerpiece of the film title created, designed, and directed by Greenberg for *The World According to Garp*. It was breathtaking on the big screen at a period when most film titles were mundane typographic afterthoughts often composed by a film's editor. The flying baby was a testament to innovative design, and with this short sequence Greenberg single-handedly reinvigorated the practice of conceptual titling, which had been dormant since the 1960s, when Saul Bass produced titles for films like *The Man with the Golden Arm, Vertigo*, and *North by Northwest* and Steven Frankfurt designed the classic opener for *To Kill a Mockingbird*. Greenberg's *Garp* was born of that tradition but also pushed the boundaries of form and technology.

To underscore its conceptual acuity, it was necessary for Greenberg to develop a white matte screen process that eliminated the telltale outline of light that surrounded objects when superimposed on blue matte screens. Without this invention the credibility of the visual illusion would certainly have been diminished. He perfected the application of programmable camera motion, using the rostrum camera to give a hyped-up sensation of movement even with inanimate objects. And he also took advantage of—indeed, greatly advanced—the computer as both a commonplace and special-effects tool. These technological coups became the foundation on which R/Greenberg Associates built its reputation for cutting-edge film design and production.

With a mastery of technology, a talent for design, and an instinct for storytelling, Greenberg created other memorable titles that wed graphics to cinematography, including such films as *Superman* (1978), *Body Double* (1984), *The Untouchables* (1987), *Altered States* (1980), *Lethal Weapon* (1987), *Dirty Dancing* (1987), and *Alien* (1986). These titles used bold images and crystalline sound effects not merely to introduce the cast but to define a movie through vivid visual narratives that were abstracts of plot.

Superman was Greenberg's first movie title, and it set the tone for his unique iconographic style. As memory of the film fades, the title sequence stays indelibly fresh in the mind. The sequence begins with curtains parting on the screen, literally setting the stage for the Depression-era movie palace in which the original Superman serial might have played; next, a Superman comic book emerges as a young boy slowly reads aloud about the origins of the Man of Steel. Gradually, the camera closes in on a picture of the Daily Planet Building, with its huge globe logo sitting atop. From comic-book drawing the globe transforms into real life, and then, as if Superman himself were ripping by at the speed of light, the title surges across the screen, suggesting the mythic quality of this story.

Like films within films, Greenberg's title sequences provided context, elicited mood, and offered clues. The baby in *Garp* was not merely a graphic device but suggested the special relationship of the *Garp* character to his unwed mother. The grainy, slow-motion, extreme close-ups of dancing couples that opened *Dirty Dancing* did more to establish the premise of this film than a half hour of disquisition. The use of a louvered grid that cut through type and image in the opening of *Body Double* isolated and abstracted the key portion of this thriller rooted in voyeurism. Each told a concise story about the story. Greenberg's title sequences were a means of allowing the audience to settle into a film and ensured iconic memorability.

Multi-Maus

DESIGNER: PETER GIRARDI

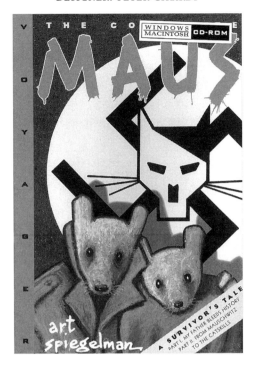

With its huge capacity for information storage, is the CD-ROM a receptacle for minutiae? This question must inevitably be addressed in any analysis of the 1995 CD-ROM *Maus: A Survival Tale* (Voyager), based on Art Spiegelman's two-volume graphic memoir (1986, 1991) about the Holocaust; the CD-ROM includes the entire three-hundred-page comic strip supplemented by thousands of pages of notes, sketches, interviews, reviews, and essays, in addition to personal and documentary photographs. Having such a wellspring of material begs a fundamental question: How much is too much of a good thing?

The CD-ROM does not enhance the reading of *Maus* itself. Given such a charged theme in comic-strip form, the printed book is much more appropriate than any electronic alternative—indeed, it's revolutionary. Yet the digital medium is an invaluable companion in that it offers heretofore-unavailable material that provides further insight on various complex levels. Although *Maus* is a completely resolved work in which Spiegelman chronicles his father's account of Holocaust survival and his own difficult relationship to his parents' tortured lives, it is also just the tip of an iceberg of artistic endeavor—the result of years of critical research, development, and introspection. For the reader who wants to learn more about the artist's motives and process, the CD-ROM provides an invaluable resource. But it is for posterity that these "papers" are in a retrievable form, which, prior to the CD-ROM, was impossible. Whether too much information is included is not the issue. If all that this CD-ROM did was to recreate Spiegelman's didactic, deconstructive 1992 exhibition at the Museum of Modern Art in New York, it would provide sufficient content, but it also reproduces so many footnotes that it becomes a biography of an artwork and a boon to present and future scholars.

The *Maus* CD-ROM must also be analyzed as to whether it sets a viable design standard for CD-ROM interfaces. These are generally rather lackluster because the real intent of CD-ROM—text, video, or multimedia hybrid—is unclear. The *Maus* CD-ROM is rooted in a conventional print environment. Therefore, while it is interspersed with limited animation (primarily of Spiegelman talking at his drawing table) and audio grabs of interviews with Vladek, his father, the disc is actually quite conservatively formatted, using print devices that are mercifully neither computer clichés nor digital extravagances. The screen is framed by an unobtrusive red band that echoes the cover package design from which the typeface, Metro, is dropped out. Navigation through the various segments or chapters is aided by an accessible table of contents that indicates which hot buttons to click on for the option screens. Spiegelman's massive notes and unedited interview transcripts with his father are set in a typical computer default face, which, though dry, is appropriate. Overall this is an invitingly transparent on-screen format.

At Voyager, back in 1995, designer Peter Girardi (b. 1966) was responsible for making the technology behave according to plan. Since the *Maus* CD-ROM's launch, the ability to both mimic the printed page and transcend its constraints have been fairly well accomplished. However, back then the state of technology was primitive, and simple functions that are taken for granted today were barely possible given the state of authoring environments. It was a struggle to make the disc that the author and producer wanted and be assured it would run on the machines of the day. "Essentially, we were figuring out how to translate something that was fine in an existing medium (print) to an interactive medium," Girardi explains. "It was early enough in the development of 'interactive media' that there were no defined rules yet. It was really important to figure out what the medium was actually good for. The mixed blessing of *Maus* was all the content was available to work with, but it made the job of creating an intuitive, navigable interface quite a challenge. We spent a long time flowcharting and storyboarding the disc. With any piece of interactive media (especially CD-ROM because of the controlled environment), linking all the content together in a structured information flow is another big challenge. This is especially true for users possibly unfamiliar with the material."

The fundamental question—Does the CD-ROM add to the experience of *Maus*?—was always a motivation for exploring the boundaries of another medium. That led to a dilemma: whether to create a documentary versus whether to embark on an entirely new form. "At Voyager we always felt that CD-ROM was the last frontier for documentary film," answers Girardi. "That idea was always in our minds as we designed and produced discs. We were always careful in presenting context and background information for any particular subject. More importantly, what the CD does well is the *relationship* between all the media types. How a piece of audio and an image relate, how a segment of video will be informed by a passage of text—that's the real promise of the interactive media. The CD doesn't exist without the books, but it also takes the books to a new place. We weren't tied to the narrative of the book."

Adapting *Maus* to CD-ROM, like adapting a novel to film, was a difficult balancing act. How faithful must those who intervene remain to the original? How much of the original will be sacrificed to another creative individual? "I was always conscious of Spiegelman's work and what he would like or dislike," Girardi says. "I figured if he liked it, I was halfway there. The part of the disc that I do feel is my own as the designer is the way that the information is constructed and presented graphically to the user. If people use *Maus* and are not conscious of the interface, then I've succeeded. Every time I approach a project where I have to translate information from one medium to another, I know that I'm also affecting the way that that particular piece of information is received. It's changed by my interpretation and translation. Sometimes this is something to be played up and made apparent. For *Maus* it was the opposite. The design and interface needed to be recessive, more like a tool, less like an aesthetic object. The real work in the interpretation of *Maus* from book to disc was done by the producer, Elizabeth Scarborough. She spent months breaking the books and the additional content down into a structured object to then be designed."

Yet navigating *Maus* was not problem-free. While the manual provided keys, reading them demanded undue patience. So until users became instinctively familiar with the subtler aspects of the interface, they likely got stuck in segments, unable to return to the main menu. On one occasion, this user was forced to click all over the screen before finding an invisible hot-button that enabled escape back to the contents menu. This and other way-finding misadventures hampered a total appreciation. The problems, however, were outweighed by the return. Anyone who heard Spiegelman lecture about his process and the structure of comics found that this experience (although perhaps not as even-flowing as a film) was the next best thing to a live performance. Yet even a real-time videotape could not present the graphic work with the same fidelity as the CD-ROM.

What does the future hold for this work? Will it survive the ages like the *Maus* book itself? Or will it be as forgotten as a Tony Orlando eight-track tape? "*Maus* continues to hold up. The technology is getting a little tired, and the disc itself runs slow, but the information architecture and interface design is still some of our best work," asserts Girardi. "No one tackles this amount of content anymore. Sure, I could take *Maus* today and recode it for the Web, but I wouldn't have to rethink the design. The information design is solid."

Cheap Thrills

DESIGNER: R. CRUMB / ART DIRECTOR: BOB CATO

A standing ovation at the Fillmore East, New York's premier music hall during the late 1960s, was reserved for rock-and-roll royalty. The Fillmore hosted the best bands of the age, and Fillmore audiences were jaded, demanding, and sometimes rude in the bargain. On one occasion, early in their career, the members of the band Sly and the Family Stone were shouted off stage because the audience could not wait a second longer for the evening's headliner, Jimi Hendrix, who received one of the longest and loudest ovations ever. That is, with the exception of the time in fall 1968 when Janis Joplin announced to the assembled fans that the cover for *Cheap Thrills,* the recent Big Brother and the Holding Company album, was illustrated by underground cartoonist R. Crumb. The audience went wild as a slide of the image filled the huge screen behind her.

Back then, Crumb (b. 1943) was as popular as any rock star. His cartoon inventions, Fritz the Cat, Mr. Natural, Honeybunch Kominsky, the Keep on Truckin' chorus line, and scores of raucous and ribald comix published in underground newspapers such as the *Bee, East Village Other,* and *Gothic Blimp Works* had earned him hero status throughout youth culture. He was in the vanguard of artists who forever busted the timidity and mediocrity that had been enforced since the mid-1950s by the industry's self-censoring organ, the Comics Code Authority. Through a combination of zany raunch and artful acerbity wed to unequaled pen-and-ink draftsmanship, Crumb's drawings of big-hipped hippie chicks, bug-eyed nerdy guys, and weird average-American white folk engaged in extraordinary (if unspeakable) acts pounded at the propriety and sanctity of an aged establishment. No wonder the union of Joplin and Crumb (who were born in the same year) was greeted with ecstatic delight when it was made public. There is no telling how many records were sold from that night's debut, but, musically, it was Big Brother's best album and graphically it was the most memorable cover art of the generation.

The *Cheap Thrills* cover was an ersatz comic strip with panels radiating from a central circle. Like illustrated liner notes, each panel contained a cartoon reference to either Joplin, Big Brother, or a song on the album. For the cut "I Need a Man to Love," Crumb has a zaftig Janis (his signature female archetype) almost bursting out of her tight clothes, fetchingly strewn on a bed. For "Ball and Chain," Joplin's classic tour de force, the same character drags along a leg iron attached to a ball and chain, as if in an endless search for the right man. For "Summertime," Joplin's masterful cover of the old standard, Crumb uses a dubious caricature of a black woman, a throwback to vintage racist mammy cartoon images from the nineteenth century, holding a wailing baby with cartoon tears radiating around its head. Separately, each panel is a slapstick gag in the comic tradition; together they form a curiously hypnotic, multi-image narrative that in retrospect visually reflects the San Francisco music scene of the day.

Aside from Crumb's bawdy humor, what made this album cover such an icon was its good timing. Produced at a moment when cultural innovations were introduced at a fast and furious pace, this was the pinnacle of sixties exuberance and invention, just prior to its neutering and commodification by marketers and entrepreneurs. Which is not to say that marketers and entrepreneurs were not already maneuvering in the wings—they were. But even the consumer outlets—FM radio, the record industry, head shops, and so on—seemed not to be constrained by market or conventions and were willing to take risks that went beyond "most advanced yet acceptable." For an all-too-brief moment, youth-hippie-alternative culture was in a state of grace when everything seemed new and unfettered. Music and art were rebellious, expressive, and instinctive. Formulas, clichés, and stereotypes had yet to exert a viselike grip on creativity. Crumb's cover for *Cheap Thrills* was not just a calculating effort to win market share; it was the marriage of two artists and two art forms that truly spoke to the gut of the same audience without pretense or conceit. Joplin's music was raw emotion; Crumb's art was pure wit.

Nevertheless, *Cheap Thrills* was a product of a well-established music industry. In the wake of the mid-1960s British pop invasion, the American music establishment responded to the popular groundswell toward psychedelic and folk rock emanating from San Francisco by quickly signing as many top local bands as possible (Jefferson Airplane, Grateful Dead, Country Joe and the Fish, and more). It churned out albums (instead of 45s, the standard music medium of the preceding generation), and with albums came a need for eye-catching cover art that telegraphed the eccentricity of the new rock. In competition with the visionary psychedelic posters that advertised San Francisco's music palaces, simple photographs of band members were no longer sufficiently engaging to attract record buyers by the late 1960s. With the art-based collage on the Beatles' *Revolution* in 1966 and the elaborate fantasy photograph on *Sgt. Pepper's Lonely Hearts Club Band* in 1967, concept album art became a viable alternative to studio photography. Record company art director/designers were unleashed to test the limits of conceptual presentation.

The veteran Bob Cato (1923–1999) was among the more conceptually astute. During ten years as an art director and, subsequently, as the vice president of creative services for CBS/Columbia Records, working with such decidedly contrasting musicians as Leonard Bernstein, the Band, Glenn Gould, and Johnny Mathis, Cato developed or directed the creation of some of the most memorable record-album covers of the 1960s. As a student of and assistant to the legendary art director and designer Alexey Brodovitch, Cato cut his art directorial teeth on the fashion magazine *Harper's Bazaar,* where Brodovitch had transformed editorial and fashion design with his innovative mixture of white space, elegant typography, photography, and modernist art. The former *New York Times* advertising columnist Randall Rothenberg says that these "were characteristics that would also define Cato's own work during the next several decades."

Many of Cato's album covers featured his own photography, but for others he enlisted some of the era's most influential painters, designers, and photographers, among them Andy Warhol, Robert Rauschenberg, Francesco Scavullo, and Irving Penn. But Cato did more than just conceive and execute album covers. "He was also intimately involved in the conception and even the naming of the recordings themselves," says Rothenberg. One of these was *Cheap Thrills.*

As was customary at CBS, Joplin came to see him about the design of her record. Originally, Cato wanted to shoot the group in a fabricated "hippie pad," but Big Brother balked at the pretentious set. Instead, both Janis and Cato agreed that Crumb's artwork was a perfect way to give the album a look sufficiently raw to match the music. Crumb worked without interference. Joplin wanted a title that was synonymous with her life and the epoch in which she lived, insisting that the album be called "Sex, Dope, and Cheap Thrills." Given her soaring popularity, CBS records executives were tempted to give in. Nevertheless, "the title didn't seem quite right to me," Cato wrote years later in an unpublished memoir. "It said too much, gave away too much. Besides, even in the sixties, the recording business was still a business, and there was only so much you could get away with."

Cato, who was no novice when it came to taming celebrity egos, calmly suggested to Joplin that the words "sex" and "dope" on the cover would limit the record's radio airplay, recommending that she use only the last two words of this phrase for the title. Joplin demurred. "Well, I've always settled for cheap thrills, anyway," she said. With Crumb's comic splash panel at the top, *Cheap Thrills* the record went on to become one of the biggest-selling rock albums of all time.

Shock and Roll

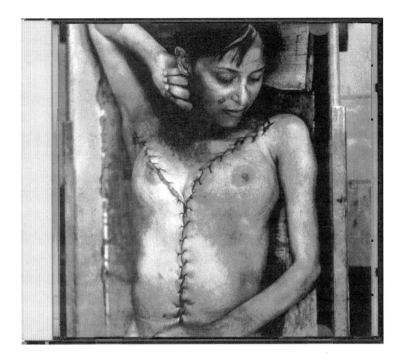

$\mathbf{F}$ear spread throughout the land when a
primitive beat rose from the melodies of rockabilly and young people began to shake, rattle,
and gyrate. Unleashed from the cocoon of civility, otherwise upstanding young Americans,
hypnotized by frenetic rhythms, rejected the music of their parents to revel in youthful passion.
Left alone, rock and roll would probably have found its own way into the mainstream without
incident, but the generational dread of rock-influenced juvenile delinquents running wild in the
streets and the exploitation films preying on such feelings contributed to the myth that rock and
roll was shock and roll.

Despite efforts by the music industry to fend off criticism by schlocking up rock with clean-
teen idols whose tepid pop covers of rock music prefigured the neutered sounds of Muzak, the
real thing was never totally squelched. Trying to cool the hot persona of rockers, record-company
image makers may have replaced leather motorcycle jackets and boots with seersucker suits and
penny loafers, but rock and roll was unstoppable. And after spending the fifties trying to tame
the beast, the keepers lost control when it escaped into the sixties.

The worst fears of the preceding generation ultimately came to pass. Bubblegum not
withstanding, shock was endemic to sixties rock. Sounds, lyrics, and album and poster art busted
taboos and defined rock's aesthetic. Vivid misogyny and overt sexuality replaced the mildly
graphic sensuality of fifties bachelor music. The Deviants' cover for their first album, simply
titled *The Deviants* (1969), featured a photograph of a nun, the likes of which might titillate even

the pope. Later, in the early seventies Roxy Music took its graphic inspiration from girlie magazines with album covers (designed by Bryan Ferry) that were aimed at the masturbatory fantasies of adolescent (and adolescent at heart) record buyers. Sacred icons of American puritan culture were routinely defiled in the name of the (consumer) revolution.

By the seventies, however, shock had become novelty, and novelty soon wore thin. Alice Cooper resorted to live snakes on stage, Kiss put on Kabuki makeup and spit fake blood, while the punks turned to body piercing, skinned heads, and ritual brawling. However, in an age when conceptual artist Chris Burden shot himself with real bullets as the ultimate artistic statement, there wasn't much left that was actually shocking.

Okay, there were still moments of shocking behavior. The very name of a late-seventies group, the Dead Kennedys, evoked momentary pangs of revulsion among members of the baby-boom generation who had been traumatized by the assassinations of John F. Kennedy and Robert Kennedy. Surprisingly, their album art was not as shocking as the name, and even that—if not on radio, then in the middle-ground club culture that had become the haven of alternative music—was contextually removed from its shocking reference point after repeated airing. Repetition reduced the "statement" to meaningless sounds.

With shock on the wane, an erstwhile shock rocker now has little recourse but to turn up the offense. Marilyn Manson's stagecraft is shockingly entertaining in the blood-and-guts department. But recent run-ins with the Christian Right over satanic lyrics and performance rituals to the contrary, the group's album art barely raises a hackle. The package suggests the contents but, in deference to the sales force, stays within the bounds of acceptability.

Of course, the definition of acceptability, like pornography, changes from decade to decade, so today the shock in rock is really a quest for that which goes way over the edge. Frontal nudity is now fairly regular on prime-time TV, and so shockers must look to truly distasteful imagery for inspiration. Where once shock had an element of sarcasm and satire, today in-your-face disgust is more the state of the art.

A brief survey of shocking album art reveals a new fascination for dismembered body parts, depictions of violent death, aberrant sexual acts, and references to Nazis. For example, the cover of Sacred Reich's *Heal* (Metal Blade Records, 1996) is a photograph of a mysterious medical contraption by Max Aguilera Hellweg, taken from his book *The Sacred Heart*. Although difficult to decipher what exactly is going on, hands wearing surgical gloves hold a machine that appears to be inserted into a pulsating human heart. It's hard to even imagine Frankie Lyman and the Teenagers using this image on their record cover back in the fifties. But in the nineties it's as unextraordinary as Pat Boone's white bucks and probably less eye-catching. (Ironically, even squeaky-clean Boone wears leather now as he covers Metalica).

Compared to Sacred Reich's clinical depiction, Unsane's album art is more violently blood soaked but no more shocking. The cover for *Singles 89–92* (Matador Records, 1992) is an overview of a bathtub splattered with blood, a reference to the apparent suicide of one of the band's members. The back cover showing a toilet stall is equally gruesome, and the CD graphic itself shows smeared blood and the razor blade that did the deed. Songs with titles like "Urge to

Kill," "Vandal-X," and "Blood Boy" reinforce the violent obsession that continues with the band's next album (Matador Records, 1994), which features a color photograph of a man lying in a pool of blood, splayed across a railroad track, his severed head cut neatly at the neck. Songs with titles like "Organ Donor," "Cracked Up," and "Maggot" suggest the band's resistance to the brighter side.

Unsane uses violence as a narrative; the group called Scheer uses it as pattern. The album *Infliction* (Warner Brothers Records, 1996) features an array of photographic close-ups of sutured and stitched skin and internal organ parts; the CD is a close-up of body hair. The images seem to illustrate songs with vivid titles, including "Wish You Were Dead," "Demon," "Driven," "Screaming," and "In Your Hand." The cover is hardly shocking to a medical student or registered nurse, but, for those who are squeamish about physical interventions, this is a painful collection of images. Yet as record art it is a voyeuristic conceit with a nod to the trend in body piercing.

The cover for Animal Corpse's *Vile* takes piercing to a stylistic extreme, with its painting of a carved-up head and torso filled with slimy worms and maggots. Unappetizing as this may sound, it's no more shocking than a few choice bug scenes in *Indiana Jones and the Lost Temple of Doom*. Moreover, the cover art simply echoes the *Heavy Metal* comic style that reached the crest of the shock wave well over a decade ago. The band's logo is suitably gothic and oozy, but, regardless of how hard it tries to shock, there is a comic-book quality that doesn't allow it to come close to reality.

Where has shock gone? Despite vain attempts to make rebellious statements through album covers using such tropes as erect middle fingers, bloody pieces of meat smeared on human heads, and even vivid scenes of enema application (such as the cover of the seven-inch vinyl for Seattle's Demolition Doll Rods), shock has become pure schlock. This is not to say that there is no chance of shocking people in the nineties; the news offers plenty. But in an age when the verisimilitude of movie special effects has so numbed us to violence, blood, and guts, the real shock in music art is a CD cover that is based on the tenets of good design instead of inept tricks.

LANGUAGE

Miami has its magnificent beachfront hotels, Hollywood its sumptuous movie palaces, and deco structures are found in Washington, Seattle, and Chicago. Even a deco hybrid known as "Navajo style" can be found in cities throughout the Southwest. As Paris and Brussels are capitals of art nouveau (owing to the profound influence of architects and designers who practiced the fin de siècle style), so New York City must be hailed as the art deco capitol of the world for its many monumental buildings conforming to this international, between-the-wars decorative style.

Two stages of the moderne manifestation—skyscraper and streamline—centered in New York. The former began during the early-1920s, postwar building boom; the latter during the Great Depression, when America retooled and redesigned its industry toward modernity. Despite the preference following World War II for architecture in the stripped-down international style, New York's art deco legacy remains virtually intact today. Although some icons have disappeared (such as Fifth Avenue's gilded traffic lights topped by statuettes of Mercury), New York's undisputed treasures—the Empire State, Chrysler, Radiator, Fuller, and Chanin Buildings, as well as Rockefeller Center—continue to define the deco cityscape.

The Empire State Building did not start out as the jewel in New York's art deco crown but was conceived so that financier Jacob Raskob could turn a real estate profit in an underutilized part of midtown Manhattan. However, what began as a stubby, thirty-story office building soon grew larger and larger as this feisty little man decided that profit wasn't really as important as breaking all the existing skyscraper records.

At a meeting with his architect, William Lamb of Shreve Lamb and Harmon, Raskob pulled out a large pencil from his desk, held it up, and asked: "Bill, how high can you make it so that it won't fall down?" This became the battle cry in a competition between the Empire State and the Chrysler Building, whose height was increased each time Raskob added new floors to the Empire State. When Lamb reached eighty-six stories, only four feet higher than the Chrysler tower, Raskob wasn't about to take any chances. He looked at the flat-topped scale model and said, "It needs a hat." With those words came the dirigible mooring mast, towering two hundred feet above the eighty-sixth floor, which gave the Empire State its distinctive "hat" and New York its art deco landmark.

Unlike other period styles that ebb and flow as tastemakers command, art deco in New York has enjoyed a rather prolonged revival, beginning in the early 1960s when the first revivalist exposition opened at the New York Coliseum at Columbus Circle. Today, there is still a preponderance of renovated art deco office and apartment buildings—including lobbies as well as indoor and outdoor gardens—replete with murals, friezes, and sculpture of the period. Deco is visible throughout the five boroughs (Manhattan, Queens, Brooklyn, the Bronx, and Staten Island) as well as at Jones Beach, where, in the 1950s, New York parks and highway czar Robert Moses built deco castles in the sand. Owing to today's revivalist and postmodern design trends, more deco-inspired structures (often with domed or pyramid tops) have been added to New York City's skyline, while street-level storefronts and scaffoldings are adorned with deco ornament.

Deco emerged as an international style of luxury and exclusivity immediately following World War I, but its gestation period began before the outbreak of war. While deco roots can be traced to the applied arts academies and workshops in *fin de siècle* Vienna, Glasgow, Berlin, and Munich, its birthplace was Paris, and one of its fathers was Paul Poiret. In 1911 he founded the Martine School of Decorative Art. As Picasso and Braque revolutionized visual language at that time through cubism, Poiret created emblematic period fashions influenced by cubism. Poiret had professed revulsion for cubist and abstract art but, nonetheless, appropriated many abstract designs for his own work, thus forging a startling union of decorative and modern tendencies into the modernistic style. Although the modern and moderne shared virtually the same chronology, the differences between them were undeniably profound.

Modernism was about the future; art moderne reaffirmed the past. Modern movements in Russia, Germany, Holland, and Italy were antibourgeois. Moderne design was created for the bourgeoisie and trickled down to the masses through inexpensive knockoffs. Early deco products were usually made from an array of opulent materials, but subsequent models were machine-made en masse using economical plastics and lightweight metals. Deco's archetypal motifs were inspired by cubism, the Ballets Russes, and even Aztec and Mayan ornament. With the discovery of Tutankhamen's tomb in 1922 near Luxor, Egypt, deco ornament was transformed into a mélange of Egyptian ziggurats, sunbursts, and lightning bolts—representing the past, present, and future. Deco forms were essentially rectilinear as opposed to art nouveau's curvilinear; they were symmetric rather than asymmetric as well. But every nation that adopted deco had a distinct decorative idiom.

The *Paris Exposition Internationale des Arts Décoratifs et Industriels Modernes,* the watershed of art moderne, was sarcastically referred to by Le Corbusier as "an international performance of decoration." Although the description was apt, it was also a celebration of a decade of invention by many of the world's leading form givers (Le Corbusier included). The United States, however, was one of the few industrial nations made conspicuous by its absence. Then Secretary of Commerce (later President) Herbert Hoover declined the invitation to participate because, he said, America had nothing of merit to exhibit. Social critic Walter Lippmann had dubbed this epoch the "American Century," underscored by America's leadership in industry and urban planning, but there was no honest American style in applied and decorative arts other than historical revivals and faux mannerisms, including neocolonial, neobaroque, and neotudor.

The 1925 Paris Exposition "revealed the isolation of the United States from progressive European design," writes Karen Davies in *At Home in Manhattan: Modern Decorative Arts, 1925 to the Depression* (Yale University Art Gallery, 1985). But she also argues that people were motivated by curiosity "and [with] the desire to become conversant with modern decorative arts, thousands of Americans visited the exhibition." In New York City, which was dubbed "the nation's style pulse," enthusiasm for the new style was on the increase, thanks to various museum and gallery exhibitions. "In the wake of the 1925 Paris Exposition," continues Davies, "growing interest in modern decorative arts generated commissions for designers in New York City—from furniture to rugs to dishware. . . ." New York moderne was so popular that John Dos Passos referred to it as "the Fifth Avenue shop-window style."

Industry and technology further influenced American twentieth-century design. Technology became a kind of religion, and the temples of American know-how—skyscrapers—were awed and envied throughout the world. In 1913 the world's tallest office structure was New York's Woolworth Building, designed by Cass Gilbert in a gothic-inspired "eclectic" mode. It vividly symbolized America's economic might—the same might that fostered multimillion-dollar investments in other architectural projects. The skyscraper was imbued with mythic power, giving new meaning to the word "metropolis."

In the 1930 book *The New World Architecture,* author Sheldon Cheney writes that skyscraper design in New York was influenced by Eliel Saarinen's second-place entry to the benchmark Chicago Tribune Tower competition: "This was a logical, powerful, nakedly impressive structure," exhibiting "that loftiness, that flowering of formal beauty out of function." In rejecting historical precedents for a building of simple rectangular masses, Saarinen's work became a model for many buildings that rightly stood under the deco umbrella. The most vivid New York example was Raymond Hood's American Radiator Company Building (1924). This structure, comments Cheney, carried traces of "devotion to picturesque effects, but marked another step out of wasteful decorativeness." It did not disguise itself in an attempt to hide its function as an office building. Its exterior color scheme was also given attention not apparent in other contemporary structures. But compared to the austere international-style glass buildings erected decades later, Hood's structure stands as the epitome of decorativeness.

The Radiator Building also exemplifies the evolution of the cityscape in the 1920s because of a zoning ordinance known as the "set-back" regulation. This and other restrictions were official safeguards against the inevitability of a dense forest of skyscrapers. Karen Davies notes that "most critics say Manhattan's rising skyline was an inspirational symbol of American achievement," but certain prescient civic leaders and social commentators saw the inevitable congestion, pollution, and loss of light as hazardous to the environment. In response to the demand for "set-backs," some unique solutions were devised by architects to maximize the limitations, resulting in the many Mayan-inspired silhouettes that dot the city.

It is fitting that New York art deco, with the skyscraper as its backdrop, was called the "skyscraper style." But had it not been for Jacob Raskob, the most celebrated deco monument might not have been unique at all. Curiously, the Empire State Building was restrained compared to other ornamented buildings. Its decorative touches were actually restricted by the financial constraints of the Depression. Only the grand entrances and aluminum spandrels connecting the windows are pure decoration in the deco sense. Even the dirigible mast, though seen as a kind of folly (and used only a few times before high winds made it impossible to employ with any accuracy), could theoretically pass as functional. At the time, the Chrysler Building, both interior and exterior, was by far the most extravagant of New York's deco palaces.

For artists touched by the modern spirit, Manhattan's skyscrapers were inspirations. Painters, sculptors, and printmakers like Georgia O'Keeffe, Charles Sheeler, Louis Lozowick, and Joseph Stella transformed the already-symbolic skyline into personal and universal metaphors. The skyscape was also a powerful inspiration for Hugh Ferriss, New York's leading architectural "conceptualizer." In addition to his commissions to render real and proposed buildings, bridges, and World's Fair pavilions, Ferriss created numerous charcoal drawings (collected in his book *Metropolis of Tomorrow*) that predicted a city of the future. Other artists drew inspiration from the past to create sculptures and murals that decorated deco interiors and exteriors. Paul Manship borrowed from mythology for Rockefeller Center's gilded Prometheus, and Alfred Janniot made a monumental limestone figure of Marianne. Also in Rockefeller Center, José María Sert's massive mural *Abolition of War and Slavery* and Dean Cornwell's Eastern Airlines mural conformed to the heroism of the deco style.

In addition, New York was home to a new breed of applied artists known as industrial designers, many of whom had their offices in and therefore drew nourishment from Manhattan. Included were Donald Deskey, Raymond Loewy, Walter Darwin Teague, Gilbert Rhode, and Egmond Arens. Among their collective contributions to the decoscape were storefronts (Loewy's aluminum front for Cushman's Bakeries and Teague's glass front for Kodak) as well as building and theater lobbies (Donald Deskey's interiors for Radio City Music Hall). These machine-age artists, working to raise American industry out of its depressionary sinkhole by promoting increased consumerism, developed the streamline style that was manifest in products and graphics most vividly displayed at the "World of Tomorrow," the 1939 New York World's Fair.

No survey of New York's art deco legacy can be complete without discussion of this World's Fair. Although it was intended to introduce the world to the march of progress, its exhibits were futuristic movie-sets, decked out with art deco conceits that symbolized the future as the contemporary designers thought it might (or should) be. Social critic Lewis Mumford reproved the architecture for, in fact, being a caricature of modernism. Indeed, some of the grand streamlined structures, like Alfred Kahn's General Motors Futurama, looked like a Buck Rogers dacha. Even Harrison and Fouilhoux's Trylon and Perisphere combination, at the center of the fair and emblematic of it, was not geometrically precise in the Bauhaus manner but rather awkward in its cartoonlike form.

The streamline aesthetic was actually a bridge between the rampant ornamentalism of art deco and the pure functionalism of the international style. Nevertheless, New York deco did not die in 1940 when the World's Fair closed; instead, it became something of an anachronism owing to new priorities brought on by a global war that would soon engage the United States. The 1939 New York World's Fair marked the end of New York's deco dominance—that is, until decomania returned in the 1960s.

Der Kampfbund für Deutsche Kultur, Ortsgruppe
Frankfurt-M u. der Deutsche Buchdrucker-Verein
Frankfurt-M laden zum Besuch der Ausstellung

Die schöne
Deutsche +
+ Schrift

im Kunstgewerbemuseum, Neue Mainzerstr. 49,
ergebenst ein. Von Montag, den 6. Oktober bis
Freitag, den 19. Oktober, von 10-2 Uhr geöffnet

"Lettering is an active and vitally needful
civilizing factor and must from henceforth play a much greater part in our life. . . . It will help to
vitalize individual capacities and hence further the development of the whole of our future
civilization," proclaimed a 1936 editorial titled "Writing and Lettering in the Service of the New
State" in *Die Zeitgemässe Schrift*, a magazine devoted to students of lettering and calligraphy. The
state was the Third Reich and the lettering was Fraktur, the traditional German blackletter that
had lost favor during the Weimar Republic years when the New Typography challenged its
dominance. Yet by 1933 the Nazis, who assailed modern sans serif type as "Judenlettern,"
brought Fraktur back with a vengeance. Such was the influence of Adolf Hitler over every aspect
of German life that lettering and typography were harshly scrutinized by party ideologues.

Joseph Goebbels, Nazi minister for propaganda and enlightenment, initially decreed that
blackletter be returned to its rightful place representing German *Kultur*. So in the early years of
the Reich, blackletter became the official *Volksschrift* (lettering of the German people). However,
they who decreeth also taketh away. After registering complaints about Fraktur's illegibility
(purportedly from Luftwaffe pilots who could not read tail markings), Martin Bormann, Hitler's
secretary, forbade the use of Fraktur in 1941 and ordered all official documents and schoolbooks
to be reprinted. Overnight, blackletter became "Judenlettern," and roman type made a
triumphant return. Although blackletter continues to evoke the spirit of Nazi authoritarianism,
this summary fall from grace only adds to the historical confusion.

Blackletter, as Paul Shaw and Peter Bain state in the introduction to their catalog for the exhibition *Blackletter: Type and National Identity* (the Cooper Union, April 1998), is shrouded in mystery, mystique, and nationalism. The polar opposite of the geometrically based roman, blackletter, they explain, "is often misleadingly referred to as Old English or gothic [and] is an all-encompassing term used to describe the scripts of the Middle Ages in which the darkness of the characters overpowers the whiteness of the page." It is based on the liturgical scripts found in Gutenberg's 1455 Mainz Bible and precedes Nicolas Jenson's earliest roman alphabet by fifteen years. Blackletter developed throughout German-speaking Europe during the fifteenth century in four basic styles: textura (*gotisch*), rotunda (*rundgotisch*), schwabacher, and Fraktur. It has been reinterpreted in various manifestations and styles. The essays and time lines that comprise Shaw and Bain's catalog trace the dialectic between blackletter and roman and set the stage for the even more fascinating ideological issues inherent in the history of the type form.

Blackletter was always much more than an alphabetic system. The most illuminating essay in *Blackletter,* Hans Peter Willberg's "Fraktur and Nationalism" offers a vivid narrative of blackletter's ideological development. Prior to the Napoleonic wars, for example, tensions between the German states and France inflamed virulent nationalism, which encouraged official recognition of Fraktur as *the* German type, bestowing upon it the same passionate allegiance as a national flag. Throughout the nineteenth and twentieth centuries, blackletter symbolized the best and worst attributes of the German states and nation. In the twenties Jan Tschichold (a leftist who briefly changed his name to Ivan in solidarity with the Bolsheviks) denounced "broken type" as nationalistic, while Rudolf Koch, who also designed the sans serif Kabel as well as his own version of Fraktur, supported, to quote Wilberg, "the 'German way of Being,' which manifested itself in the 'German Way of Writing.'" Other considerations, such as rationalism versus romanticism, later entered the debate for and against blackletter. The German left used Fraktur almost as much as the right, yet the type has been criticized most for being "Nazi-letters."

Given the negative perception of blackletter, one might presume that, after the Nazis' defeat in 1945, the type would have forever fallen into disrepute. But, as Yvonne Schemer-Scheddin explains in her essay, "Broken Images: Blackletter between Faith and Mysticism," an astute analysis of past *and* present usage, the type was retained by those businesses for whom conservative or traditional values could best be symbolized through Fraktur (including those in the fields of gastronomy and beer production as well as newspapers, for their mastheads) and as a fetish for those loyal to neo-Nazi ideologies. Since German federal law forbids any display of the swastika, blackletter continues to serve a ritualistic and symbolic role for extremists. At the same time, not all blackletter revivals are the property of skins or neofascists. Contemporary typographers from Jonathan Barnbrook, to Zuzana Licko, to Michael Worthington have reinterpreted blackletter in a variety of ways, and their quirky alphabets adorn gothic novels, heavy-metal CDs, and countless magazine and television advertisements for hip products. Probably most young designers have not even considered the ramifications of blackletter. Despite its ancient history, does blackletter's short stint as the face of evil shroud or inhibit its continued application? Indeed, this type, and type in general, is not just a vessel but a catalyst of meaning, message, and ideology, and as such, it poses questions still unanswered.

During October 1925, members of the German Printers' Association based in Leipzig opened envelopes containing *Typographische Mitteilungen (TM),* the organization's monthly journal, and were shocked by the contents. Founded in 1903, as a chronicle of information, news, and "current awareness," *TM* showcased conventional German typography and used a variegated array of spiky Fraktur, or black letter, typefaces common to German publication design at the time. Occasionally, examples of au courant mannerisms, including decorative art moderne typefaces and logotypes, were reproduced in the magazine. However, the October issue, guest-edited by Jan Tschichold, a typographic prodigy who authored *The New Typography* in 1928, was not only a departure from the norm but a revolution in form, style, and content that would have a huge impact on twentieth-century graphic design. Nevertheless, at the time it was published, this scandalous issue of *TM* was an anomaly—a blip in the continuum of typographic convention. Neither the issues before nor those that followed were so dramatic.

Tschichold admired and collected experimental work from Russia, Holland, Czechoslovakia, and Germany. (Decades later he donated his collection to the Museum of Modern Art in New York.) In a decidedly uncharacteristic liberal act, *TM*'s otherwise conservative editorial board invited him to guest-edit and "summarize and introduce a few special pages" of recent developments, which Tschichold titled "Elementare Typographie" (elementary, as in returning to basics). To the *TM* editors' surprise, the magazine (which never really conformed to a single format yet was nonetheless rather proper) lost its Fraktur (except in the paid advertisements in the back) and was entirely redesigned with sans serif, lower-case gothics to frame a sampling of the most austere and ascetic "modern" compositions, which are now considered the classics of the New Typography. Although such work was featured in arcane avant-garde publications, this was the first time that the German printing establishment had a full dose of what was construed as anarchic type and layout produced by socialist and communist radicals.

In fact, this issue of *TM* not only was an aesthetic deviation but ignited political debate as well. The postwar twenties were a critical period in German politics. The advent of the Weimar Republic gave rise to major polarities on the political spectrum among right- and left-wing as well as centrist parties, all vying for governmental dominance and popular support. Revolutionary modern design was perceived as a product of the left; Russian constructivist, Dutch de Stijl, and German Bauhaus ideals were suspected of harboring political agendas. The Germans were rather unusual in allowing ideology to influence design as they did. It is nonetheless clear from the political broadsides and posters of the Weimar period that sans serif typefaces did have a symbolic connotation and, as the left critics of the day described it, "breathed the new."

Since *TM* was distributed not only to members of the Printers' Association, which was apolitical in nature, but also to all printing and design professionals throughout Germany, Austria, and Switzerland, the inherent ideological issues caused some alarm. Throughout the twenties, Austrian and Swiss designers eschewed this trend as qualitatively unacceptable. Only intense lobbying forced a sea change in design attitudes. Although *TM* never intended to lobby the design industries to change attitudes or radicalize them, the political side of the New Typography did wash over into literary publications and organizations that supported book design, such as the social democratic–leaning Büchergilde Gutenberg, which encouraged using sans serif and other novel (for the time) typography in books. Aligning themselves along political lines, different German publishers directed their in-house design departments to work in either the modern or traditional manner.

TM was careful to discuss experimental typography without taking sides or showing preference for any style or trend. Its responsibility was to report, not to criticize. However, its editors often did speak out about the frequent poor imitation of the so-called Bauhaus style. The editors accepted Tschichold's authority in this area, and, in showcasing the so-called form-givers—Lazar El Lissitzky, Kurt Schwitters, Theo van Doesburg, Karel Tiege, and others—they felt justification for devoting an entire issue to the subject. Yet other trade magazines, including *Gebrauchsgraphik, Reklame,* and *Archiv,* were apparently less reticent in offering ongoing coverage to the Bauhaus imitations. After Tschichold's October 1925 issue, *TM* hardly revisited elementary typography with such vigor again. The following month, and for many subsequent years, Fraktur remained the typeface of choice, although the layouts gradually became a little more contemporary. *TM* continued until 1933, when it was absorbed into *Graphische Nachrichten* (Graphic News, founded in 1922). By then, the Nazis had gained power, and the New Typography was declared degenerate anyway.

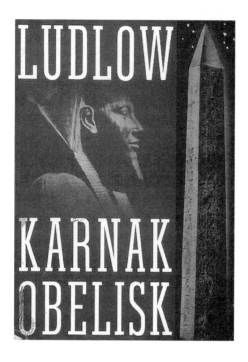

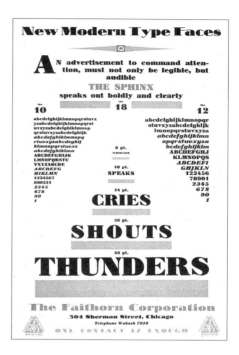

Type specimen sheets from the mid-1920s through the early 1930s were exuberant displays of a new commodity. Type was not merely a neutral means of transmitting the word, it was the lead-cast embodiment of ideas and ideals—the symbol of newness and improvement—of industrial nations that saw few economic bounds. More than a graphic product, it was a weapon of sorts in the consumer revolution between the world wars.

With the advent of mass advertising in early-twentieth-century newspapers and magazines, novel (indeed, novelty) letterforms—some revivals from antiquity, others resolutely of their own time—were all the rage. Under the banner of modernism, a slew of typefaces (and dingbats too) with mystifying names—Vulcan, Cubistic Bold, Novel Gothic, and Chic—were promoted as heralding a new age. Job printers, commercial artists, and designers were assured through trade journals that advertising was the vanguard of progress. But, in truth, progress was a fetish: an aura of cosmopolitan culture and avant-garde style manifest in hot metal, imbued with the power to attract and hold consumer attention.

Specimen sheets were not new to the modern (or moderne) era. Type designers from the fifteenth century composed showings of partial or complete alphabets, often in aesthetically pleasing displays, to give printers a sample. During the late nineteenth century, many of these showings used quotes from the Bible or other literature. Sometimes the compositor, perhaps an erstwhile poet, set sample lines of doggerel. By the turn of the century, type founding was a big business; the catalogs, booklets, and specimen sheets of the day were no-nonsense rosters of form and style. But with the Jazz Age, modern era, and modernistic epoch after World War I, the makers and distributors of type were impelled to borrow the same marketing conceits of the advertising industry that they serviced, selling families of type as if they were clothes or cosmetics.

Type specimens announced the latest fashions. "Three Larger Sizes Now Ready" screams a notice for a new mammoth cut of Ultra Bodoni; "A Colorful Showing of Beautiful French Types" exclaims the heading over a selection of au courant imports. Type specimens were the sheet music of the printing industry. Covers featured striking designs and colorful images, often in moderne decorative, geometric styles. For the perfume faces (so called because they advertised sundries and fragrances), designs were complete with ornamental flourishes and swashes. Inside lines of letters were systematically composed according to their relative weights. Sandwiching these showings were examples of type both at work and at play. Mock advertisements, calendars, flyers, letterheads, and logos revealed in two or three bright, flat colors the conjugal bliss of letter and image. These were not, however, total flights of fancy or even impeccable design. Specimen sheets were required to convey a considerable amount of information and were often cluttered with the designed effluvia that today typify the age.

As novelty wore thin by the 1930s, most specimen sheets followed the same trend toward simplicity. But moments of design inspiration could still be found in dingbats, sectional dashes, and other printer "jewels." In Bauer's "Futura Schumck," the equivalent of a child's set of blocks, geometric forms were used to construct abstract and representational images for the modern layout. In the American Type Foundry "Broadway Series" calender, silhouettes dance along the pages. Cubistic dingbats, including an array of stairstep and sawtooth ornaments printed in bright pastels, seems contemporary by today's standards.

Most leading international type foundries issued specimens, including American Type Foundry, Continental Type Foundry, Deberny and Peignot, Flinsch, and Bauer; they were distributed through type shops. During the Great Depression, elaborate type specimen sheets became an unnecessary extravagance, and type was ultimately sold primarily through simple type catalogs. Notices of new arrivals would be done through rather ordinary postcards or flyers, and the high art of the specimen ultimately atrophied.

Typography, like the hemline, changes as fashion dictates. So, in the 1960s, a growing trend in universal typography began to outstrip the utopian ideal that had provoked missionaries of the modern to establish rules governing the use of limited type families and compositions. While the masters of this form, Paul Rand, Rudolph de Harak, and George Tscherny, expertly practiced the art of typographic neutrality to frame strong visual ideas, others, who designed with blind adherence to those tenets, produced bland compositions that typified the mediocre in corporate communications.

In the 1950s, the distinction between quotidian commercial art and sophisticated graphic design was defined by a high standard of typographic craftsmanship. In the period before the widespread application of phototype, hot-metal typesetting required considerable refinements to avoid horrendous results. Skilled typographers rejected faces that led to disaster, like the novelty and poster faces common in print advertising. The remnants of bygone eras were summarily dismissed. Systematic type composition was the key to design purity. But, by the 1960s, a reaction to what had become the rigidity of the overarching international style—in addition to a distinctly natural, creative urge to move ahead of the curve—prompted designers to push the boundaries of type.

Push Pin Studios revived Victorian, art nouveau, and art deco letterforms for display and body copy in reaction to the rational Swiss approach of the late 1950s and 1960s. Returning typography to a period of exuberance before Jan Tschichold's *The New Typography* (published in

1928) imposed its revolutionary strictures on modern design, Push Pin Studios advanced the notion that graphic design ran the gamut from serious to playful while solving a wide range of problems. Type did not have to be a neutral element on a pristine page but, rather, could be an expressive voice—a means of giving the written word character and nuance. This was possible by the shift toward phototypesetting, which, in turn, encouraged typographic revivals. So by reintroducing passé commercial art styles and reviving forgotten letterforms, Push Pin introduced an individualistic typographic language rooted more in graphic ornament than precisionist grids.

Late modern typography, distinguished by the clean and simple compositions of both classical and modern typefaces, was changing the look of advertising from chaotic to eloquent and at the same time was more expressive too. Through Westvaco's *Inspirations,* Bradbury Thompson promoted "talking type." By tweaking traditional letterforms into visual puns, typeset words became both verbal and visual. This concept was further pursued by Robert Brownjohn, who imbued letters with sound and motion, making them visual components of a word or phrase. Ivan Chermayeff made otherwise static type appear kinetic in a print prefiguration of today's on-screen typography. The letterform as pun was further tested in advertising layout by Gene Federico, Lou Dorfsman, and Herb Lubalin. With precision, Federico made type and image into total compositions. Dorfsman used type not only to convey a message but also to be part of rebuslike compositions. Lubalin exploited the type-as-sound idea and further explored the sculptural eccentricities of letterforms to their communicative advantage. He demonstrated that the shape of letters signified as much as their content; he would set excruciatingly tight lines of text, smashing bodies together as if to animate the forms. For these designers, typography was, in fact, illustration, sometimes complementing and often substituting for pure imagery.

As type directors and graphic designers were convinced to switch to phototype, typography became more stylistically and compositionally eclectic. The large variety of typefaces available on Typositor made typographic experimentation more commonplace. Although the grid was still a sacrosanct element of modern design, the liberties that designers were taking was beginning to affect the dominant ways of working. And, with the advent of psychedelic typography in the late 1960s, characterized by radical optical exaggerations in historical faces from the Victorian and secessionist periods, it appeared that the language of typography was in for a reevaluation.

Typography in the 1960s was transitional, a word that connotes flux but not necessarily instability. The classical or orthodox moderns established a true standard for "good typography," but standards ultimately beg to be challenged. The critical response of the revivalists and eclecticists was an alternative that became yet another style. Bridging these groups were those individuals who took from both extremes to create a design language that became the quintessential expression of the times.

Bell Centennial

DESIGNER: MATTHEW CARTER

ABCDEFGHIJKLM
NOPQRSTUVWXY
&Z123450678–
acdefghijklmnop,
rstuvwxyz.

Despite the PC-era popularization of the word "font," few aspects of graphic design are taken for granted by the general public more so than type design. As Beatrice Warde, a type scholar of the 1930s, cautioned in an essay titled "The Crystal Goblet or Printing Should Be Invisible" (1932), type is a servant of communication and must not draw attention to itself and away from the message. Like a crystal goblet, type should be elegantly designed yet must never be anything more than a vessel.

Among the most quotidian and disregarded typefaces, but probably the most critical of any type families or systems because of their effect on daily life, are those faces designed exclusively for use in telephone directories. While cramming countless names, numbers, and addresses onto tightly packed pages is doubtless one of the most challenging of all typeface applications, its very functionality ensures that it is less appreciated than more commonly referenced commercial text and display faces. The type commonly found in the white or yellow pages is so matter-of-fact, so lacking in pretense, artifice, or style, that it is one of the most obvious examples of Warde's invisibility principle. If it is well designed, it just gives the facts—and nothing but the facts—in a manner that is readable, legible, and timeless.

Yet not all telephone directory typefaces are created with perfect attributes. Over time, not all type designs have withstood the difficult demands placed upon them to function efficiently in this unique data environment. In the early 1970s, for example, when AT&T was growing at breakneck, monopolistic speed, as both its customer base increased and new technologies were introduced, the time came for a reevaluation and overhaul of directory design, stimulating a new efficient type design for telephone directories. Type designer and digital-type pioneer Matthew Carter (b. 1937) was commissioned to create a system based on his analysis of the technical and aesthetic deficiencies of the existing Bell Gothic.

One of the catalysts was a new method of composition: AT&T's regional Bell companies were beginning to compose directories on cathode-ray-tube typesetters. This electronic technology greatly increased production speed, but, as Carter reports, it "had the bad side-effect of causing the existing directory typeface to print lighter than it had as metal type." To counteract the loss of weight, printers ran more ink on the presses, which darkened type on the page but also tended to cause inkblots within and between letters—"a remedy that had a worse effect on legibility than the problem it was meant to solve," adds Carter. On the aesthetic front, Saul Bass had redesigned AT&T's corporate identity using the essence of neutrality, Helvetica. As a consequence Bell Gothic, derived by Linotype in 1937 from sturdy nineteenth-century American gothics, clashed with the newer Swiss style of sans serif.

Carter was challenged to design a face that balanced utility and aesthetics while addressing the new typesetting technologies. "The previous type," says Carter, referencing obsolete technology, "was designed as brass line caster matrices for Linotype hot-metal machines. Linotype matrices were 'duplexed,' which is to say that each matrix was stamped with two letters to make it easier to change between pairs of faces from the keyboard. The matrices of Bell Gothic coupled the primary face, used for names and numbers, with a secondary face used for addresses. The address face was made lighter and smaller than the name-and-number face, but, because the two were duplexed, it was impossible to make it any narrower." By the 1970s the mechanical constraint of duplexing was obsolete, and Carter had to find a means to achieve variation within strict boundaries.

The uncomfortable realities of directory production—printing tiny type at high speeds on very thin newsprint—made the development of Bell Centennial an exercise in what AT&T called "design for printability." The overriding concern was to make the directories more legible. In ordinary reading of continuous text, the brain recognizes words by grasping their overall shapes not by deciphering individual letters. "Readability" is the efficiency of this process, and it relies heavily on the context of meaning. Telephone directories are for reference, not for reading. There is little or no context of meaning in a directory entry to help with interpretation. A familiar name might be understood if a single letter is obscured, but six legible digits in a telephone number give no clue to a seventh that is illegible. "In a normal text type, where 'readability' is the issue, the designer's concern is to make the letterforms combine well into distinctive word-shapes," Carter explains. "In a directory face the issue is 'legibility,' which is governed entirely by the discriminability of its individual letterforms. The difference is between cohesion and clarity. Legibility, the more objective quality, can be tested by, for example, visually degrading alternative designs of the same character to the point where one or other version becomes unintelligible."

The original requirement for a typeface that would be more compatible with Helvetica lost ground during the development phase of Bell Centennial. Helvetica was not designed to be at its best at six-point size, as it is used in telephone directories. Many of its features, clean-cut and elegant at text and display sizes, tested badly for legibility when miniaturized. "The rounded lowercase letters and the figures in particular were problematical: 3 and 8, and 5 and 6, for example, were easily confused. More articulate forms had to be devised," says Carter. "In the end the functional imperatives of 'design for printability' outweighed stylistic concerns to the point that it is rather hard to categorize Bell Centennial typographically by reference to general-purpose sans serifs."

Digitalization allowed for greater flexibility. "In a digital design the name-and-number typeface could afford to be wider, as was appropriate to its importance in the directory entry," Carter explains: "while the address face, which was subsidiary in purpose, could be made narrower. This freedom—to give the two faces independent metrics—together with a designed-in gain in overall weight were the starting points of the new design." One of AT&T's requirements for the new type was that it must "provide an equal content on a page as presently achieved" by Bell Gothic. "In practice it turned out that un-duplexing the name and address fonts resulted in an aggregate saving of space and in fewer two-line entries," Carter adds. "Because the multipliers in directory production are so huge (entries, columns, pages, copies, editions), this small saving in the type achieved a significant economy in paper consumption." Today, with the AT&T monopoly disbanded, this typeface is used at the discretion of individual telephone companies; most do, some do not. Likewise, at its inception, the decision to use the new face was left up to the individual Bell companies; however, in 1978 all American directories adopted Bell Centennial, whose name refers to the centenary celebration of the first directory.

TONEELSCHUUR

SMEDESTRAAT 23, 2011 RG HAARLEM

TONEELSCHUUR

SMEDESTRAAT 23, 2011 RG HAARLEM

TONEELSCHUUR

Style is not a four-letter word, yet it does imply superficiality, conformity, and a foolish enslavement to fashion. The moderns condemned these attributes as detrimental to clear and efficient communication. And although the postmoderns reveled in stylisms, they insisted that theirs were not merely fads or fancies but rather necessary stimulants to ensure more engaging communications. The pendulum swings, and today the naysayers warn that obvious style must be avoided because it relegates the designer to a prison of the ancient or recent past. Hence, style is condemned as a tool of obsolescence.

However, style is also a signature that need not be insincere or bankrupt. It can also be a cue for an underlying visual persona born of complex aesthetic and conceptual issues. Remember, graphic design is as much about signaling a message to a receiver in a unique, sometimes idiosyncratic, way as it is about neutrally conveying ideas and information. When style is efficiently used, it serves as an identifier and entry point. At its most successful, style modifies language as an accent indicating from where and perhaps from whom the message derives.

As style goes, the graphic narratives and distinctive hand-lettered typography by Dutch designer, illustrator, and cartoonist Joost Swarte (b. 1947) is a tapestry of twentieth-century influences as viewed through a visionary's lens. Swarte's style draws directly from one of the century's most ornamental epochs, between the 1920s and 1930s, when art moderne (or art deco) reigned supreme as a commercial alternative to utopian modernism. But Swarte's interpretation of these fundamental modernistic attributes, among them rectilinear letterforms and ziggurat/sunburst printers' ornaments, are adapted as elements of a personal vocabulary. Swarte's routine references to the past are so consistent that his ownership is undeniable. Despite déjà vu among those who know the origin of his most common hand-lettered faces, over the course of his development they have become inextricably wed to his own hand. Letters that were used over half a century ago are revived not simply for the sake of pastiche but rather to express his own aesthetically playful urges.

Swarte's is a seamless weave of both moderne and comic influences. His work is multi-dimensional and relies on letterforms to complement his narrative drawings. Regarding the latter, the influence of the simple linearity of the cartoon character Tintin by the Belgian artist Hergé is most apparent. "In the beginning I drew in Hergé's style to study how he did it and I found it suited me well because I could draw so many details in architecture and objects," explains Swarte, with a nod to his passion for buildings and ephemeral design objects. Swarte coined the term "clear line" to describe Hergé's approach and his own. Yet he is quick to affirm that the line alone is only a means to achieve an end.

Swarte uses lettering and line drawing like personal speech. His singular vision emerges through a combination of dramatic, witty, and absurd comic images within a total narrative. As a designer, he enjoys artifacts of the past, but as storyteller he starts from zero. And where he diverges from his main influence is clear in this statement: "Hergé tries to take the reader to the real world, I take the reader into *my* world."

The galaxies for Swarte's world are comic strips, children's books, record covers, posters, wine labels, shopping bags, ex libris, magazine covers, postage stamps for the PTT (the Dutch postal service), and architectural interiors. He has published his own comics magazines including *Tante Leny* (Aunt Leny), and *Vrij Nederland* (Free Netherlands, which originally began as an anti-Nazi [real] underground newspaper); in addition, he served as a contributor to *Submarine* (a Belgian counterculture journal), *Charlie* (a French humor paper), *Humo* (the Belgian TV and radio guide), the Dutch comics magazine *Jippo,* and *RAW,* through which he was introduced to the American public. Whether a publication contains an exclusive collection of his work or the occasional contribution, there is no mistaking a "Swarte" for the work of any other artist. Style combined with conceptual mastery are his virtues.

Swarte's style is ultimately secondary to the tales he tells. Six stories originally published in *Charlie,* for example, are collected in the 1979 book *Modern Art,* of which the title story is a satire on the nature of style and art. It stars Anton Makassar, one of Swarte's cartoon alter egos about whom Swarte says: "As always with comics, you invent your character out of your character so that parts of yourself come out of a character *in extremo.*" Another Swarte stand-in is the character Jopo de Pojo (he chose the name because it sounded so pleasing), who reflects Swarte's shy and isolated side, while Makassar (named after the city in Indonesia) suggests the artist's self-proclaimed professorial side. "He is a bit of an inventor. He always comes up with crazy ideas, and is proud of himself. That's me, too." The third part of the personality puzzle is Pierre Van Ganderen (which, translated, means "of simple mind"). "He is a working man who does what he has to do, who is a bit childish and sometimes naïve."

Swarte is not wed to conventional cartoon situation comedies but, rather, varies his story lines as much as he pushes the technical boundaries to transcend any hint of nostalgia. For example, although the adventures of Makassar resemble 1920s comic artist George McManus's "Bringing Up Father," it is clearly synthesis not revival. "A young artist must grow out of the past to build up a solid background," he says. "But one must find one's own way out of nostalgia and stop looking too much over the shoulder." When 1930s type design and early-twentieth-century cartooning converge, a certain timelessness is evoked. Of Swarte's mastery, Art Spiegelman, former *RAW* editor/publisher, explains that he "has a refined visual intelligence wed to a sense of humor and history. He experiments within a tradition, and is always trying things that are so daring yet made so simple that by the time they are accomplished it looks so easy that it betrays the courage involved."

Every part of Swarte's lettering and drawing is meticulously rendered. His clear line may be reduced to the necessary strokes, but his images are flooded with ideas. Ironically, in an era when coarse, expressionistic *art brut* is in vogue, Swarte's circumspect precisionism is often called retro. Yet attention to detail is not stylistic conceit, it is timeless.

In the 1930s, typefaces were announced with the same hype and hullabaloo as a popular song. Contempo names like Ultra Modern, Streamline, Cubist Bold, Broadway, Vulcan, and Novel Gothic appeared like song titles on the covers of specimen sheets designed to look like sheet music. But, because of wartime shortages of hot metal, by the forties type specimens became austere and by the fifties they were densely packed line or word showings. The exuberant prewar spirit returned only somewhat in the sixties, when Photolettering Inc. introduced its alphabet encyclopedias stuffed with hundreds of new photofaces on pages that approximated old Victorian theater bills, but even these did not totally recapture the energy of the thirties. For most of the seventies and eighties specimens were more or less functional and usually lackluster, but the dawn of type's digital age in the mid-eighties marked a new inventiveness as a handful of digital foundries started to compete for market share.

In 1984, Emigre Fonts announced its original typefaces in applications designed to capture the type buyer's attention and imagination. Emigre Fonts has announced new faces over the years—first through brochures, later on the pages of *Emigre* (as ITC does through its magazine, *U&lc*), and also via broadsheets (double-sided, folded posters). On the broadsheet front, a typographic composition presents the face in a free-form manner, while half of the verso is often an additional type specimen designed to accentuate the quirky characters of the face. The other half of the verso, the business side, includes the mailing panel and ordering information. Emigre's specimen sheet for a face called Not Caslon offers a showing of this classically inspired but decidedly experimental face on the front and includes on the back an essay on the history of type founding, which explains why liberties have been taken. As a collection of documents, these posters are not merely salesmen samples but, as well, a distinct history of digital type founding of the past decade.

Inspired by Emigre Fonts, Elliott Earls, an independent type designer in Connecticut, creates specimen sheets that announce his own eccentric digital-type designs and markets them almost exclusively through a series of large broadsheets mailed out quarterly. Like Emigre, these are one- or two-color posters, which on the front have an abstract assemblage of his latest face(s), often combined with Photoshop-manipulated images containing references to both the inspirations for and origins of the face. As an introduction, for example, to his family of eroding types— Dysphasia, Dysplasia, and Dyslexia—the poster announces: "3 fonts in the family. 3 states of duress." But rather than a conventional sampler of functional options, the poster shows the face(s) as texture or pattern in a virtual type painting. The verso side shows off complete alphabets presented in original, sometimes rambling essays, or what Earls refers to as "events" of typographic form, as well as references to other faces in his humorous font folio, including Heimlich and Heimlich Maneuver, Hernia, Turnbuckle and Turnbuckle Bland, Klieglight and Klieglight Dark. Although they are part of a marketing strategy, Earls's specimens are a kind of typographic performance art that may ultimately inspire a type buyer but are designed first and foremost to express his own vision.

Less art-based, but no less eccentric, are the specimen sheets designed by House Industries of Wilmington, Delaware, whose typeface names all begin or end with, you guessed it, the word "house," as in Blockhouse, Coffee House, House Trained, Stakehouse, Splitlevel House, and their industrial-strength stencil, Warehouse. Printed in two colors, including either a metallic copper or silver, on heavy cardboard or rag colored paper stock, House Industries' specimens suggest a botched printer's makeready. Borrowing from the same stock printer's vernacular that influenced Charles Spencer Anderson, these type manifestos have a camp quality that both Emigre Fonts and Elliott Earls eschew. The front sides of House Industries' specimens are a collage of layered, mundane commercial cuts and logos, while the versos offer a deceptively traditional showing of their faces in the manner of the ubiquitous 1970s dollar-a-word Typositor line chart. A recent specimen for a new "Scrawl Font Collection" of handwritten lettering—the kind that one might doodle while on the telephone—is at once a mélange of visual effluvia and a disciplined showing of silly letters. These specimens do attract attention and provide the desktop designer with a wide range of witty typographic options.

Some fanzines and magazines, such as *Ray Gun, Erzatz,* and *KGB,* offer their own custom fonts for commercial release. *Plazm,* a Portland, Oregon–based digital type foundry and culture magazine of the same name, issues a variety of specimen sheets, from simple line showings (one with the headline, "Heavy Breathing for Your Eyes") to poster-sized broadsheets in the manner of Emigre. Plazm Fonts are ostensibly display and novelty faces designed by local fontographers that build upon the idea of the degenerating font originally developed by Erik van Blokland and Just van Rossum, whose Beowulf is distributed by FontShop International. Faces such as Dave

Henderlieiter's Pulsitallia, Doe Man, and Dizzy Spell, which are some of Plazm's featured specimens, are among the most compelling of this group for their technical ingenuity.

Like Elliot Earls, independent designers are also branching out into the type market through specimens and other printed ephemera. Chicago designer Rick Valicenti's Thirst Type catalog is a display of conceptual experiments with contemporary form. While others toy with eroding type, Valicenti uses anamorphic mechanisms to achieve strange contours and curvilinear relationships. The catalog itself is one of the most ambitious of the smaller specimens. Printed in full color, this booklet shows full-page examples of his signature layered and gauzed imagery used as backdrops for his Thirst Type alphabets, which sometimes get lost amid the visuals. What's most curious is that the Thirst Type catalog is like a video frozen in print, wherein the type specimens seem to be waiting to be placed in a screen environment.

Indeed, many of today's typefaces appear to be designed with the screen environment in mind, which is probably why the next generation of innovative type specimens will not be found on paper. Following *Fuse* magazine's pioneering efforts, Emigre Fonts already has a large collection of entertainingly animated showings on its First Class software and Web site locations. Elliott Earls recently added a CD-ROM to his repertoire, which like his posters features pictures of types in motion, not functional showings. And in Amsterdam Erik van Blokland and Just van Rossum currently display their designs in computer-generated type animations that dance to music and sound effects. This curiously brings the art of modern type specimens back to its starting point in the early 1930s, when typefaces had a unique cache and the sheet music style provided a suitable context for display. Today it's not enough to show elegantly set line samples; owing to the proliferation of home computers, desktop publishing, and screen-based media, type is such a highly competitive activity that it necessitates a larger stage on which to audition and perform.

Pussy Galore

DESIGNERS: TEAL TRIGGS, LIZ MCQUISTON, AND SIAN COOK

During the late 1960s, when the feminist movement was in full tilt, two women writers known for their satiric essays in *Bitch*, a New York–based underground newspaper that they edited, decided that the English language was the principal tool of male oppression against women. Therefore, their publication would not include any word that had a gender-specific prefix or suffix, such as "man" or "son." Instead, the neutral word "one" was substituted so that the word "person" became "perone," and the word "woman" (which they deemed was most subjugated of all words) became "woperone." They applied the new spelling to common nongendered words as well, like "many" (peroney), "season" (seaperone), and "manifold" (peronefold), which forced readers to examine the so-called masculine dominance in the English language. However, the editors ultimately admitted that these linguistic alterations were unwieldy in their own writing, and after an issue or two they reverted back to standard spellings.

The point, however, was clear. Woperones were afforded second-class citizenship in ways that were matter-of-factly ingrained from birth in the minds of both genders. And although certain habits, such as written language, were not going to change overnight—or as easily as the popular acceptance of the alternative Ms. instead of Miss or Mrs. (which, in fact, did not happen overnight)—it was important to expose cultural and societal absolutes that were prejudicial and detrimental toward women. Even if the spelling experiment was just a satiric exercise that reached a small number of readers of an arcane alternative newspaper, it was a good lesson in how archetypes and stereotypes are retained through inertia. It was also an indication that other confrontations were in the offing.

Gender issues have not been ignored by the graphic design profession—which prior to the 1980s was predominately a men's club and today is weighted more toward women in designer and design management roles. Yet, although female graphic designers have increased their overall presence and individual prestige within the field, few have used their design and communications skills to redefine or restructure visual language. The editors of *Bitch* realized that while it was not easy to alter basic lexicons, it was important to raise fundamental issues about gender inequities that had been simmering below the surface for ages.

Toward this end, yet with greater determination to make a substantive (and educational) impact, members of a design collective in England called the Women's Design and Research Unit (WD+RU)—founded in 1994 and including Teal Triggs (b. 1957), Liz McQuiston (b. 1952), and Sian Cook (b. 1962)—sought means of addressing continuing inequities within the design field. They targeted the once-arcane yet newly democratized digital realm of font design as both a forum and medium for altering values and perceptions. They decided to create a font comprised of symbolic pictographs and word-bites that were engaged by using conventional keyboard strokes. This, they hoped, would be an effective way to both enter and engage the consciousness of users.

The resulting font, Pussy Galore, named after the bombshell heroine of James Bond's *Goldfinger* film and memorably played by the actress Honour Blackman, was begun in 1994 and completed in early 1995 (although it continues to be somewhat open-ended in terms of final form). It was commissioned by Jon Wozencroft, the editor of *Fuse* (the experimental-type magazine published by FontShop International), for publication in *Fuse 12: Propaganda* (winter 1994), but only a portion of the entire typeface was published at that time due to a variety of technical reasons.

Pussy Galore, the fictional character, was what McQuiston and Triggs call a "femme fatale with a mission," who maximized her sensual endowment as a tool of power rather than of subservience. "She was wonderfully sexy and at the same time strong and in control," says Triggs. "We hope by appropriating Pussy Galore as a term and typeface title that it will get people to think twice not only about its use but also about other words that usually denote [the] negative. . . concerning women. We also wanted to use language which celebrated women— hence the ambiguity of the term."

So, whatever contemporary or nostalgic images or ideas that Pussy Galore evokes in the minds of beholders—cocksmanship or Blackman's sexual omnipotence—the font offers unique independent frames of reference that reveal numerous myths about women. In this way, Pussy Galore is a "conceptual typeface" designed to help explore the roots of misconceptions about women propagated through contemporary vocabularies of Western culture. As Triggs explains in *Baseline: Issue 20* (1995), "Pussy Galore is an 'interactive tool' which invites response and urges you to talk back, challenge, and reassess, not only [about] how women have been constituted by language, but also the structure of language itself."

Pussy Galore is not, however, a typical typeface—in fact, "typeface" may be the preferred description because it functions in relation to a keyboard but an inaccurate one because Pussy Galore bares no relation to a conventional alphabet. Rather, it is a clever commingling of Otto Neurath's Isotype system of the 1930s and a sampling of printer's cuts and dingbats. The pictographs and word pictures that comprise the Pussy Galore font are fragments of narrative that individually serve as stop signs and, when fashioned together, as vehicles for various archetypes and stereotypes.

The keyboard is employed to create pathways in order for the user to make references and associations with the characters of the font. It acknowledges the conventions of language (e.g., vowels, consonants, upper and lower case) and uses shift, option, and normal keys to launch functions that allow for additional layers of exploration. For example, conventional "level one" keyboarding of any word will render a string of ideological statements (graphic picture boxes that frame such words or sayings as "sisters," "rights," "grrrls," "mother," "power," "Thelma & Louise"). Progression through each additional keyboard level takes the user through a journey into what Triggs describes as a multilayered web of associations and representational sets of ideas about women, such as the following:

Level 1 normal = empowerment of women
Level 2 shift = ugly stereotypes
Level 3 option = personal choices
level 4 shift+option = vulgar and sexual language

The complex layering of messages embedded in this font, including fragmented line drawings of the female anatomy, gives users the chance to make serendipitous juxtapositions through random access or specific polemical statements by deliberate applications. Asterisks appear on selected icons/words indicating additional strata of information, such as textual quotes or images-sequences, which are accessed through other operating programs contained in the disc's suitcase. Accessing these alternative strata, the user is allowed to highlight, among other things, a selection of "Hidden Heroines" who have made important contributions to art, design, and film. In addition, other elements are likely to appear throughout, including a witty animated sequence of women's hands ranging from a revolutionary raised fist to a diamond-clad glove. Humor is an effective mediator in the communication of Pussy Galore's decidedly ideological messages.

Although Pussy Galore was created for an experimental design venue, it is not intended for a visual elite of sophisticated graphic designers alone. The digital nature of the font is accessible to anyone with a minimum of computer savvy. It serves both as a graphics tool for those who choose to integrate some or all of its forms into layouts or as a game of digital hide-and-seek for those who choose to uncover all the hidden messages. "Through the user's 'personalization' of the typeface," Triggs adds, "Pussy Galore's aim of embracing democratization is underscored, removing any reliance upon 'artistic' sophistication which might render it alien to popular use."

The "letterforms" have indeed been created as simple shapes or pictograms for the user to reconstruct or redesign, and the possibilities are numerous: Through certain keyboard configurations a picture of Eve's snake might be juxtaposed to a floppy "dumb blonde" hairdo. Likewise, strings of characters or words develop accidentally depending on the user, "but each connection is heavily charged with meaning and value," says Triggs. "In this way technology is used to help users assemble their own visual languages, bringing to the typeface unique experiences, individual prejudices, and interpretations."

It is not likely that Pussy Galore will be bundled with the iMac or any other personal computer, at least not in the near future. But there is no reason why it should not be. Although conventional wisdom might argue that an essay in the *World Book Encyclopedia* (which is bundled on many computers) on feminism is a more straightforward method of conveying factual information, Pussy Galore's interactivity ultimately invites more questions and presumably greater engagement in the issues it raises. What began as an attempt to challenge typographic principles in an experimental context has become a model of how new media encourages novel methods of communication. "The old gal has fared really well!" Triggs concludes. "We are really surprised that Pussy Galore has taken on a life of its own. What is really satisfying is when we get correspondence from students in New Zealand, Brazil, Mexico, and the USA who want to explore further the ideas we propose in research essays and in their own use of the typeface. We always said if we reached just one student/designer, the whole project was worthwhile!"

Mrs Eaves

DESIGNER: ZUZANA LICKO

A B C D E F G H I J K L M N O P Q R S T U V W
a b c d e f g h i j k l m n o p q r s t u v w x y z 1 2 3 4 5 6 7 8 9 0
A B C D E F G H I J K L M N O P Q R S T U V W
a b c d e f g h i j k l m n o p q r s t u v w x y z 1 2 3 4 5 6 7 8 9 0
A B C D E F G H I J K L M N O P Q R S T U V W
a b c d e f g h i j k l m n o p q r s t u v w x y z 1 2 3 4 5 6 7 8 9 0
A B C D E F G H I J K L M N O P Q R S T U V W X Y Z 1 2 3 4 5 6 7 8 9 0
A B C D E F G H I J K L M N O P Q R S T U V W X Y Z
↜ ↢ © ↧ ↥ ↦ ¼ ½ ¾ ⅛ ⅜ ⅝ ⅞ ⅓ ⅔ ℗ ✳ ® ✿ ✴ ↑ ff fi

F or those who experienced firsthand the digital-type revolution that began in the mid-1980s, it was nothing short of liberating. For the first time since Gutenberg, the means of creating complete alphabets for repeated text and display application was not limited to rarefied specialists but was available to anyone possessing a little beige box called a Macintosh—anyone, that is, inclined toward letter design. At first the characters made for the computer screen were blocky and bitmapped, as if they were boxes inked on graph paper, which indeed they were in the digital sense. The constraints imposed by nascent computer software, seventy-two-dot-per-inch computer screens, and dot matrix printers gave rise to letterforms that were both functional and aesthetically limited. Nonetheless, the very idea that designers could compose *and* create their own type spurred an initial frenzy for custom alphabets that ranged from sublime to ridiculous.

One of the pioneers of the new fontography is Zuzana Licko (b. 1961), who started designing typefaces in 1985 for use in *Emigre,* the homespun culture tabloid founded in 1983 by her husband Rudy VanderLans (b. 1955), a former page designer for the *San Francisco Chronicle.* Designing on the early Macintosh before the advent of sophisticated page-layout programs, WYSIWYG, and Hypercard was itself a feat of ingenuity, but seeing beyond computer limitations required a vision born of that proverbial mother—necessity. Licko's plunge into the design of coarse-resolution type was prompted by a need to overcome the conformity of Mac default faces and to create a distinct identity for the fledgling magazine (not, at that time, recast as the clarion of postmodern graphic design, which is its legacy today). What *Emigre* became for graphic design culture is underscored by Licko's contribution to the history of digital-type founding; the Emigre venture proved trailblazing on two fronts. Licko's early designs—including her initial typefaces (c. 1985) called Emperor, Universal, Oakland, and Emigre—further helped launch the unique type business Emigre Graphics (later Emigre Fonts), which spawned today's indy digital-type industry.

Licko's education in graphic design and typography (she received a B.A. from the University of California at Berkeley) included one course in calligraphy, which, as she recalls, "was nightmarish" because the instructor insisted that calligraphy could be done properly only with the right hand. Licko has what she calls "the gift of being left-handed," and so she did her homework assignments with her left hand while pretending to use her right during class time. She admits that "the results were awful!" and, ultimately, she rejected calligraphy entirely. Nevertheless, Licko recalls that she marveled at the functional beauty of typefaces while studying graphic design. "I was blown away when I realized the power that typeface designs have on a typographic piece of design. Without touching the layout, [just] change the typeface design, and voilà! you have a completely different design."

However, the process of designing typefaces remained a mystery until Licko laid hands on her first Macintosh. "As it turns out, bitmap fonts were the perfect place for me to start learning about type design because I love the building-block approach," she says, referring to the puzzlelike way in which letterforms were constructed by linking squares (or bits) together. From that moment on, her experience and skill with more sophisticated typeface designs evolved at a pace commensurate with the Macintosh's ability to produce more complex font programs. However, when she began using her new Macintosh for *Emigre,* mastering the new tool, not sophistication, was the primary issue. She continues: "As graphic designers, we enjoyed the newfound ability to test and implement the faces directly within our design work." Of course, the results were primitive and decidedly of the moment. Yet, *at* the moment, few could predict whether or not Mac-generated bitmap type would slowly wear thin. Eventually, a new standard emerged.

Within what then seemed like a blink of an eye, the introduction of high-resolution PostScript outline technology enabled Licko to develop several high-resolution designs based upon her earlier bitmaps, including faces called Matrix, Citizen, and Lunatix. Although these were based fundamentally on classical forms, given the computer's limited memory, Licko had to compensate by limiting the characteristics of each face to the bare essentials. Thus even the most traditional-looking face, such as Matrix, retained sharp edges that gave it the appearance of a stone inscription on the one hand and a novelty form on the other.

For Licko, overall appearance was less important than how a face functioned within technological constraints. Her mission at the time was to work within limitations, which meant that her faces took on certain characteristics endemic to the computer, which, in turn, caused an alternate appearance in layouts that used the faces. Incidentally, in 1999, she revisited and successfully reworked some of her early bitmap ideas through new fonts called Base 9 and Base 12, which offer compatible screen and printer fonts to solve the current dual need of low-resolution screen display and high-resolution printing with an integrated typeface design.

Licko's inspiration usually comes from the particular medium that she's involved with at any given time (and the needs posed by that medium). "I search out a problem that needs to be addressed or a unique result that a production method can yield, such as my early experiments with bitmaps, and later purely geometric forms." The results were faces that have become emblematic of the digital epoch. "My latest interest in creating somewhat more traditional text faces," she continues, "is a result of *Emigre* magazine's increased publishing of in-depth articles, which require fonts appropriate for lengthy text setting."

Having one's own magazine to design typefaces for offers untold advantages. Most type designers create faces on commission for a publication or an institution, with little opportunity to make certain that they are truly seaworthy; some produce speculative faces for others to sample, thus ceding control of the typography. But with the opportunity to actually flow new type into a vessel such as *Emigre* for testing in layouts by a sympathetic designer (in this case, VanderLans), Licko has been allowed to check the tolerance of her work under the stress of real-world conditions. In turn, *Emigre* has been the ultimate proving ground and specimen sheet.

For the first decade, when *Emigre* was a hothouse, Licko (and other designers) showcased often quirky work. But when the size of *Emigre* decreased with the thirty-third issue (winter 1995) from a luxurious tabloid to a standard magazine format, and when the content switched from highly visual to heavily text, a changed occurred for Licko and *Emigre*. Licko relays: "We needed a typeface appropriate for lengthy text setting; this presented the opportunity to take on the challenge of doing a revival." For Licko, this was uncharted territory.

Revivals are common fare for most type designers, and the classics are fair game for update, renovation, or rehabilitation. Type designers—a critical lot to say the least— are always finding flaws in original designs that "drive them crazy." In Licko's case, she became fascinated with Baskerville, the popular alphabet by the English founder John Baskerville (1706–1775), who influenced the "modern" designs of Didot and Bodoni but had his work severely criticized during and after his lifetime for being what type historian D. B. Updike referred to in *Printing Types* (Harvard, 1922) as "sterile." "From personal experience, I could sympathize," Licko wrote in her 1996 introduction to her own revival of Baskerville, the typeface Mrs Eaves (named after Sarah Eaves, the live-in housekeeper who became Baskerville's wife and later ran his printing business).

Originally revived in 1917 (owing to an interest by Bruce Rogers) and later reissued by Monotype and Deberny & Peignot, Baskerville often plays second fiddle to Caslon. But Licko selected it for its familiarity as well as for its formal features. "Since Baskerville is a neutral and well-known design," she explains, "it allowed me significant leeway in the interpretation, while retaining the familiarity of a classic." Baskerville was also chosen because it is the ultimate transitional typeface, the category between old-style and modern types. Licko states: "I ruled out old-style models for the idiosyncratic reason that I'm personally not attracted to typefaces which are reminiscent of calligraphic influences (probably for the opposite reason why calligraphers tend to dislike bitmap or geometric designs)." She adds that "an old style would not have been a natural choice, given my experience and sensibilities." Her subsequent revival was Bodoni, but for *Emigre*'s first-ever text revival, Licko wanted to avoid the austerity of the thick and thin strokes of early modern design.

Revivals are curious beasts. A designer is usually faced with the dilemma of either making minor adjustments or radical renovation. Arguably, the former is what the originator might have done if technology or other factors were different; the latter challenges the dotted line between fealty and reinvention. Licko says that there are no conventional limitations because every type designer brings his or her own perceptions to a particular face. And, about her own effort, she admits: "Perhaps some would say that Mrs Eaves is far removed from Baskerville's basic model and may question it being a true revival. The fact that Mrs Eaves is not a slavish replica is one of the reasons why we chose an original name, rather than calling it Emigre Baskerville."

Revivals are, of course, about critical reevaluation and then change—in perception, typographic needs, or technology. Licko notes that "the idea of fixing, or improving, a classic is relative to usage. Some typefaces are more appropriate for certain uses than others and some may have a wider use than others, but there is no absolute measurement for typeface designs that calculates good versus bad." The fixing done to a classic typeface that makes it suitable for one use may make it less suitable for another. Moreover, adds Licko, "A revival also exemplifies the idiosyncrasies of the type designer doing the revival. If two designers do a revival of the same typeface, each designer's interpretation will be unique, based upon . . . relative sensibilities, vision, and skill."

With Mrs Eaves, Licko's point of departure was one of the most critiqued characteristics of Baskerville's original—the sharp contrast between stems and hairlines, which naysayers in his day believed was a hindrance to legibility. Licko wanted to understand the criticism, if not as well disprove it, so she opted to "explore the path not taken. After all, the sharp contrast evidenced in Baskerville was new at the time of its creation due to recent developments in printing and papermaking technologies. In his pursuit of 'perfect' printing, John Baskerville developed ultrasmooth and brilliant white papers, as well as intensely black printing ink." Ultimately, Licko's analysis forced her to conclude that she should retain the overall openness and lightness of the face. So she reduced the x-height, relative to the cap-height, which gives Mrs Eaves the appearance when set of being one point-size smaller than it really is. In roman, bold, italic, small, and petite caps, Mrs Eaves is a very readable face that is also quite elegant, not unlike a hot-metal impression. It turned out to be one of Emigre's best-selling font packages ever.

Crossing over from "original" to revival, Licko learned an unexpected lesson. "I've found that doing a revival is in many ways easier than designing a typeface from scratch. Because the fine details, which can be very time-consuming, are prescribed by the model, there are fewer stumbling blocks in the development." Of course, she continues to pursue new designs as a means of exploring the unexplored. But her subsequent revivals have given her the opportunity to study and better understand the details that she would never fully appreciate by merely observing, studying, or using the typeface. In light of Mrs Eaves, Licko asserts: "In subtle ways, a revival forces me to accept certain design decisions that I would not have made myself, to integrate a different way of thinking."

The Area Code (Parenthesis)

DESIGNER: LADISLAV SUTNAR

Sample Directory Introductory Pages

$\mathbf{I}$f recognized at all, graphic designers earn cultural kudos for work that has a direct impact on society. Yet even under these circumstances the world is usually oblivious. Which is why Ladislav Sutnar (1897–1976), a Czech modernist graphic and product designer who emigrated to the United States in 1939 and worked in New York until his death, has not received even a modicum of credit for a unique graphic innovation that has had far-reaching effect. Although it may well be considered arcane, his invention was the parentheses around American telephone area-code numbers when the system was introduced in the early 1960s.

Sutnar is not credited for the appearance of the area code because the concept was so integral to the design of the Bell System's new calling apparatus that it was instantly adopted as part of the vernacular. Moreover, Ma Bell never offered or gave Sutnar credit; for this company, graphic designers—like the functional graphics they produced—were invisible. Nonetheless, Sutnar's other contributions to information architecture, the commissions that brought him to the Bell System's attention in the first place, are milestones not only in graphic design history but of design for the public good. Sutnar developed logical and hierarchical graphic systems for a wide range of American businesses that clarified and made accessible vast amounts of complex, often ponderous information. He took on the thankless job of transforming routine business data into digestible and understandable forms.

Before most designers focused on the need for information organization, Sutnar was in the vanguard, driven by the missionary modern belief that good design applied to the most quotidian products had a beneficial, even curative effect on society. In his role as a pioneer of information design and progenitor of the current trend in information architecture, Sutnar's sophisticated data-management programs, which he designed during the late 1950s and early 1960s for America's telecommunications monopoly, allowed customers to scan directories more efficiently. The Bell System was engaged in the technological upgrade of its huge network, and Sutnar's brand of functional typography and way-finding iconography made public access to both emergency and regular services considerably easier while providing Bell with a distinctive identity. But in the history of graphic design, Saul Bass received more attention for his late-fifties/early-sixties redesign of the Bell System logo, which had little direct consequence for the public, than Sutnar did for making user-friendly graphic signposts. In recent years information architect Richard Saul Wurman has also utilized Sutnar's model in developing the California Bell telephone directories known as "smart pages."

Although it was a small part of the overall graphic system, the parenthesis was one of Sutnar's signature devices, among many used to distinguish and highlight various kinds of information. From 1941 to 1960, as the art director of the F. W. Dodge Sweet's Catalog Service, America's leading distributor and producer of trade and manufacturing catalogs, Sutnar developed an array of typographic and iconographic navigational tools that allowed users to efficiently traverse seas of data. His icons are analogous to the friendly computer symbols used today and were inspired, in part, by El Lissitzky's iconographic tabulation system in Mayakovsky's 1923 book of poems, *For the Voice*. In addition to designing grid and tab systems, Sutnar made common punctuation, including commas, colons, and exclamation points, into linguistic traffic signs by enlarging and repeating them, which was similar to the constructivist functional typography of the 1920s. These were adopted as key components of Sutnar's distinctive American style.

While he professed universality, he nevertheless possessed graphic personality that was so distinctive from others practicing the international style that his work did not even require a credit line, although he almost always took one. Nevertheless this graphic personality was based on functional requisites not indulgent conceits and so never obscured his clients' messages (unlike much of the undisciplined commercial art produced during the same period).

"The lack of discipline in our present day urban industrial environment has produced a visual condition, characterized by clutter, confusion, and chaos," writes Allon Schoener, curator of the 1961 *Ladislav Sutnar: Visual Design in Action* exhibition, which originated at the Contemporary Arts Center in Cincinnati, Ohio. "As a result the average man of today must struggle to accomplish such basic objectives as being able to read signs, to identify products, to digest advertisements, or to locate information in newspapers, books, and catalogues. . . . There is an urgent need for communication based upon precision and clarity. This is the area in which Ladislav Sutnar excels." If written today, this statement might seem like a critique of current design trends, but in 1961, it was a testament to progressivism. Sutnar introduced the theoretical constructs that for him defined "good design" in the 1940s, when such definitions were rare in American commercial art. Design was one-third instinct and two-thirds market convention, and the result was eclectic at best, confused at worst. Such ad hoc practice was anathema to Sutnar, who was stern about matters of order and logic, fervently seeking to alter visual standards by introducing both American businessmen and commercial artists to "the sound basis for modern graphic design and typography," which he asserts in his book *Visual Design in Action* (Hasting House, 1961) is ". . . a direct heritage of the avant-garde pioneering of the twenties and thirties in Europe. It represents a basic change that is revolutionary."

Sutnar synthesized European avant-gardisms, which he says "provided the base for further extension of new design vocabulary and new design means" into a functional commercial lexicon that eschews "formalistic rules or art for art's sake." While he modified aspects of the New Typography, he did not compromise its integrity in the same way that elements of the international style became mediocre through rote usage over time. "He made Constructivism playful and used geometry to create the dynamics of organization," observes designer Noel Martin, who in the 1950s was a member of Sutnar's small circle of friends. Despite a strict belief in the absolute rightness of geometric form, Sutnar allowed variety within his strictures to avoid standardizing his clients' different messages. Consistency reigned within an established framework, such as limited type and color choices as well as strict layout preferences, but within those parameters a variety of options existed in relation to different kinds of projects, including catalogs, books, magazines, and exhibitions as well as the Bell System's instructional materials.

In the field of information design, it is arguable that contemporary missionaries Edward Tufte and Richard Saul Wurman are really just carrying the torch that Sutnar lit decades before. Many design students, either knowingly or not, have borrowed and applied his signature graphics to a postmodern style. Nevertheless, Sutnar would loathe being admired only as a nostalgic figure. "There is just one lesson from the past that should be learned for the benefit of the present," he wrote in 1959, as if preempting this kind of superficial epitaph. "It is that of the painstaking, refined craftsmanship which appears to be dying out."

Little Blue and Little Yellow

AUTHOR, ARTIST, DESIGNER: LEO LIONNI

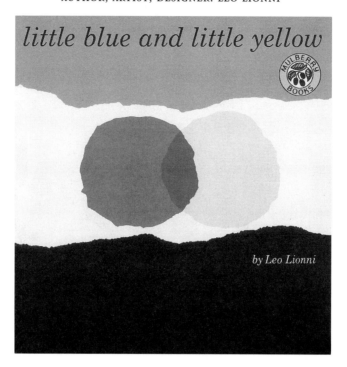

Leo Lionni's first children's book, *Little Blue and Little Yellow,* began as the act of a desperate grandfather trying to calm down his rambunctious grandchildren during the one-hour train ride from New York City to Greenwich, Connecticut. The year was 1959, and Lionni, then the art director of *Fortune* magazine as well as design consultant to Olivetti and the Museum of Modern Art, was transporting the two usually well-behaved children to his suburban home when they developed a case of the restless willies. Unable to quiet them, he pulled out an advance copy of *Life* magazine from his briefcase and tore into small circles a page dominated by the colors blue, yellow, and green. Next, he improvised a story that captured their attention and, apparently, that of the other commuters.

The tale, told in Lionni's basso voice, was about two circles—Little Blue and Little Yellow—the best of friends, who went on a hike together. While playing hide-and-seek in a forest, they lost sight of each other and searched everywhere to no avail. Then suddenly, behind a large tree, they were reunited. They hugged and in so doing became . . . Little Green. "The children were transfixed," Lionni recalls in his autobiography, *Between Worlds* (Alfred Knopf, 1997), "and I noticed that the passengers who were sitting within hearing distance had put down their papers and were listening too. So for their benefit I had Little Green go to the Stock Exchange, where he lost all his money. He broke out in yellow and blue tears, and when he was all tears he was Little Blue and Little Yellow again and their stock rose twelve points. The children applauded, and some of the passengers joined in."

A week later, Lionni created a refined dummy of his ad hoc story. He wrote the improvised script, only this time with attention to the rhythm and flow of the narrative. He retained the original abstract shapes rather than giving them overt human features and kept their torn appearance rather than cutting them with scissors. "While I was placing and gluing them down with rubber cement," he recalls, "it occurred to me that I was repeating in story form the little games I used to play during my first weeks at N. W. Ayer [the Philadelphia advertising agency where he was an art director from 1939 to 1947] when I experimented with positions in space to evoke moods and even to express meanings." The book also mentions a promotional booklet that he had developed entitled "Design for the Printed Page," a collection of abstract designs to show advertisers how exciting the creative use of the large *Fortune* format could be.

Lionni showed *Little Blue and Little Yellow* to his friend, Fabio Coen, the newly appointed children's book editor for MacDowell Obolensky in New York. After a long perusal, Coen announced that he wanted to publish it. Lionni was stunned. "I couldn't imagine any publisher would have the courage to publish what looked like a defiant object designed to *épater le bourgeois*," he remembers. He accepted the offer, further refined the narrative, and in no time finished the artwork for reproduction. "It would take more than one evening with Fabio before I could fully understand how much the simple little tale of two blobs of color would affect my soul, my mind, and my way of life," Lionni adds. But eight or so months later, what seemed like ages for the expectant first-time author, *Little Blue and Little Yellow* was published and became the first of over thirty books that Lionni has produced since 1959.

As an advertising and editorial art director for over a quarter century, and a painter and sculptor for even longer, Lionni has always searched for the means to combine craft and invention as well as applied and fine art into a single entity. But he was surprised to discover through this fortuitous accident that children's books were the perfect métier for such fusion. The medium not only allowed him the freedom to be an auteur but also served as a conduit between his inner psyche and the outer world.

This is not to say that Lionni aimed his genius only at children; his intense intellectual rigor is ultimately expressed in many more complex ways as a painter, sculptor, teacher, and author. But, in his books for children (and particularly the fables), he found the key to unlocking decades of personal fear, joy, insecurity, love, and longing while presenting ideas about life through accessible metaphors. His children's books, for the most part, are the clearest windows into the depths of what he would call "the soul" as any art form could possibly be. In fact, even more than Lionni's own elegantly told autobiography, children's books like *Little Blue and Little Yellow, Swimmy, Frederick, Nicolas, Where Have You Been?* and *Matthew's Dream,* to name the most introspective, both fire the child's imagination and provide a catharsis for their maker.

Leonard "Leo" Lionni was born in Holland in 1910, into a world on the cusp of social, cultural, and technological revolution. His father was a skilled diamond cutter, and his mother was an opera singer whose melodic voice filled his childhood with joyful memories. Lionni's uncle Piet, an architect, allowed young Leo to play with his drafting tools; two other uncles, both collectors of modern art, fed Leo's artistic inclinations. In fact, one uncle deposited Marc Chagall's *Fiddler* directly outside the boy's bedroom.

After World War I, Amsterdam was governed by socialist leaders who supported a progressive educational system, which Lionni used to great advantage. He recalls there was an emphasis on nature, art, and crafts, and in an early grade, he was taught to draw from a big plaster cast of an ivory leaf. "There was something magical about it," he notes in an interview. "I can still draw that leaf today, and probably not better than I did then." He was also permitted to draw at the Rijksmuseum, where he copied the plaster casts, and recalls feeling that Rembrandt, Van Gogh, Mondrian, architecture, and music were "one big mood to me." Here was the root for his rejection of cultural hierarchies and fervent belief that "art is as important as design."

At age fourteen, Lionni briefly resided in the United States when his father secured a job in Philadelphia with the Atlantic Richfield Company. A year later, he was relocated to Genoa, Italy, where he attended a "commercial" high school. He learned Italian and became conversant with Italian art, literature, and poetry. At sixteen he met Nora Maffi, who later became his wife and lifelong companion. Her father was one of the founders of the Italian communist party and was placed under house arrest by the fascists after their rise to power in 1922. The sight of this man whose freedom was denied by blackshirt militia guards was enough to raise Lionni's radical political consciousness.

By the late 1920s, Italy had spawned a number of significant poster artists and a distinctive typographic style. Lionni was interested in commercial art and created his own advertisement proposals for Campari, the liquor company that already had a very progressive graphic policy based on the work of futurist designer Fortunato Depero. Lionni was also inspired by futurist art, and, by 1931, he found himself painting turbulent abstractions typical of the era and movement that celebrated speed and industry. Somehow his work caught the eye of F. T. Marinetti, the leader of the futurists, who proclaimed that the twenty-one-year-old Lionni was "a great Futurist" and encouraged exhibitions of his paintings. Lionni, however, was ambivalent about this recognition. Futurism celebrated fascism, and its chaotic and anarchic character conflicted with Lionni's rationalistic sensibility. "I am really Dutch," he wrote at the time. "I feel closer to DeStijl, and respond to the patterns and symmetry of the tulip fields."

He left the futurist orbit to work in Milan as an advertising designer, "simply for the joy of putting good imagery onto pages," he reports. At the same time, he attended classes at the University of Genoa and received a doctoral degree in economics after completing a thesis on the diamond industry. A year later, however, one step ahead of a fascist crackdown, he returned to Philadelphia, this time with Nora and their two sons, Manny and Paolo, as a designer for N. W. Ayer under famed advertising art director Charles Coiner. Lionni's early jobs included designing advertisements for *Ladies' Home Journal* and the Ford Motor Company. The latter gave him considerable prestige, and other job offers came his way. Before leaving the agency in 1947 he had worked on campaigns for the Container Corporation of America (the "International Series"), assigning work to Willem de Kooning, Alexander Calder, and Fernand Léger; Comptometer, assigning work to Saul Steinberg; and Regal shoes, assigning a young Andy Warhol to render loose sketches.

All the time, Lionni continued to paint, and he took a year to learn mosaics. In 1947 he moved to New York to open a small office. One of his first calls was from *Fortune* magazine, looking for a new art director. Although he had never designed a magazine before, he says, "it fit me like an old shoe, because I brought everything that I learned with passion to some kind of concrete manifestation." Lionni relished giving assignments to illustrators and painters who authored visual essays and graphic journalism. True to his own career, he encouraged artists to "do things that they were not accustomed to doing."

Lionni termed what he did "civilized and human" art and design, which was a marriage of equal parts rationalism and serendipity—every element, type and image, had a reason for being, but each entity was a new discovery. During this fertile period Lionni also consulted with Time/Life's Henry Luce on the prototype for *Sports Illustrated;* for the Museum of Modern Art, he designed the catalog for Edward Steichen's milestone photography exhibition *The Family of Man;* he served as design consultant for Olivetti and designed the American Pavilion for the 1958 Brussels World's Fair, which addressed the unsolved problems of American society. In the mid-1950s Lionni was coeditor and art director for *Print* magazine, where he replaced the typical shoptalk with commentary and criticism.

By his fiftieth birthday, Lionni accepted that he was on a professional par with Paul Rand, Lester Beall, and Alvin Lustig, yet he realized that the majority of his life had been in the service of others. "Everything I had done was a happy compromise that I've never felt ashamed of in the least," he says. But he was ready to devote himself to his own muse—to embark on new challenges and radical change. Leaving the sinecure of Time/Life, he returned to the hills of Tuscany in Italy to live, work, and immerse himself in art.

While preparing for this seismic shift, Lionni stumbled into the field that would consume a big part of his soul. For almost forty years now, he has authored close to one book a year and has crafted characters that are indelibly etched in the consciousness of millions of children (and former children) who have read the numerous translations available throughout the world. Lionni's midlife success is significant when seen against the backdrop of millions of books produced annually (most of which have the life span of an anemic fruit fly) and at least equally numerous authors who try and fail. Indeed, to capture the hearts of children and the trust of parents and teachers is a fairly remarkable accomplishment. As the psychiatrist Bruno Bettelheim proclaims in the introduction to Lionni's anthology, *Frederick's Fables,* "It is the true genius of the artist which permits him to create picture images that convey much deeper meaning than what is overtly depicted."

Little Blue and Little Yellow was something of a fluke, its abstractness something of an anomaly in the representational world of children's illustration. But it was matchless as a synthesis of sophistication and naïveté—a confluence of a seasoned artist's experience and a neophyte author's ignorance. "I don't think Leo knew anything about publishing, about who the audience would actually be," says Frances Foster, Lionni's editor, first at Knopf and currently at Farrar Straus and Giroux. "He did it in a strictly instinctive, intuitive way. He never really considered himself a children's author, particularly back then."

When Fabio Coen asked him for his second book, Lionni began doodling a sequel and quickly abandoned the idea, realizing that he'd done the Little Blue thing and didn't want to get trapped into, as he calls it, "Little Blue Goes to the Zoo." Ever the restless artist, Lionni decided that his second book had to be very different from the first: The result was *On My Beach There Are Many Pebbles*, a collection of drawings of different pebbles (fishpebbles, peoplepebbles) hidden among the real things, realistically rendered in pencil. "I still consider it with pride to be one of my handsomest achievements," Lionni said before an audience at the Library of Congress in 1993. "Perhaps it wasn't a children's book at all."

Lionni insists that the third book, *Inch by Inch,* is really his first. "For unlike *Little Blue* and *On My Beach* it seems to have embodied all the qualities I later demanded of my work." This book is the prototype of his animal fables, told in words and images that are clear and simple, underscored by a stylistic coherence and a sense of humor. "Although it doesn't have an explicit moral, it invites search for meaning," Lionni explains. And Foster adds that, with *Inch by Inch,* he found his voice. "Leo really was interested in saying something, and his books all had a point. Later on it became a moral or political point." The point of *Inch by Inch* is that through ingenuity, a helpless little inchworm outwits the stronger, more powerful bird. And this is key to one of Lionni's recurring messages, that the imagination can transcend all obstacles.

Similarly, his classic book *Swimmy,* which was made into an animated film, is about a diminutive fish who bamboozles its predator, a giant tuna, by organizing other smaller fish into the shape of a large one. When Swimmy says, "I will be the eye," it is clear that this is also a portrait of the artist as seer. "Anyone who knew of my search for the social justification for making art, for becoming or being an artist," Lionni observes in his autobiography, "would immediately have grasped what motivated Swimmy, the first embodiment of my alter ego, to tell his scared little friends to swim together like one big fish." Swimmy's memorable line in the book, "Each in his own place," is said as he becomes conscious of the ethical implications of his own place in the greater crowd. "He had seen the image of the large fish in his mind. That was the gift he had received: to see," says Lionni about the idea of seeing clearly and, by extension, helping others to find a vision. "I think that's certainly the way Leo saw his role as an artist, seeing for people," notes Foster.

Lionni uses the children's book to metamorphose himself—and his alter egos— into animals (such as Frederick the poetic mouse and Cornelius the upright alligator) that embody his own passion and desire, wit and wisdom, sophistication and innocence. He uses the fable as a means to reveal his and, by extension, the world's moral complexities. "With Leo's work I would use the term 'fable' quite loosely," explains Foster. "In the beginning his fables were just stories. But as he matured he got very interested in conveying deeper messages." *Tillie and the Wall* (1989), a book about seeing beyond impenetrable barriers, was published in Germany around the time that the Berlin Wall fell (and indeed it sold very well there). Lionni was so excited by the potential of this book to impart worldlier ideas that he decided from then on that everything he did had to have some sort of political message. "He felt that the world was in such a state that he really couldn't afford not to use the picture book as kind of soapbox." Yet Lionni's political messages have more to do with human kindness and understanding than realpolitik. "He actually wasn't thinking of the Berlin Wall when he did *Tillie and the Wall,*" says Foster. "That was after the fact. He was thinking of the wall as symbol. So when Leo says 'political,' I think he really means social responsibility."

Whatever Lionni's deeper agenda, children always find different meanings in his work. No kid (or adult for that matter) would fathom that *Matthew's Dream,* in which a mouse fantasizes about making great art and romancing the girl mouse of his dreams, is about Lionni and his wife, Nora. For children, it could mean any number of things: that dreams come true, art has great power, or love conquers all. "I think it's hard to know what it is that children take from a story," says Foster. "I am sure they do see Frederick sort of as a dreamer. But I don't think they see Swimmy in all of his dimensions. I think they basically see this little fish who is spared, who is not eaten by the bad tuna, and then shows the others how to trick the tuna. But on some levels, I think there is a kind of residual that's left when children are read a story over and over again. And if it's something that does resonate, even if they don't know exactly what it means, it stays with them, and they sort it out in time, either consciously or unconsciously."

Children do recognize, in some sort of basic way, their lifetime in these stories; "Leo is dealing with conflicts, problems and solutions, and is really navigating life," adds Foster. Such is Lionni's gift for igniting the imagination that kindergarten teacher Vivian Gussin Paley has written a book, *The Girl with the Brown Crayon* (Harvard University Press, 1997), about a year that she spent exploring with her young students the lessons of Frederick and his friends. Curiously, Lionni knew nothing about this until her book was published and he received an advance copy by mail.

"Without delving deep into the distant memories of their own childhoods, authors could not find the mood, the tone, the imagery that characterize their books," Lionni said, describing his own inspiration at his Library of Congress lecture. "They could not create convincing protagonists were they not able to fully identify with their heroes. . . ." Lionni accidentally fell into children's books but found that it became a significant part of his creative life because it has allowed him to reveal meaning that he might not have been able to express through his other art. "There's narrative in everything he does," concludes Foster. "You know, he doesn't just do a sculpture for the sake of a sculpture. It's in some way part of a larger story." Lionni creates fiction from life. Yet it does not matter how his books are understood; ultimately, they inspire—and that is his gift.

Ancient Life

DESIGNER: BRAD HOLLAND

When Brad Holland (b. 1943) was in kindergarten, the writing—or, rather, the drawing—was on the wall. Even then he was a prolific artist, scribbling dinosaurs and cavemen in crayon on whatever surface he could find, including the walls of his parents' home in Fort Smith, Arkansas. His mother frowned upon his attempts to recreate the cave paintings of Lascaux yet proudly bound the drawings on paper into a little book titled "Ancient Life." Hidden in an attic for decades, a few years ago the book was unearthed; the fifty-five-year-old veteran illustrator was surprised to find that today he is drawing the same way and, coincidentally, the same subject matter, that he drew back then.

By 1971, Holland was a successful editorial illustrator, known for his precisely rendered surrealist painting for *Playboy* and linear graphic commentaries on the op-ed page of the *New York Times*. But he was also drawing in a very free-form, stream-of-consciousness, childlike cartoon manner. "It always went hand in hand with the other stuff," he explains. This decidedly noncommercial work was so loose and anarchic as to appear done by a different artist. So Holland decided to keep it under wraps, except for occasional use in underground newspapers and personal correspondence, preferring to focus on his more formal, linear and painterly work. "I figured the other stuff would just confuse people," he adds.

Yet the primitive drawings are arguably Holland's most original métier and the foundation of his conceptual method. "All my ideas look like this when I start out, and then I objectify them," he says. "Some ideas never improve beyond this stage." So drawing like a child is not a manu-factured conceit but the natural way he creates his art.

Over the years, however, Holland has despaired about an increasing number of illustrators imitating his style—what he refers to as "seeing the ghosts of my paintings" in too many magazines and advertisements—and has sought out alternative methods that others could not possibly claim for their own. Gradually, he found that primitive pastel scribbles were showing up in his paintings as visual counterpoints to his more formal conceptual methods. A battle, of sorts, ultimately raged between formality and informality: The childlike scrawls were beginning to dominate many of the paintings. As if possessed, Holland couldn't seem to stop the scrawls from taking over.

Somewhat timidly, he began approaching selected assignments in this manner. One of the first was an ersatz portrait of the poet Sylvia Plath for the cover of the *New York Times Book Review,* which looked nothing like her but represented her tragic life through the primitive quality of the rendering. "Actually, this method allows me to extend ideas that I couldn't do in a more realistic way," he confides.

Many art directors have given Holland the license to experiment with this approach, which some have compared to the cartoonlike forms of the abstract painter Philip Guston. In fact, Holland was given a huge assignment to design the cover and divider pages of the 1997 annual of the Swiss art directors' club with a score of these absurdist images (which won a silver medal at the New York Art Directors Club). Yet he has found it incredibly difficult to convince the editors of most American magazines (even those that he has worked for) to publish this new work. "Thirty years ago they [editors] thought my paintings were unfinished," he opines. "Of course, over time they got used to them, but now they say that these are unfinished."

Holland may be weary but not discouraged. "I just have to talk more people into using these things," he says. Indeed, he was commissioned by a California winery to do one of the childlike drawings for the label of their white wine, but they had decided to assign their complementary red wine label to a different, more realistic artist. Holland had to talk them into letting *him* do the realistic painting for the red wine too. Such are the vicissitudes of commercial art.

Grandma

The jacket of the Japanese children's book
Grandma (Balloon-sha), written by poet Syuntaro Tanikawa and illustrated by Shigeru Miwa,
shows a drawing of an old woman with antennae sprouting from her head as she leans on a cane,
standing against a blue and yellow surreal landscape. In the background, off to one side, is a
cherubic-faced boy, maybe five or six years old; on the other side, farther away, with their backs
toward the old woman, are two adults peering into ominous space. This old lady is the little boy's
grandmother, and this is his story.

"My grandma is like a baby. She stays in bed all day long," he says in the bilingual (Japanese
and English) text. "She wears a diaper. She can't eat by herself. But when she's hungry, instead of
crying like a baby, she cries out, 'Is dinner ready?'" The accompanying drawings, rendered in a
primitive pen-and-ink style (with two flat somber colors, gray and brown) vividly illustrate the
emotionally complex, yet simply written story about the strain placed on an entire family when
the household revolves around the care and feeding of a loved one suffering from Alzheimer's
disease.

Set in modern-day Japan where elders are not routinely warehoused in nursing homes, the
attendant anger and resentment harbored by the family is seen through the little boy's eyes and
expressed through his plaintive words. As the narrative jumps from the past ("Grandma's father's
mother. She was pretty when she was young.") to the present ("Grandma sometimes asks father,
'Who are you, mister?'"), the little boy reveals his own growing anger toward a being, whom he

cannot ever know and, therefore whom he finds impossible to love ("When I say, 'I wish Grandma was dead!' Mother hangs her head and says nothing").

Upon learning that nothing can cure Grandma, the boy concludes that she must be an alien creature. And in one of the most powerful illustrations of the book, he is shown holding on to a huge, disembodied tree-trunk of an arm while he laments, "It's difficult to live with an alien creature. It looks just like us humans, but it's different in some way."

Children's books can neutralize or reconcile the angst and anxieties of children, such as monsters under the bed, fear of the dark, even anger toward parents or siblings. In recent years, more social and cultural issues have also been addressed, from divorce to homosexuality. Alzheimer's disease has also emerged as a prevalent theme. Yet the tone of most children's books is optimistic, offering happy resolutions as a counterpoint to an increasingly pessimistic world. In American books, for example, "there are none of the unpleasant details about senility and mental disease," notes Dr. James Fraser, a librarian and children's book scholar. "There is a certain amount of whimsy regarding behavior quirks, such as 'grandfather put a necktie in the refrigerator,' or the observation that 'grandmother is acting like a child.' Ultimately, the grandparent dies or goes to the nursing home, or there is some other antiseptic disposition without the mess or the details given in *Grandma*."

In Japan, it is rather unusual for personal matters to be so openly discussed in public. However, according to Richard Thorton, professor of design at the University of Connecticut and expert in Japanese art and design, Japanese children's books have become much more open insofar as expressing otherwise personal issues that can be fictionalized. "I see this story as a way to help children understand why their grandparents are acting they way they do," Thornton explains. "In Japan it is the responsibility of the oldest son or daughter to bring his or her parents into the family to live. This story is not a radical departure from the typical family structure." Fraser, who spends considerable time working in Japan, adds that "when I visualize the comparatively small homes in which Japanese families live, I presume that the kind of living arrangement presented in *Grandma* is very difficult, and this book vividly reveals the intense pressures below the surface."

According to Eden Ross Lipson, children's book editor of the *New York Times,* even in Japanese culture, where "children's books routinely address what in America is taboo subject matter (notably a recent spate of books on bodily functions)," this is a groundbreaking approach. The story of *Grandma,* she adds, is not how children's editors in the United States would approach a similar theme. In this book the ultimate wisdom of the child belies his young years, especially when the boy says, "When mother and father get old, they are going to be alien creatures, too. I am going to be one someday."

Grandma is one of a series of psychologically sophisticated books that Balloon-sha, a fairly traditional children's book publisher of picture and chapter books, which has produced with emphasis on "the feelings and interactions of children and adults as they confront the problems and weak points of modern society." The other volumes are also illustrated by Shigeru Miwa in the same almost-artless, primitive manner and include *Why Don't They Ever Ask Me* by Kikaru

Kataoka, which concerns the thoughts of a little girl, an only child, who wants a younger brother but whose parents are constantly fighting with each other and turn their rage on her. ("If only Daddy would read to me or Mommy make me some cocoa. They've begun to fight again tonight as if they're enemies.") Another such title is *Only One Me* by Suntaro Tanikawa, about a young boy who prefers to be alone, except for his fantasy friends. ("This is my face. My name is Yoshio. That kid is Yoshio, too, but we're different. We only have the same name, that's all.") Still another is *Playing War* by Suntaro Tanikawa, involving a boy's realization that war is not a game. ("Oh, Mommy's dead. Oh, no! Father! Daddy's dead too, and Sis and even my dog, Goro.")

These books are not distributed in the United States and Fraser thinks that *Grandma* may be just beyond the realm of acceptability here, unlike the Japanese children's books devoted to bodily functions, which are available in American editions. Presented simply in a truthful and emotionally wrenching manner, the Balloon-sha books have had a strong influence not only on children's attitudes but also on Japanese parents, if only as reminders that under the surface their children must cope in a world that can be frightening to the uninitiated.

Jambalaya

DESIGNER: STEFAN SAGMEISTER

Design organizations are the short-order cooks of printed ephemera, and the posters and flyers that they produce announcing myriad events—from competitions to conferences—are the graphic designers' equivalent of two eggs, bacon, and side of down. Served up at such a prodigious pace, design for designers could constitute its own industry within an industry. Since members of these organizations are asked to donate their talents, their payback is a license to experiment. But despite the latitudes in designing for designers, one requisite is absolute: the need to visually represent *design* itself. Can anything be more mundane?

Unfortunately, unique solutions to this problem have diminished as clichés have risen. And the most common of these are the tried-and-true, including light bulbs, pencils, T squares, drawing tables, loupes, and computer monitors—as well as combinations thereof, such as pencils with light bulbs as erasers, or computer monitors with light bulbs on the screen, or light bulbs with pencils for filament. Add to this a lexicon of somewhat more abstract symbols—like babies (birth of ideas), rainbows (variety of ideas), sunbursts (the dawn of ideas), and picture frames (framing ideas)—and it is reasonable to conclude that design creativity is difficult to represent creatively.

As Mies van der Rohe once said, being original is not as important as being good. But to be good under these circumstances a designer must find alternative ways to express the nature of design without resorting to hackneyed concepts. This, of course, is the very essence of creativity:

creating something unexpected. However, surprise is not always a virtue. Sometimes it can be as cloying as a cliché and as annoying as any distraction. Effective surprise—the kind that does not merely shock but influences perception and understanding—is not as simple as shouting *Boo!* in a dark room.

Stefan Sagmeister (b. 1962), a native of Austria with a New York design studio, encountered this problem when he was commissioned to design a mail-poster announcing Jambalaya, the 1997 AIGA National Conference in New Orleans. Although designers covet such assignments for the visibility and prestige afforded them within the design community, the requirement to pack both an iconic image and an enormous amount of information onto the front and back of the missive creates challenges that often limit license. Information architects may be stimulated by the problem of clarifying layers of names, times, and places, but often the results, though well ordered, are too reductive to be stimulating. Finding a balance between clarity and the unexpected is difficult. And since this particular AIGA conference situated in the mecca of Mardi Gras was a veritable gumbo of speakers and events, the pressures to accommodate *and* innovate weighed heavy. Sagmeister's art school training taught him discipline, but his instinct demanded raucousness.

After starting his own New York studio in 1994, Sagmeister, who worked for two years at the Leo Burnett advertising agency in Hong Kong and later for eight months at M&Co. in New York, earned attention for CD covers for the Rolling Stones, David Byrne, Lou Reed, and others that were conceptually startling and eschewed stylistic consistency. "Style = Fart" reads a banner over Sagmeister's desk, which for him means that trendy surface alone is hot air. Instead of adhering to contemporary conceits, Sagmeister builds his design on ideas that, although quirky and contentious, are very logical, ultimately producing work that grabs the eye and disrupts the senses while satisfying his own atavistic need to agitate.

When considering the metaphors for this AIGA poster, Sagmeister made lists of various design references and New Orleans clichés—everything, he notes, "from silly jambalaya recipes to stupid Mississippi steamboats. And I hated them." But when the conference coordinator gave him a list of the eighty participants speaking in eight different auditoriums over three days, Sagmeister says, in his lilting Viennese cadence, "it sounded like one big happy chaos that had everybody running around like headless chickens." This reference to domestic fowl was the egg that hatched into an idea. Indeed, a picture of a couple of headless chickens with its reference to voodoo ritual was just the perfect off-center illustration that Sagmeister needed as the focus for a wealth of information on a dense but dynamic poster.

The probability that such an image would be offensive to some, including the client, did not really concern Sagmeister, who prostrates himself to avoid making things good, clean, and ordinary—or what he dismisses as "nice design." "There is so much of this well-done, competently designed fluff around," he observes, "that doesn't bother anybody, doesn't annoy anyone, and is rightfully ignored." He refers to design in which form rather than concept prevails and ornamental layering triumphs—like slick paper-company promotions where designers are engaged in orgies of stylistic excess. "Tons of this stuff was given away by paper manufacturers in New Orleans," he chides, "gorgeously produced beautiful fluff designed by people who have no opinions on nothing whatsoever."

Sagmeister objects to experimental work that is really dysfunctional. While some may apply the word "experimental" to Sagmeister's own work, he insists his design solutions are built on equal parts intuition, play, and the desire to rise above the mundane. For example, he once defiantly designed the logo, labels, and shopping bags for Blue, a chain of blue-jeans outlets in Austria, using only gold and black. Sagmeister maintains that he has no interest in hiding in a laboratory while his work is tested; rather, he is on a crusade to pump untried ideas into the real world. The Jambalaya poster was one way of announcing that he was an enemy of the safe and sanctioned.

"I refused to do it in any of the 'hot' mannerisms, like Euro-techno, the new simplicity, or tiny type in boxes," he explains. In fact, his real influence comes from a Swiss outsider artist named Adolf Wölfli, who in the 1920s covered his own imagery with bits and pieces of found detritus. Sagmeister acknowledges that at the time he was given the AIGA poster assignment, he was also working on album covers for the Rolling Stones and the Pat Metheny Group, which demanded very exacting effort. The Stones cover required months of tiresome research and the Metheny cover involved creating very intricate visual codes. As a respite, he says, "I was happily and mindlessly doodling."

In addition to the headless chickens, which were deliberately composed so that they would emerge as the poster was unfolded, the front and back of the piece is comprised of hundreds of small labels featuring the handwritten names (and self-portraits) of the conference speakers. Some were pasted ad hoc on top of the image on the front side, while the rest (along with all the registration information and sender's reply coupon) were affixed willy-nilly on a board that was photographed and used as the back side. Sagmeister asked all the participants to sign their names in ballpoint pen or draw comic portraits. Naturally, scores of mistakes were made, which, after copyediting, were corrected in a rather unorthodox manner. "Some of the corrections were done directly on the poster while on the phone with the client," Sagmeister says, explaining how he crossed out words and phrases and replaced them with his own handwriting. Rather than leave empty space, Sagmeister wrote additional text as much to enhance the chaotic nature of the poster as to offer conference lore. "I hid a lot of small inside jokes and stories all over the poster, and I actually talked to a number of people who read the whole thing start to end." In fact, now it can be told: One of the small hidden images, Sagmeister confesses, "is a photograph of my testicles (I told the client that it was a picture of a monkey's knee)."

When the poster arrived in AIGA members' mailboxes, it caused the stir that Sagmeister had hoped for. Some recipients were enraged that the AIGA, long the keeper of America's modernist design tradition, condoned such abhorrent, anarchic work. National headquarters in New York received a few letters of protest, and even a membership was canceled. But positive sentiments far exceeded the dissent. Viewed as an enticement for prospective conferees to register for an event that promised to broaden the design discourse, the poster served its purpose well. It effectively promoted AIGA's Mardi Gras and signaled that the event was not just a staid congress of self-important old-timers. But most the "headless chicken poster," as it has come to be known, proved that when designing for designers nothing is worse than resorting to clichés.

COMMERCE

Russian Film Posters

DESIGNERS: VLADIMIR AND GEORGII STENBERG

Most contemporary posters for feature films adhere to rigid formulas designed to capture the fleeting attention of the average pedestrian. Typically, they contain a strong central image—often a picture of the star or symbol of the plot— a bold title or logo, the stars' billing, a blurb or two, and a bank of scrunched-together credits, ratings, and other theater information. Given this cacophony, movie posters are rarely masterpieces of graphic design. But the genre was not always so artless.

From 1923 to 1933 the brothers Vladimir (1899–1982) and Georgii (1900–1933) Stenberg, Russian avant-garde graphic designers, created innovative posters that promoted the new Russian cinema and revolutionized graphic design. As proponents of a radical, new art form called constructivism, which was rooted in a marriage of technology and abstraction, the Stenberg brothers changed the look and feel of poster art and movie advertising. By introducing montage, the mechanical juxtaposition of disparate elements into a new entity, they created compositions of unusual grace and exceptional power. Using bold colors, simple geometry, and stark typography, their work caught the eyes of the largely illiterate Russian masses. Like the films that they advertised, the Stenbergs' posters had a visceral effect on the viewer. Although the posters did not reveal the plot, they provided clues. So, like a temptress, a poster would entice its audience. Today, these posters are just as powerful and visceral, and they continue to have influence, not so much on contemporary movie posters, but on other forms of graphic design— including packaging, posters, and record and book covers.

When viewed together the posters exhibit a dominant visual style that draws as much attention to the designers as to the design. These posters may be artifacts of an eighty-year-old political, social, and cultural revolution, which has since gone sour, but they have not turned into mere nostalgia in the same way that both art nouveau and art deco have become quaint over time. The Stenbergs used a visual vocabulary and graphic wit that did not rely on fad or fashion. Remarkably, their ideas remain fresh.

The Stenbergs' primary goal was to shock. "We deal with material in a free manner . . . disregarding actual proportions . . . turning figures upside down; in short, we employ everything that can make a busy passerby stop in their tracks," they wrote in 1928. Theirs was a synthesis of avant-garde philosophy and eccentricity applied in the commercial arena. In a nation where strong iconography propagated the Soviet message, the Stenbergs rightly reasoned that commercial art was the best tool for reaching the proletariat. In fact, constructivism and its utilitarian offshoot, productivism—the primary avant-garde movements in the first few years subsequent to the Russian Revolution—were in large part serving commerce in ways that brought visual art to the greatest number of people. The Stenberg posters expanded this notion both individually and together with the work of like-minded artists.

The brothers' emblematic style developed from 1918 to 1922, during the so-called laboratory period of constructivism, when the leaders of the avant-garde—Aleksei Gan, Varvara Stepanova, and Alexander Rodchenko, among them—founded the First Working Group of Constructivists, which issued manifestos that pronounced the utilitarian purpose of art. Constructivism was typified by experiments that explored the kinetic quality of geometric and linear form and the compositional dynamism of two and three dimensions. In this spirit the Stenbergs "constructed" their posters by building up layers of visual material to a point where it appeared to explode on the poster's surface.

Their pioneering efforts with photomontage, vibrant and vibrating color, and stark typography influenced the early modernists and continue to influence designers of the computer generation. Furthermore, and perhaps most important, the Stenbergs contributed to the popular notion that commercial design is dictated by many of the same principles that govern art in general.

"It is noteworthy that the brothers' most significant achievements came in the theater and film," writes Christopher Mount, a curator of design at the Museum of Modern Art, New York, and a Stenberg scholar, "two drama-based mediums in which their designs were subservient to another art form." Yet in servicing these media, the Stenbergs also helped to define them. They used montage to create effects that simulated the cinema. And by combining fragments of still photographs their images approximated the simultaneity of film. At the same time they added an additional level through redrawing and repainting their photographic compositions in a technique that Mount describes as "magical realism."

Initially done to avoid the technical constraints then common in reproducing color photographs, magic realism evolved into a distinctive personal mannerism. And to achieve this, the Stenbergs introduced an array of abstract graphic devices, including various outlines, spirals, and concentric circles, which implied movement and further allowed them to mix reality and fantasy into a single graphic image. To cap their compositions, they used blocky, sans serif Cyrillic letterforms to accentuate the mechanical quality of the posters.

The avant-garde artists called themselves "engineers," because they produced mechanical art in a mechanical age, but Mount explains that the Stenbergs thought of themselves more as tinkers. Play was just as important as the more formal methodology. Busting the rigid framework of fine art was one of their missions, and commercial art was the principal vehicle. "The poster provided for us pure enjoyment during our creative work process," explains Vladimir Stenberg. In this spirit the brothers invented a special projector that was capable of distorting photographic images to their specifications. They also said: "We could distort a vertically-organized image . . . to make it look like a diagonally-oriented image." While traditional painters and sculptors saw technology as somehow opposed to the purity of their work, the Stenbergs embraced it for it allowing great compositional freedom.

They worked on a wide variety of films, from comedies to propaganda documentaries. The images were likewise quite varied—frequently humorous, sensual, and often psychologically complex. By using dramatic close-ups, the Stenbergs focused on characters' darker personalities; sometimes multiple personalities of the same character were depicted. Faces rarely appeared joyful, but rather anxious or fearful and often in distress. This ability to comment upon, even critique, a particular film through visual means further revealed the artists' autonomy from the film studios and commissioning agents—autonomy of a magnitude unheard of today in the demographic-driven, committee-dominated film marketing system, where movie poster designers are subject to untold interference.

The Stenberg brothers worked together intimately on the conception and design of every poster until Georgii's untimely death in 1933. In 1934 Stalin instituted the doctrine of social realism, which effectively ended the experimental work of the constructivists, thus forcing the leading experimentalists into a more official style of art. Vladimir adapted to the new dictates on art and design. He later held the post of chief of design for Red Square until 1964, during which time he collaborated on film posters with his sister and son. He died in Moscow in 1981.

Movie poster designers must fight to retain even a semblance of artistic integrity today. But from 1923 to 1933, the Stenberg brothers' film posters were unfettered by the caprice of movie distributors, the egos of actors, and the tired conventions that render contemporary posters instant clichés.

The film poster was a unique genre that developed its own conventions. Akin to the figures in religious art or political propaganda, film stars were portrayed as icons and mythic heroes (or villains). During the twenties, the standard American film poster was copied throughout the world. But different countries reinterpreted or adapted the model. An inventive genre of constructivist-inspired Soviet film posters artfully introduced collage, while a Japanese variant emphasized type and letterforms. In 1914, when the first Jewish movie house in Palestine, the Eden, opened in Tel Aviv, yet another variation was introduced, whereby linocuts mimicked photographs. Ultimately Hollywood's visual and verbal advertising language was translated into Hebrew.

During the early years of the first European immigration to Palestine (or Eretz-Israel), Tel Aviv became a totally Hebrew city down to its minute details, including signboards, advertisements, public notices, and newspapers. Gradually, American and European movies were imported, but according to designer and film-poster scholar David Tartakover, "they threatened the leaders of the Zionist-Hebrew cultural revolution, who believed that foreign films would somehow interfere with the revivification of the Hebrew culture." Cinema was considered a "foreign body, an external influence which was importing the values of a decadent culture, the same culture they had abandoned. . . ." By the twenties, a newer wave of lower-middle-class immigrants, mainly from Poland, who did not fervently embrace the Zionist ethos, had arrived. In attempting to recreate their European lifestyles in the Middle East, among other things, they encouraged the importation of large number of foreign films—first silents and then talkies. Although the "Defenders of the Hebrew Language" feared that the talking film was an "instrument for the dissemination of foreign languages in the Land," they came to accept that cinema had come to stay, and the only retaliatory measure was the creation of Hebrew-speaking cinema.

Nevertheless, the Hollywood style (paradoxically, the work of Jewish immigrants who became film moguls in America) was dominant, and so were the techniques used to advertise and market films in Tel Aviv. Posters for such American hits as Howard Hawk's *Hell's Angels* and *Dawn Patrol* (both 1930), David W. Griffith's *Abraham Lincoln* (1930), and Raoul Walsh's *The Yellow Ticket* (1931), among many others, were composed just like the Hollywood variety but with two notable differences. The first change was to Hebrew lettering, mainly faces such as the "Sephardic Character" harking back to sacred texts, which in some posters assumed art moderne characteristics. Second, the romantic painted and photographic portraits of the stars found in the Hollywood originals were replaced by crude linocuts printed in flat colors. These were cheaper to produce than full-color lithography and gave the posters an exotic, primitive look.

The posters were created by three key commercial artists: Israel Hirsch, David Gilboa, and Zaslevsky, called by design historian Yaacov Davidon "those advertising wizards of the screen," who used to rework the imported material into "exaggerated confections according to the taste of that romantic period, preparing the public to see the monumental creation the like of which had not been since the creation of the world . . ." They further translated some of the film titles into superlatives that had little to do with the original. While some of the interpreted images echoed the painting style found in Soviet film posters, most were considerably more naïve, indeed some were so lacking in anatomical precision that they looked as if a child had roughly traced a photograph.

Because of the temporal nature of the linocut, the posters were produced in very limited editions and were hung on the fifty or so notice boards placed around the then small city. Films played for two weeks at a time, and the posters were changed accordingly. Until 1926, Tel Aviv was a one-movie-theater town, but with a sharp rise in the immigrant population in the late twenties other theaters opened: first the Beitan (a silent film house), and later the Ophir and Opera Mograbi (both talking film theaters). In the competitive climate, the one-sheet poster evolved into a larger, four-sheet variety. Soon Tel Aviv was awash with colorful graphics that announced film openings months in advance.

The linocut genre continued through the mid-thirties, when it was replaced by order of the Association of Movie Theater Proprietors, which instituted a standard of identically formatted notices, printed in letterpress and using only text. By the end of the decade Tel Aviv theater managers employed the American method of "selling points," huge paintings or cardboard-mounted photographs of a film's stars or scenes on the facade of the theater. The golden age of posters in this "West Asian" frontier town was over.

The show card (or sho-card) was the quintessential form of early commercial art. It embodied essential design attributes of balance, harmony, and proportion that enabled unsophisticated designers, primarily job printers, to produce effective advertising. But even such modern pioneers as El Lissitzky, Jan Tschichold, E. McKnight Kauffer, Herbert Bayer, and Paul Rand adhered to the same design truth associated with the show card: Primary colors and sans serif typefaces resulted in eye-catching design.

Starting in the late nineteenth century, the show card was a piece of bristol board on which a letterer or artist would draw or paint a message or image. The quantities that were produced were invariably limited. Eventually show cards were printed on multilith presses, and stereotype plates were designed by art service agencies, which distributed to printing companies large and small. Standard show cards were produced by printers and sign makers, who inserted their own wood and metal types into the empty mortised sections on the printing plate.

Various styles filled sample books, but around 1920 the now classic format was initiated by Empire Litho, a printing firm in Massachusetts, and was quickly adopted by job printers throughout the nation. These predominantly type-based posters printed against one or two stark primary colors became the most ubiquitous medium of advertising for all kinds of regional events, including county fairs, vaudeville and movies, prize fights, square dances, and political campaigns.

Functional design was essential: gothic type, flat colors, and sometimes the split-fountain technique—where two colors at the top and bottom of the card mix in the middle to give a multichromatic effect. The occasional stock line cut or halftone might be used for decoration, and a variety of eye-catching borders were required. "The border demands full consideration in card design," wrote F. A. Pearson in the 1925 edition of "Ticket and Showcard Designing." "Its effect is that of a frame round a picture. It limits attention within its bounds." In addition, bull's-eyes, stripes, and other geometric patterns, not unlike Russian constructivist and Bauhaus compositions, guided the viewer's attention to the message.

The genre has been both parodied and used as inspiration for contemporary work. Paula Scher's New York Public Theater posters, for example, with their bold gothics of varying sizes set against yellow or red backgrounds, are admittedly influenced by the show card. In its original form, it is still used for carnivals, circuses, auctions, and concerts. The classic show card has survived shifts in trend and fashion because it is the essence of good design.

"How can one describe those incredible times," wrote Stefan Lorant in *Seig Heil* (W. W. Norton & Co., 1974) , a personal history of pre–World War II Germany. "In the morning a newspaper costs 50,000 marks—in the evening, 100,000. The price of a single pair of shoelaces would have bought an entire shoe store with its entire inventory a few weeks before. Beggars threw away 100,000-mark notes as they could buy nothing with them."

Never in the history of industrialized nations did an economic crisis have such ruinous short- and long-term effects as the German inflation of 1922–1923. Five years after Germany's ignominious defeat to the Allies in the First World War, Germany's immense war debt and punitive reparations had virtually depleted its treasury and drained its resources. But even more crippling were the large sums (40 million *gold* marks) spent daily by the Weimar government to support "passive resistance" in the Ruhr, a major industrial area of Germany then occupied by French troops. The mark took such a nosedive that its value in the world market and buying power inside Germany changed virtually minute by minute. At the beginning of 1923 the American dollar was worth 7,424 marks. By August the rate had risen to over a million, in November the rate increased to 600 billion, and by December the figure skyrocketed to 4,210,500,000,000 marks. The thirty-five Reichsbank printing presses working night and day could not print the new denominations fast enough to satisfy demand or keep up with inflation, and so a flood of unofficial Notgeld, or emergency scrip, was issued daily by towns and businesses. Wages, though handed out almost every day, could not keep up with the rising cost of living. Individual salaries in the billions (which in German was equivalent to trillions) could barely pay for the needed staples. Savings were ruined, pensions were worthless; the bedrock of this once-mighty industrial nation had turned to dust.

We are familiar with the famous black-and-white wire-service photographs of Germans pushing wheelbarrows piled high with cash to the local bakery to buy bread or carrying trunkloads of bills to the grocery for butter. People actually baled the Reichsbank notes into wastepaper, since the smaller denominations of these otherwise-impressive-looking bills had no purchase power. Their only tangible use was as heating fuel. This untenable state of affairs continued for over a year until the government, led by the chancellor Gustav Stresemann, issued a proclamation ending passive resistance in the Ruhr and introduced the Rentenmark (a more manageable denomination that literally knocked nine zeros off the mark, bringing the exchange rate from 4.2 billion marks to 4.20 marks per dollar). This was the first step in stabilizing the ravaged economy. By 1924, other firm-fisted measures helped slow the downward slide. But, as history vividly reports, the economic condition fueled other hatreds and resentments, for the Weimar Republic was doomed by the power of German nationalism.

The only minor bright spot to emerge from this devastatingly critical period was the exemplary artistic quality of the emergency (Notgeld) and substitute (Ersertzgeld) paper money issued by cities, states, banks, political groups, and businesses to ease the burden on Reichsbank presses and, more importantly, to provide some semblance of economic stability for individual citizens, who were naturally panicked by the state of economic affairs.

Practically speaking, since official Reichsbank notes were virtually worthless, most emergency money issued by municipalities was worthless save for an investment of faith. On the other hand, since they were used as instruments of barter, Ersertzgeld and Notgeld issued by businesses were redeemable for goods or services (and even entertainments such as films). In fact, Notgeld began as a kind of redeemable coupon in prisoner-of-war camps during World War I as an instrument for paying wages to Allied prisoners laboring outside their camps in service to the local community or private industry. Officially, these vouchers had value only for POWs in the camp kitchens and with ersatz wheeler-dealers, but despite government regulations, some bills managed to circulate among civilians, causing problems that lead to strict rules on the official use of Notgeld.

The issuance of "civilian" substitute money (which preceded the large-denomination emergency money) began a few years before the inflationary vortex began to spiral. With the permission or, in most instances, the silent agreement of the government ministry of finance, local and private institutions could cheaply print bills on rag paper or cardboard, usually on newspaper presses (or in the case of coins, at locksmiths or machine plants). Since these printers were not subject to government standardization, the sizes, shapes, and designs were wildly inconsistent. The images reflect a variety of talents and technology, ranging from artful to primitive execution. Though many of the bills were beautifully rendered by professional artists and designers, many were simply scrawled by rank amateurs. Since a majority of the printing is inferior to the standards of government printing offices, false money was easy to produce as well as difficult to police.

In addition to its worth as redeemable scrip to workers and citizens, municipalities found that substitute money had inherent value to collectors. Akin to small European nations, such as San Marino, whose economies are literally dependent on the export of their artful postage stamps, various German provinces garnered extra needed income by selling series of decorative bills directly to dealers and collectors for prices higher than face value. In fact, dealers advertised and sold albums to erstwhile collectors from all over the world. The examples shown here are culled from three such collections recently purchased in different parts of America but originally sold in the late 1920s by a Den Haag stamp and coin dealer named Lij Lieban, who included in each impressive Notgeld album a brief history of the form available in Dutch, French, English, and German.

For many German and Austrian graphic designers and poster artists, the design of Notgeld was a commonplace assignment. Thousands of different variations were produced between 1918 and 1924. The genre was even recognized in issues of *Das Plakat,* Germany's most influential advertising-arts magazine. Lucian Bernhard, Germany's premier poster artist, was among the most renowned designers to create Notgeld (though examples of this work were apparently destroyed during the war). Comic artists for the various German satiric weeklies, such as *Simplicissimus,* were also used in such design, since forms of Jugendstil and expressionism were the dominant styles. As for imagery, virtually any theme was a fair subject, so some were satirically ribald, such as one in which a donkey eats grass and shits gold. A few are religious, like that showing a cripple able to walk after swimming in a pool of redemption. Most common were local scenes and local fables. Some commemorated German heroes (such as Goethe), great battles, architectural masterpieces, and so on. As is the Nordic proclivity, many of the most intricate notes were replete with images of death. Sporting and political groups used their own iconography, such as the steel helmet that appears on the notes issued by the Stahlhelm (a nationalist group that would later merge with the Nazis). Some of the notes included stylistic lettering, while others were rooted in classicism. Many were vibrantly colorful, others somberly monochromatic.

Though substitute money was officially illegal tender, by 1922 the German government found it difficult to forbid what was referred to in government circles as "the money folly." By 1923 the government itself was so busy printing new money (even Herbert Bayer designed some Bauhausian Reichsbank notes) that Notgeld was taken for granted. Not even forgery of official banknotes was taken too seriously, since the speed at which people had to dispose of large quantities of cash to avoid hourly price increases made it impossible to monitor. Actually, money—real *or* counterfeit—was essentially worthless at the moment of printing.

By the summer of 1923, paper money wasn't even accepted as having value. Only real products (actual material goods) had any worth. Notgeld became a generic term for any kind of emergency "currency." Leather-producing firms gave out their salaries in the form of shoe soles, brickworks in bricks; food processors offered sugar or margarine. The suppliers of electricity, gas, and water issued vouchers, but even these vouchers had to be redeemed on the day of issue— waiting even one moment meant risking a dramatic increase in rates. Given the paucity of gold marks and the worthlessness of paper and coin, raw materials could not be purchased. The country was indeed desperate.

Stresemann's conciliatory stance with the Allies and his government's attempt to regain control of the railways and other vital industries—which were relinquished to private owners as conditions of unconditional surrender—helped stabilize the German economy but, as well, ignited further acrimony among left and right factions who were tired of paying and suffering for the war. Somewhat effective were certain Allied plans that reduced the costly reparations, returned some resource centers, allowed the mark to have some parity in the world market, and otherwise improved domestic conditions. But civil war between communists and nationalists would trap Germany in a political vortex even more tragic than its economic plight, with Adolf Hitler democratically gaining dictatorial powers in 1933.

The history of Notgeld briefly picks up again in 1944, when, certain of Germany's defeat in World War II, the Allies printed new currency for the occupied German nation. But the denominations were small and ineffective. Because all bills and coins with the swastika were outlawed, towns and business had to help themselves by producing Notgeld once again. Since 1939, it had been illegal to produce substitute money, but by the same law the Reichsbank would provide the proper "value signs." In 1945, with the war over and the nation in disarray, the Reichsbank was in no position to forbid anything, nor could it produce enough currency on its own. After a short period of crisis, the Allies quickly stabilized the currency and began its denazification and recovery programs.

Though much of the Notgeld issued throughout Germany was destroyed by the war, the artistry of these bills inspired some to maintain collections that, until quite recently, were little known. Today Notgeld documents a critical economic and political epoch in German history and reveals how artists in this nation of tragically conflicting morals and ethics ironically made a crisis look good.

Decorative Book Jackets

DESIGNER: W. A. DWIGGINS

In the early 1920s, when William Addison Dwiggins (1880–1956) was in his forties—an age by which many of his contemporaries had already done their best work and were ossified in their ways—he was at the peak of his form and open to all possibilities. He did not subscribe to avant-garde theory or any other theory that held sway in the twenties or thirties. He was never dogmatic regarding the ideological rightness of form. On one occasion he wrote disparagingly about the typographic antics of those modern American designers he referred to as the Bauhaus boys, while on another he attacked the rigidity of narrow-minded traditionalists.

Dwiggins, WAD, Dwig, or Bill—take your pick—grew up in Cambridge, Ohio, and at nineteen studied lettering with Frederic Goudy at the Frank Holme School of Illustration in Chicago, Illinois. He was weaned on the ideals of the aesthetic movement, of which proponents imitated fine printing of the past. In 1912, Dwiggins and T. M. Cleland were singled out by the preeminent posterist and typographer Will Bradley for work that had brought taste and skill back into a field that had "sunk to the lowest possible depths before their appearance."

But Dwig did not follow the rules. His longtime friend and collaborator Dorothy Abbe once said that he had arrived at his own determination of fine printing, and it differed very considerably from that of Goudy, Updike, and Rogers. While these stalwart keepers of the classical rejected mass production as anathema to fine design, during the course of his life Dwig witnessed the passing of individual craftsmanship and the substitution of bigger, faster machines in all phases of typesetting and printing. He saw no reason why new technologies should not produce quality work, and he proposed that photoengraving, for example, made calligraphy more widely available, which would increase popular appreciation of good design.

Dwiggins practiced advertising design, type design, book design, and marionette design. He even designed a working puppet theater in his clapboard studio across the street from his home in Hingham, Massachusetts. But to appreciate Dwig's obsessions for work and therefore his contributions, one must know that he was driven to accomplish as much as possible before succumbing to the dire prediction of an early death. "He was handicapped by the clock and the calendar," says a biographical notation. Diagnosed with diabetes, an often fatal disease at that time (1922), Dwiggins exhibited an intense drive to get on with life. Dorothy Abbe explained: "He resolved thenceforth to satisfy himself." A year later Dwig announced to the world: "Me I am a happy invalid and it has revolutionized my whole attack. My back is turned on the more banal kind of advertising and I have canceled all commissions and am resolutely set on starving. . . . I will produce art on paper and wood after my own heart with no heed to any market." However, fate intervened: Insulin soon became available, giving Dwiggins another thirty-three years of life.

Tossing aside his lucrative advertising accounts, he concentrated on the not-so-profitable business of book design and page ornament. His earliest book commissions were from the Harvard University Press, for whom he designed the now rare volume *Modern Color* (1923), and from Alfred A. Knopf, for whom, beginning in 1924 and continuing for almost two decades, he designed 280 books of fiction and nonfiction as well as almost 50 book jackets. "Bill enabled us to produce a long series of trade books that for interest and originality of design are unequaled," writes Mr. Knopf.

In addition to his uniquely composed (and sometimes illustrated) title pages, two features characterized his design: The text was always readable, and the bindings (and especially the shelf backs) were adorned with his calligraphic hand lettering and neo-Mayan ornament. Every piece of lettering and typography—down to the minutest graphic detail—was rendered by hand; given the extant physical evidence, many were done without a single mistake (when mistakes did occur, he simply redrew them rather than touching up the errors). Dwiggins's calligraphic display letters, a marriage of classical typefaces and invented scripts, set the standard for Knopf's books and influenced many other publishers, who employed Dwig or one of his many imitators.

Book jackets, however, fell into the category of advertising that Dwiggins initially wanted to avoid. Yet, due to his special relationship with Mr. Knopf, when asked, he did them. Nevertheless, his method was a form of denial. He refused to pictorially illustrate most covers, as was the common practice, but rather applied Dwigginsian ornament and calligraphic lettering. Hence, there was a great formal similarity between all his jackets. The image area of his most common jacket format was cut in half, with the title on top and a subtitle or other type below. Sometimes he used an excessive amount of ornamentation, but only with his self-authored books did he ever use a drawing. A typical approach—found in his jacket for Willa Cather's *Lost Lady*, which includes a hand-lettered title and byline and characteristic Dwigginsian ornament printed in pink, green, and brown—is something like a souped-up title page. Compared to the designers of many of the lettered jackets of his day, Dwiggins had a unique flair, wedding balance and harmony with quirkiness. The jackets rarely evoked the plot or theme of the book but were essentially decoration—a "dust wrapper" in the purest sense of the word. One of his most alluring jackets—for James M. Cain's *Serenade* (1937), the design of which is a bouquet of abstracted flora—is akin more to beautiful wrapping paper than an advertisement for the book.

Given the choice, Dwiggins preferred using his hands to make things; hand lettering was more satisfying than type design. He did not begin to design complete type alphabets until 1929, when, at the urging of C. H. Griffith, marketing director for the Mergenthaler Linotype Corporation, he designed his first typeface for continued reading. He did not attempt to replicate his calligraphy. In fact, the initial undertaking (the first of eighteen typefaces), had no relationship whatsoever to his lettering. Metro Black was a uniform sans serif letter that Dwiggins designed because he saw a need for a strong gothic that did more for display advertising than Futura and other European gothics. Ironically, Dwig never used this typeface on any book jacket.

"There are few American designers whose work can be revisited after decades with more pleasure and instruction," an admirer wrote about Dwiggins a decade after his death. When viewing examples of his printed work or the original drawings that surface at exhibitions, much of Dwig's work stands up not as nostalgia, but for its invention. Even the book jackets, which are stylistically locked in time, could, with some typographic modifications, be used today. By the fifties, however, with the advent of the international style and the sweeping success of corporate modernism, Dwig was virtually ignored. Moderns, who tended to disclaim as crass commercial art anything that preceded modern design, eschewed Dwiggins for being folksy, arts-and-craftsy, and, of course, passé.

Though he challenged tradition, he attempted to reform the old school not abolish it. Curiously, his work, including the book jackets, is gaining appreciation among makers of so-called distressed type; even Emigre Fonts sells Dorothy Abbe's book of Dwig's stenciled ornament, the same decorations used in his book and book-jacket design.

Book Covers

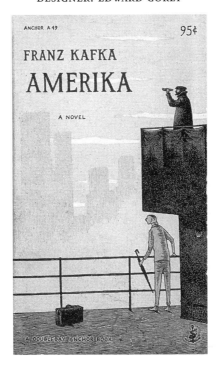

The public knows him for his animated titles for the PBS television series *Mystery!* and the sets and costumes for the Broadway productions *Edward Gorey's Dracula* and *The Mikado.* Through his numerous books and theatrical productions, Edward Gorey (b. 1925)—illustrator, author, playwright, theater and ballet set designer—has carved out a unique place in the world of arts and letters. The imaginary tableaux in his books and stage plays are replete with turn-of-the-century appointments (lace curtains in windows, marble mantelpieces, four-poster beds, vases of aspidistras, and ornate funeral urns) and peopled by a cast of eccentric and sinister gents, dames, and tykes as well as a menagerie of autochthonous hippos, birds, alligators, bats, and cats. Through his macabre crosshatched drawings and staccato linguistic rhythms, Gorey (the name is certainly appropriate) has created a world that transcends all sense of time and place. His surreal black humor is literally a study in light and dark in which the unspeakable is spoken, the unthinkable is thought, and the horrific—murder, mayhem, and unexplained disappearances—is comic.

In 1953, he published his first book, *The Unstrung Harp,* an odd thirty-page tale illustrated in a satiric Edwardian manner, about the trials and tribulations of the mythical author Clavius Frederick Earbrass, a pathetic figure in a fur coat who lives alone in a stately house full of portraits and statuettes that look exactly like him. That same year, he accepted a position in the art department of Anchor/Doubleday, where he did pasteups and lettering. He also designed about fifty book covers before leaving in 1960. These illustrated covers comprise a small but significant chapter in the history of paperback cover design and in the legacy of the white-bearded, fur-coated man who made them.

All but forgotten today, these covers established a visual personality for a company that was founded to reprint many of the world's classic texts, some of which were previously published in paperback versions during the late 1930s and 1940s, when virtually all mass-market books were adorned with prurient covers designed to pander to the voyeuristic reader. Then the style was to cover such literary classics as Tolstoy's *War and Peace* or Dostoyevsky's *Crime and Punishment* with bosomy damsels in distress, but by the late 1940s, cooler, more rational heads prevailed. In the 1950s, certain paperbacks aimed at serious readers were given more sophisticated cover art by such modern designers as Alvin Lustig, Paul Rand, Rudolph de Harak, and Leo Lionni. Gorey's covers for Anchor/Doubleday were not orthodox modern design but they were astute interpretations of the texts, handsomely designed, and smartly composed.

Gorey's involvement began inauspiciously. He had known Doubleday editors Barbara Zimmerman and Jason Epstein from his days at Harvard. He visited New York just before Christmas of 1952, when they were starting Anchor Books, and did a few freelance covers for them. In turn they offered him a job in their small art department. "At first I turned it down," Gorey recalls, "because I didn't want to live in New York. . . . So much for that. I realized that I was starving to death in Boston and took the job the next year."

Gorey was born in Chicago, where he graduated from high school in 1942. He applied to the University of Chicago, Carnegie Tech (as it was known as in those days), and Harvard. "I went to this kind of fancy, intellectually (so to speak) reputable private school in Chicago, so in those days it was fairly easy to be admitted to Harvard," he explains. "I couldn't get in now if I crawled on my hands and knees from here to Cambridge." After he was discharged from the army in January of 1946, he received his acceptance to Harvard and attended on the GI Bill. "So I trotted off to major in French, without bothering to discover whether they had a particularly good French department or not."

At that time Gorey was drawing pictures, "if that's what you want to call it," he quips about his seeming lack of motivations, "with the intent of nothing at all, I assure you. I've never had any intentions about anything. That's why I am where I am today, which is neither here nor there, in a literal sense." So he took the job in the publishing-house art department, which, he admits, wasn't too taxing. "In fact, when I saw some of the pasteups that other people did, I thought that these well-known artists [like Ben Shahn and others who did covers] really were all thumbs. I never had much patience with having to redo other people's pasteups, which looked like they'd just flung the lettering on the page."

In addition to this menial work, he designed covers. His first, *Lafcadio's Adventures* by André Gide, revealed Gorey's aptitude for classical drawing with an idiosyncratic twist. The style was rooted in nineteenth-century representationalism but was not so easily pigeonholed into a specific time frame. His second cover was what he describes as "a kind of tacky little drawing of the Globe Theater from the air, which I found someplace and copied for a book on Shakespeare by Mark van Doren." In addition to the linear drawing style, Gorey's finished lettering looked as though it were a comp or a sketch of hand lettering that approximated real type. At that time, paperbacks either had calligraphic or typeset covers, but Gorey's style was betwixt and between: "I was stuck with hand lettering, which I did very poorly, I always felt—but everybody seemed to like it," he says. In fact, when he published his own books, all except the first were hand-lettered in the manner of his earlier book jackets.

Gorey was not the first to employ hand-drawn letters. Paul Rand initiated the practice because typesetting was too expensive and deducted from his overall fee; hand lettering ultimately became a defining characteristic of his book-cover design. Gorey was not concerned with the costs; rather, "I didn't really know too much about type in those days, and it was simply easier to hand-letter the whole thing than to spec type. Eventually, though, I did a lot of things that weren't hand-lettered, as far as book jackets were concerned." But lettering became a trademark of his own work, and he also rendered it for other designers who, he says jokingly, "were even less competent in lettering than I was."

In addition to his regular diet of French literature, he also enjoyed reading British novels and had an admiration for British book-jacket illustration, which influenced his overall style. A voracious reader his entire life—"I was much better-read than most of the people who were doing artwork"—Gorey did not, however, do a lot of preparation for his covers. "I was usually handed the assignment, and there would be some little paragraph summarizing the plot," he explains. It rarely mattered anyway, since his style was so individual that the covers themselves did not illustrate the respective plots as much as they evoked moods.

Gorey developed stylistic and compositional conceits that recur throughout this work. "There were certain kinds of books where I followed a routine," he admits, "such as my famous landscape, which was mostly sky so I could fit in a title. Things like *A Hero of Our Time* by Mikhail Lermontov, *Victory* by Joseph Conrad, and *The Wanderer* by Henri Alain-Fournier tend to have low-lying landscapes, a lot of sky, sort of odd colors, and tiny figures that I didn't have to draw very hard." He also maintained a muted and earthy color palette—rather surprising, given that paperback convention demanded covers that were miniposters, able to grab a reader's eye in an instant. Explaining his palette, he says, "It was partly because you had to keep it to three [flat] colors, plus black. I guess I could have picked bright reds or blues, but I've never been much for that. My palette seems to be sort of lavender, lemon yellow, olive green, and then a whole series of absolutely no colors at all." One of these so-called no-color covers was Gorey's interpretation for Kafka's *Amerika,* which shows a Goreyesque character—an almost-skeletal silhouette standing on the closely cropped deck of a ship entering New York harbor. With only a hint of pink in the clouds, this otherwise-dark, lugubrious image is not the typical prequel for Kafka's critical vision of America but rather a snapshot of every new immigrant's fears upon entering a strange land.

For someone who professed not to know where he was going professionally, Gorey's covers reveal a skillful and unique sense of composition. He created not only a strong identity for Anchor but also memorable icons for the books themselves, regardless of his opinion about their contents. Notable is his work for the Henry James novels published by Anchor, which Gorey insists was "all a mistake" because this is one author "whom I hate more than anybody else in the world except for Picasso. I've read everything of Henry James, some of it twice, and every time I do it I think, 'Why am I doing this again? Why am I torturing myself?' Everybody thought how sensitive I was to Henry James, and I thought, 'Oh sure, kids.' If it's because I hate him so much, that's probably true."

Most of Gorey's work was illustrative, but for a few books he designed only lettered covers (what he insists on calling "tacky hand-lettering"). One such was Kierkegaard's *Either/Or*. The reason, he admitted, was fairly simple. "Was I planning to sit down and read Kierkegaard at that point? No, I wasn't! And it wouldn't have helped if I had, I'm sure. I probably would have been completely paralyzed."

Gorey left Anchor in 1960 when Jason Epstein started the Looking-Glass Library with Celia Carroll. "The idea was that it was going to do for children's books what Anchor had done for the parents," he explains. "The books were not paperbacks but rather paper-over-boards, and it was really quite a good series. Well, the paper was perfectly dreadful, but, then, the paper for everything in those days was perfectly terrible." Gorey illustrated a few books, including *War of the Worlds* ("the less said about those, the better"); he was both art director and an editor. The books conformed to Gorey's taste in nineteenth-century British literature, including *Spider's Palace* by Richard Hughes and *Countess Kade* by Charlotte M. Young. After two years the imprint folded and Gorey moved more into his own realms.

The drawings for his stories and books (many of which are anthologized in his three *Amphigorey* collections or archived at the Gotham Book Mart in New York City) are rooted in the visual language that developed while designing covers for Anchor/Doubleday. These covers are, therefore, artifacts from both a transitional period in paperback history and the formative years of Gorey's unique career.

Food packaging is as common as food itself and, therefore, raises few questions and causes little controversy. With the exception of the current concern about recycling solid waste and the food industry's attempt to address that issue, food packaging is viewed as a natural outgrowth of our natural consumables.

But like Velveeta and Spam, food packaging is not natural. In fact, as is the case with simulated food, the mother of this invention is war. Although a package is undeniably utilitarian, modern packaging is a function of a war that is fought daily, a war that many of us don't even realize is being waged. Yet it affects both our pocketbooks and our consuming habits. Before you complain that "this guy's thesis sounds like a load of by-products," allow me a modicum of strained metaphorical license.

In addition to offering protection from the elements and a convenient way of transporting goods from store to table, food packages are indeed weapons in an ongoing war to win consumer loyalty. With the huge financial investment required to develop new products and, therefore, to compete with older brands, packaging strategies that would rival many military operations are employed. In fact, for every victorious new product, scores of enemy products are defeated. For every popular brand, armies of tacticians—including brand managers, marketing experts, and product, graphic, and advertising designers—expend a huge amount of resources devising the perfect attack.

Think about why: The average supermarket is stocked with so many competitors (and these are the products that make the cut) that a typical consumer has to be conditioned, indeed brainwashed, to desire a specific brand. This allegiance, or brand loyalty, is not easily won. Only after unrelenting barrages of pitches, discounts, and testimonials will a shopper even so much as consider trying something new. We are all such creatures of habit that only the most invasive (or diabolically brilliant) marketing plans will dislodge us from the redoubts of our predictable patterns.

So, to soften the beachhead (sorry, there's that war metaphor again), the common marketing strategy involves a three-pronged attack of advertising, promotion, and packaging.

The first—advertising—introduces, positions, and establishes the brand or product through continuous media exposure. The second—promotion—ensures that the brand name becomes a household word through special direct-mail offers, bonuses, prizes, coupons, and samples. The third—the package—seduces the shopper through visual and tactile lures. In this equation, the package serves not simply as a vessel but as a signpost or billboard.

Although sustained purchase of a brand is inevitably determined by its inherent quality, a product is as good as invisible without the benefit of these combined forces. What this strategy must ensure is engagement with the eye and all the senses through what is commonly known as *appetite appeal*. But before discussing the concept of appetite appeal, let us sample a little history to whet the appetite.

Package design evolved from terra-cotta vessels of antiquity to the recycled paperboard, plastics, and tins of today. Graphics have come a long way since papyrus labels were used to identify contents three thousand years ago. But packages are still fundamentally rooted in the fifteenth century, when paper could be produced inexpensively and product *marking* began. While the form has varied, the function was ostensibly the same then as now.

From the 1500s to the late 1700s printed labels, produced on handmade paper from impressions on wooden presses, were primarily used for bales of cloth and drug vials. Production changed in 1798, when the Frenchman Nicolas-Louis Roberts invented a papermaking machine, while around the same time the Bavarian Alois Senefelder developed the lithographic process. Labels soon became a common feature on packages. They were colored by hand until 1835, when the Englishman George Baxter developed a process to print multiple colors from wood engravings onto a monochrome base. He patented this method, and by 1850, his process of chromolithography enabled printers to print twelve different colors on a single label.

There was an explosion of printed items throughout America after the Revolution. Every wooden box of peas or oysters was branded with a company identity. This kind of packaging flourished for over a century, although it was not until 1935, when an American named Stanton Avery created and produced the self-adhesive label, that a key development in packaging history took hold. Labeling became a huge industry within an industry, and anything that was not printed on a box was emblazoned with a label. These paper labels—with pictures of produce, trade characters, or happy consumers—tended to stain and peel, and so, over the years, they have been replaced by those that repel oil, water, and grease.

Back in the nineteenth century, illustrations of distant lands and exotic people lured buyers into believing that a common product was imbued with mystery, indeed romance and adventure; such an item was not commonplace but precious and rare. In addition to the exotic graphic conceits, testimonials from ersatz experts attested to a product's nutritional benefits. Even then, health concerns were an issue. Although these popular sales ploys were bogus, no trusting consumer could ignore the wisdom of a doctor or professor, even if these experts earned their degrees from correspondence schools. The method may be different, but many mainstream contemporary food packages continue the tradition of paid celebrity testimonials. Hey, who wouldn't eat Jell-O gelatin after Bill Cosby admonishes us to do so? It would be almost un-American to refuse.

With the advent of mass consumerism in the late nineteenth century, packages were transformed from quaint decorative objects into no-nonsense tools of persuasion. They were not merely commercial receptacles but containers of truth—indeed, discovery. When individual packages replaced huge bags and bushels that once filled the old general stores, the physical package itself symbolized progress. It gave allure to a product on both conscious and unconscious levels. It provoked the consumer to take pride in his consumption. It made the consumer desirous to consume.

"For manufacturers, packaging is one of the crucial ways people find the confidence to buy," writes Thomas Hine in *The Total Package, the Evolution and Secret Meanings of Boxes, Bottles, Cans, and Tubes*. "It can also give a powerful image to products and commodities that are in themselves characterless." The package, label, and bottle are at once the totem, icon, and reliquary of great essences.

In addition to improvements in packaging, notions of advertising changed from emphasis on the word to reliance on the pictorial. Throughout the second half of the nineteenth century the technological developments in printing that allowed for text and image to be printed together expanded the potential for images to have widespread distribution and influence on the American public through mass periodicals, posters, and advertisements. By the late 1890s and well into the early twentieth century, paintings and drawings evolved as the quotidian tools for conveying complex messages in accessible forms. Food advertisements with paintings of delicious food shared the same stage with drawings of friendly trade characters.

By the early twentieth century, as newly developed national brands of packaged mixes, preserved foods, crackers, and cereals competed with one another, advertising agencies invented mascots (as well as trademarks and slogans) to encourage a personal identification of consumer with consumable. As people became more detached from the actual production of food and less familiar with the essence of the particular animal or plant it came from, food became more abstract. A brand name was not always enough to stimulate devotion; products had to have deeper roots in the common psyche. In addition, new products had to be imbued with a history or genealogy. Depending on the nature or personality of the mythical trade character, some or all of these ideals were met.

Such characters as Aunt Jemima, the Cream of Wheat man, the Campbell's Soup twins, and hundreds of other cartoon and realistic/idealistic characters became the most common mnemonic devices lending a modicum of humanity to manufactured commodities. Everyone recalls characters like Tony the Tiger, Chef Boyardee, or the Frito Bandito, even if the manufacturer has long since retired its mascot, because they were as ubiquitous as their advertising budgets would allow. And, of course, trade characters are such a powerful advertising tool that they are not limited to foodstuffs. Many of the most popular characters were born of comic or cartoon lineage (some were borrowed from popular comics of the day, like Impy, the African in *Little Nemo in Slumberland,* who hawked Impy Cocoa). Some were total fantasies, inventions of the advertising agency's image makers, others were depictions of real or generalized peoples whose images were ostensibly taken without permission and who never received royalties or residuals.

Aunt Jemima of pancake fame was borrowed from an African-American minstrel character and eventually evolved into the mammy stereotype, which has, in turn, been transformed into the housewife on today's packaging. Back around the turn of the century women were hired to play the part of Aunt Jemima, traveling to events throughout the country and promoting the product as their own homespun invention. Other more generic—and indeed, by today's standards, racist—African-American "types," such as field hands, house servants, and picka-ninnies, were also used for so-called indigenous products or products that related to the work of black people, like chefs, porters, and fruit pickers. Likewise, Native American "types" were used for products that were directly or tangentially related to their culture, such as tobacco, corn, and corn oil. Often the depictions were cardboard caricatures of noble savages that parodied their dress and languages. In most instances these were extremely popular products, if not because of the food itself, then for the character that represented it. The advertising trade journals of the day reported that "Negro" and "Indian" characters, as though they were human, were very welcome in the homemaker's kitchen. The mammy character was the most popular of all because she was the loyal house servant.

Trade characters ran the gamut from silly (and, doubtless, insulting) depictions of different ethnic and racial groups, to the occasional broad-brush gender representation, to anthropomorphized animals, plants, and vegetables that somehow made the product attractive. In humanizing food products—many of which were made from brutally butchered animals—marketers sought to both detach food from reality and, at the same time, attract consumer loyalty. Who, indeed, would reject a household friend for a stranger? Who would shun, say, the Pillsbury Doughboy for a competitor? Whoever devised the original promotional concept should be self-content regardless of final destination—Heaven or Hell—because the idea has worked to this day, with many characters becoming cultural landmarks in the pantheon of consumerist history.

Yet food cannot be sold by friendly or comic pitchmen alone. Certain products demand the kind of additional persuasion that comes only from mouthwatering depictions. Modern packaging and package designers are, therefore, challenged to link the taste buds to the pocketbook.

In the 1950s, Chase and Sanborn coffee rented a Times Square billboard that, like the famous sign for Camel cigarettes a few blocks away, spewed steam into the street at regular intervals. In addition, a few times a day (at breakfast, lunch, and dinner, to be precise) coffee scents wafted into the air. A city ordinance was ultimately passed that limited advertisers to using scentless steam, but the point had been made. Everyone has experienced the seductive sway of an aroma. The unmistakable smells of fresh-brewed coffee, sizzling bacon, and hash browns make the mouth water so uncontrollably that restaurants have been known to set their exhaust fans to high, thus filling the adjoining streets with delicious breakfast emanations designed to entice the hungry customer. Likewise, a food package must appeal to the part of the brain where appetites reside and where you and I are most susceptible to suggestion.

The task facing the contemporary package designer is, therefore, how to make paper, tin, cardboard, cellophane, and glass into something that seduces our most primal urges. Yet it is not easy transforming inherently unappetizing materials into a banquet of the mind.

Numerous conventions remain in place from the time when the modern commercial package was introduced about a century ago. And the most common is the ultrarealistic illustration of a particular prepared food. A stack of pancakes soaked in butter and syrup, a steaming bowl of soup, and a plate of spaghetti topped with a delectable sauce excite the salivary glands more than the powder, liquid, or stiff strands in the packages. Reproductions of fruits—a freshly sliced apple, orange, or pear on a container of juice, or dew-soaked berries on a jar of jelly or jam— have incalculable overt *and* subliminal powers. The transformation of the contents of a box or tin into what it should become does not take genius to figure out, but talent is required to do it well. Which is why specialists called "food stylists" work closely with photographers to create the ideal representation.

In the absence of real aromas—thank heavens, no one has yet produced scratch 'n' sniff packages—images like the wedge of chocolate layer cake on the cake-mix box or smiling sunny-side-up eggs on the powdered egg package are alluring substitutes. The fact is, without these pictorial representations, the supermarket would be little more than a warehouse of generic staples. With them, it is a cafeteria of beckoning displays.

Food packages do not, however, show only cooked foods or nature's bounty. Packages today are designed to infiltrate the consumer's psyche on a variety of levels—appealing to the shopper's lifestyle as well as social and health concerns. These days a product cannot be merely mouthwatering or thirst-quenching; the package must announce that it is *indispensable* for the body, mind, and soul. Food is much more than mere sustenance, it has cultural connotations. It is also a code or symbol for class and social strata. Decades ago, we were told that we are what we eat. Today that credo motivates the food packaging industry.

Sophisticated design codes have become more accepted in many strata of our society; as we've been introduced to exotic and foreign specialties, food has become much more of a design medium than ever before. Of course, food producers—such as farmers and butchers—don't look at their wares as anything but essential dietary raw material, but food distribution conglomerates have been convinced by MBAs and Mad Ave experts that value derives from image. And image makeovers are exactly what food and food emporia have received during the past decade. Indeed, the marketing spotlight that illuminates food has far more impact than the threat of irradiated meat. How packagers have approached food as style and fashion has changed the way many people—certainly in the upper-middle- and upper-income bracket—perceive it, buy it, and consume it.

Supermarkets around the country have had facelifts to look more stylishly contemporary and also to offer more services and shelf space to a wider variety of what might be called "food for the masses and food for the classes." In addition, specialty food shops or food boutiques have increased demand for premium and novelty foods, which are not only made with more attention to fashion than mass-produced items but are also packaged in more novel ways. The combination of a general upgrade of mass products and the introduction of more upscale products, not to mention the addition of food-style magazines and radio and cable television food programming, has markedly increased the status of food in contemporary society.

Advertisements for average bottled waters claim to quench thirst, but packages for the higher-priced premium brands presume to satisfy social impulses. To impress one's guests, the theory goes, seltzer is too plebeian; so spend more for a bottle that will stand alongside a decanter of the choicest Beaujolais nouveau. For example, with its elegant cobalt blue bottle, Tynant water is perhaps even more stylish than the most fashionable wine. And the price is accordingly high. In the eighties, specialty foods—once the province of small, exclusive caterers and food boutiques—found their way into the supermarket, where shoppers are able to choose between the quotidian and the premium. Sometimes the only difference between these two genres is the look of the packages, and so design has become a tool in positioning the brand.

Packaging is key to this process. Over the years, old packaging conventions have been challenged, taboos have been shaken, and standards have been altered in an effort to restructure the relationship between consumer and product. Sure the majority of foodstuffs are packaged to be *un*packaged and used, with containers discarded, but increasingly packages are designed to be saved. Food tins, boxes, and jars are designed not only to distinguish them in a crowded market but also to be displayed in private homes. Like vintage advertising posters, certain food packaging is meant to become an instant artifact. Food packaging representing a lifestyle is a status symbol every bit as charged as a Mercedes emblem or as commonly displayed as the Nike swoosh.

In the 1950s, virtually all supermarket brands, regardless of the product, looked basically the same: bold gothic type or custom script lettering, loud primary colors, and friendly (often goofy) trade characters on a label or box. They were designed by commercial art studios that specialized in either local food-industry packages or national supermarket package design, and all adhered to marketing conventions that limited color palettes and type options. Packages followed a few models because they were tried, true, and successful. Indeed, some of the best-known packages were not altered for decades, and some particular brands, like Hershey's chocolate or Golden Blossom Honey, are still packaged more or less with the same design as when they were introduced. Change came slow to food packaging because marketers were terrified of confusing and, thus, losing their loyal consumers. When an incremental change was made, they saturated the media with advertisements about how new and improved a product was.

And one can't blame food producers, either. The public *is* easily confused when the familiar becomes unfamiliar and new items are introduced. In recent years, however, the package design field has grown to include those who do not follow convention and clients who allow them to be bolder, within reason. Today, a wide range of graphic designers (many who do not consider packaging to be their specialty) apply themselves to packages as one part of a general practice. Because of these designers, the old-school conventions have been challenged, and taboos have been busted.

In the eighties, graphic designers who were concerned more with the aesthetic value of their design than with market-tested truths turned from eye-catching gothic typefaces to both classical and new-wave typefaces; loud primary colors were replaced by subtler pastels; and trade characters were either streamlined, diminished, or retired. Yet despite changes in graphic style, in the final analysis food packaging is still the least experimental and probably the most conservative of any graphic design form.

Consumers insist that they want novelty as a respite from daily routines, yet an analysis of the average shopping cart reveals that few purchases are novelty or impulse buys. Consistency is the watchword, if not the hobgoblin, of food industry graphics. Once a shopper is hooked and loyal to a particular brand, the emphasis of design is on maintaining their loyalty. Venerable brands may have periodic makeovers, but few manufacturers are sufficiently foolhardy to threaten their hard-earned equity by tampering with success. Only those older products facing a diminishing consumer base engage in radical cosmetic surgery, and only after extensive market research determines that it is feasible and necessary.

Consumers really want their brands to be loyal to them. They don't want surprises that interrupt their basic routines or, more importantly, strain their budgets. And one aspect of packaging that has not been adequately addressed is the cost passed down to the consumer. Every national brand pays a price to be so famous, and ultimately, those who consume the brand share in the cost.

In the current market, food packaging can be divided between the staples (which will always be constant) and the impulses—fashionable or fun foods, the area where new brands with quirkily designed packages have a chance of winning market share. In recent years, salsas, bottled waters, fruity soft drinks, and "natural foods" have invaded and staked out territory, first in the specialty food shops and next in many larger supermarkets. This is where shifts in package trends begin to occur. If smaller, offbeat brands are successful in capturing consumers, larger brands may be influenced, too. This is also where contemporaneity is a virtue; the more fashionable the package, the more likely it is to attract the impulse buyer.

Package design does not exist in a vacuum but is one component of a system that controls consumer behavior. "Advertising leads consumers into temptation. Packaging is the temptation," observes Thomas Hine. What makes a tempting package? In the course of researching my book *Food Wrap* I decided that the majority of mainstream products no longer have this quality, although presumably they once did. Most venerable packages have become little more than visual bells that stimulate Pavlovian responses. A box of Kellogg's Special K, for example, no longer has the same surprising allure as it did when first issued decades ago, but it still engenders immediate recognition. The same is true for scores of other well-known brands whose packages are as effective as traffic lights in telling the consumer to stop and go. But are they really tempting? Or are they so endemic to shopping ritual that the consumer selects them without thinking?

In a marketplace overstocked with familiar packages, only the novel, unique, or out-of-the-ordinary offers any real excitement. And since these packages are appealing to a new breed of consumers distinguished by economic and social class, it is important to keep them excited and buying. Food packaging of the past decade falls into the following six thematic categories:

1. Natural: packages that either focus on the natural benefits of the product or use natural or recycled materials
2. Homespun: packaging for products simulating those made in the home
3. Vernacular and Nostalgic: packaging similar to the homespun but more specifically trading on fashionable or kitsch, once-passé design style
4. Joke and Jest: packaging that uses humor as a tool for capturing the impulse buyer
5. Classical: packaging that exudes elegance based on the traditional tenets of typography
6. Postmodern: packaging that exhibits the most contemporary, convention-busting applications of graphic design

Returning to the war metaphor . . . Like defense strategies since the fall of the Soviet Union and the end of the cold war, food packaging strategies have radically shifted. Instead of big national wars to win hearts and minds, food products are launched in local theaters of operation—not just geographically but also according to class, age, and cultural divisions. Big battles are still waged for the ubiquitous mass-produced staples and snack foods, but smaller products and brands are definitely making inroads. It seems ironic that while many in the world are starving, American food manufacturers spend huge amounts of money devising novel packages and launching costly advertising campaigns for ever more products. But just think about where the food industry would be without all that improved packaging. It's as ridiculous as total disarmament, isn't it?

Hard Sell versus Soft Sell

DESIGNER: LOUIS DANZIGER

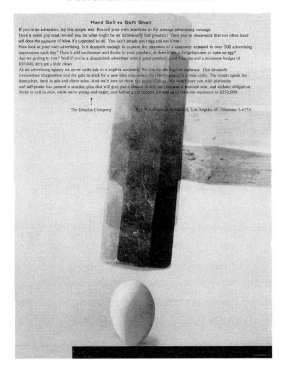

Louis Danziger (b. 1923) was raised in a generation that believed that the mission of the modern designer was to impose order, beauty, and utility on a crassly commercial world. Through his own achievements he extended the reach of modernism as an American design ethic; his work exemplifies the diversity of modernism, while his teaching promotes the diversity of design.

To look at his printed output from the fifties through the seventies is not an exercise in modernist nostalgia. The advertisements, brochures, catalogs, and posters that fill his extensive oeuvre reveal certain formal, architectonic, and conceptual characteristics of their respective times, but they also stand as testaments to his individuality. In Danziger's hands modernism was not simply a cold, formulaic template invented to universalize corporate messages; rather, each of the problems presented to him demanded and received unique attention. His common-sense approach to the needs of business led him at all times to seek the "elegant solution," which he explains as "taking a minimal amount of material and a minimal amount of effort—nothing wasted—to achieve maximum impact." His work may have promoted current products or timely ideas, but the design intelligence with which Danziger made a page structurally sound while piquing the audience's interest underscores a timelessness that defies the parameters of style or epoch. Danziger's work challenges the notion that all graphic design is ephemeral.

Ironically, though, the most ephemeral of popular mass media, print advertising, is where Danziger triumphed in creating some of his most enduring images and ideas. Among the scores of jobs he completed for many clients, perhaps his most elegant pieces are two 1956 advertisements, titled "Hard Sell vs. Soft Sell" and "The Light Touch," designed to attract business to the Dreyfus Company, a small advertising agency in Los Angeles. Each was photographed in black-and-white and composed as a full-page bleed with a simple text block framing the image; the ads showed, respectively, a sledgehammer in motion on the verge of smashing an egg and a shoe precariously resting atop of another egg.

By that time, the "Big Idea," the by-product of advertising's Creative Revolution in the mid-1950s, the introduction of wit and metaphor through a marriage of visual and textual means, had gained momentum. Danziger was one of its leading proponents on the West Coast. He preferred photography over drawings because "by and large photographs are more believable, more persuasive than drawings, which are perceived as contrived." At the outset he did not shoot his own photography, but, finding he was often dissatisfied with the work of freelance photographers, he later acquired the skill.

Harold Dreyfus ran his agency by himself, and as Danziger notes: "Single proprietor agencies were rather typical of the Los Angeles scene in the early 1950s." There were some major agencies, such as Young and Rubicam, Foote Cone and Belding, and Erwin Wasey, which handled the few large West Coast accounts, but most businesses in Los Angeles at the time were fairly small. In fact, the major industries in that part of the country prior to World War II were agriculture, tourism, and motion pictures. Only after the war did aerospace begin to burgeon. And, although the West was growing at a fast pace, the majority of companies included small manufacturing plants, clothing producers, and building industries. Danziger recalls that $50,000 ad accounts were extraordinary. All West Coast businesses were generally serviced by small advertising agencies that relied on freelancers for creative services. Among them the Dreyfus Company was one of the best, and Harold Dreyfus was "the most intelligent ad man" Danziger had ever worked with.

Dreyfus was an aficionado of good design, with a passion for furniture, architecture, and graphics. He was a subscriber to the progressive West Coast magazine *Arts & Architecture* and was aware of Danziger through his contributions to it. About their earliest encounter Danziger recalls: "We were mutually impressed, immediately simpatico, and I agreed to design an ID system for him (cards, letterhead, billing and agency forms)." But in addition, Danziger offered Dreyfus some invaluable free advice that would bond them in a unique designer/client relationship: "I told him that he was wasting his time and talent on the $10,000 accounts which took a lot more time to service than a $100,000 account. And, frankly, to my surprise he listened *and* acted.

Together they developed strategies for attracting more profitable business to the firm. Dreyfus, for example, decided to accept only clients who could be billed a minimum of $50,000 annually; he notified his existing accounts that they would have to increase their budgets to meet that criterion or find another agency. One account, American Electronics, did agree to the billing change, which encouraged Dreyfus to produce the two advertisements that ran as full pages in *Media, Agencies, Clients* magazine (the *AdWeek* of its day).

Danziger and Dreyfus decided on the egg as a symbol of creativity, which in hindsight seems to be a rather dubious concept. "We were trying to sell the agency on its ability to produce truly creative work, and yet the egg is probably the most clichéd image for creativity," acknowledges Danziger about the obvious paradox. "Of course, showing an egg and making a claim about our creativity was not very creative, so the problem was to find ways of using this symbol in an active way, that is, to make it a principal actor in the telling of the agency's story." The egg was to be a unifying device in several ads that were planned. The first ad, with the sledgehammer, visually compares the efficacy of "Hard Sell" versus "Soft Sell" while the text argues for the lasting advantage of creating a customer rather than a sale. The egg-and-foot ad deals with the thin ice that one often walks on when using humor—great if it works but really bad if it bombs. "You have to know what you're doing," Danziger observes. Nonetheless, the recasting of this visual cliché activated the symbiotic relationship of an arresting image and provocative copy.

"We felt that it was very important to visually dominate the publication," Danziger continues. "If we couldn't get attention for ourselves, how could we claim to get it for others?"

A subtle, though very important, aspect of the ad design is the black band at the bottom of both. It is an element (along with the egg) that establishes a visual mnemonic relationship between the ads in the campaign. "If you cover up the black band," notes Danziger, "you will find that the ads are stripped of their power. It is astonishing how important such a small, seemingly unimportant element can be." Indeed, what happens is that the black band serves as an anvil against which the egg threatens to break. Without it, the egg simply gets pushed out of the page. With it, there is enormous visual tension that validates the content.

These sales pitches proved to be so persuasive that Dreyfus quickly added several new clients to his roster, including Ajax Hardware, which was a $100,000 account, and Gelvatex, which billed at $300,000. Danziger did significant work for these accounts and attests that the root of his success was Dreyfus: "He was so decisive that we often did four or five ads (the conceptualization, not the execution) in one afternoon." Ultimately, the agency expanded and eventually was bought by the behemoth Ogilvy and Mather, which retained Dreyfus as a consultant until he died of lymphatic cancer in 1986. The egg ads designed by Danziger that put Dreyfus on the map are, of course, artifacts of another time. But for conceptual acuity and design strength they remain milestones of advertising in the early period of the West Coast's rise.

Bus Shelter Posters

She was a beauty–a Professional Beauty
Sundays at 9pm
Begins March 11 Channel 13 PBS
Masterpiece Theatre   Mobil

The life expectancy of an average infantry soldier on the battlefield is twelve seconds. Although likened to a battlefield, New York City's streets might not be as dangerous for people, but the average longevity of advertising posters is certainly comparable. Bills that are illegally posted on construction sidings and scaffolding are routinely defaced, pasted over, or torn down within hours. Postings on legal hoardings in public spaces fare slightly better, but few stay unscathed until the end of their official hanging periods. Such a limited life expectancy demands that advertisers think like military strategists. They must hold as many key positions as possible, accept massive casualties in the process, and generously reinforce when needed. Given the prevailing trends and the discouraging averages, only then can a campaign succeed to win consumers' hearts, minds, and discretionary incomes.

Despite these street-imposed ravages, posters continue to be an important advertising medium for entertainment, fashion, products, and services. Despite the fate of the individual posters, a well-orchestrated and intensive saturation campaign can be extremely effective in piquing the interest of New York's often-oblivious passersby. But what has made the war against the vandals and the citigoths a bit easier to cope with are the protected bus (or transit) shelters featuring illuminated display capabilities that have been springing up for more than a decade throughout the five New York boroughs. This kind of shelter is not unique to New York—the design was developed for Parisian bus riders decades ago. But until its introduction in the late 1970s, New York bus passengers waiting at their stops were not protected from the elements, and street advertising was limited to large exposed billboards and illegal "Post No Bills" hoardings. In addition to clearly demarcating transit stops, the three thousand–plus shelters at present provide a relatively secure space for over six thousand posters. And six thousand illuminated posters have had a decisive impact not only on the public's consciousness but on designers too.

Although this new venue has not sparked a full-blown poster renaissance, it has made it possible for certain advertising agencies to at least challenge the mediocrity of contemporary mass-market or mainstream poster concepts and aesthetics. During the past few years, transit shelters have factored significantly in a resurgence of narrative and teaser posters, the most well known being NYNEX's series of riddle/puns related to entries in their business yellow pages. At the fulcrum of the campaign were odd and quirky images, such as a blue rabbit or Barbie and Ken dolls in nurse and doctor outfits, first posted as teasers without any headline or text, hanging for two or three weeks before being replaced by the same poster *with* text. The copy was an absurd pun on a real yellow-pages entry, like "Hair Coloring" (illustrated by the blue rabbit) or "Plastic Surgeons" (illustrated by Barbie and Ken in medical garb). The campaign ran in bimonthly cycles, with approximately six different ideas presented over the course of a year. The public was thoroughly engaged in this game of wits.

NYNEX's ads prove that clever and aesthetically superior advertising has great power, even with frenetic New Yorkers, and the bus shelter is a tremendous vehicle for such ads. Another success story is Mobil Oil's *Masterpiece Theater* (and, to a lesser extent, Texaco's *Great Performances*) on the Public Broadcasting Service, long promoted through bus shelter posters designed and illustrated by some of America's finest posterists, notably Ivan Chermayeff, Seymour Chwast, and Milton Glaser, many of whose efforts have become sought-after collectibles. Some of the same posters have illegally been hung alongside other posters on hoardings, but when framed and backlit in the bus shelter environment they enjoy a certain majesty, perhaps not unlike the Chérets, Toulouse-Lautrecs, and Muchas of the last century.

Not all bus shelter posters are as conceptually or aesthetically exceptional. For a long time American advertising has been rooted in a "more is better" ethos that has resulted in hard-sell, type- and image-laden posters, which are little more than blown-up newspaper and magazine ads—not posters in the classic sense. Many bus shelter posters suffer from this malady, and yet the bus shelter has also inspired advertisers and designers to simplify. Large single images have, in keeping with the velocity of street traffic and consistent with the opportune format of the shelter, begun to dominate. And monochrome posters or those that exploit negative space have become an unofficial standard of shelter advertising, in contrast with the colorful surroundings.

In New York, as in other American cities, many shelters are maintained by Gannett Outdoor (and its subcontractors), who also rent a high percentage of the nation's billboard space. The shelters are a standard size: 47½ inches (wide) by 68½ inches (high), with a glass partition on the back side, open on the front and one side. The posters sit in a frame with a viewing area of 46 by 47 inches. Two posters fit in one frame (front and back). The preferred stock is 82-point Opalaine—silk-screen or offset—or styrene. When lithographed the poster is printed on two sides for greater color intensity. Posters are hung in four-week cycles in four categories: Saturation

(240 displays citywide), Intensive (180), Impact (120), and Standard (60). Since New York is a multicultural town—with 25 percent black, 24 percent Hispanic, 8 percent Asian, and 48 percent white—Gannett also offers "Ethnic Targeting Capabilities" that direct advertisements for specific goods or services to New York's ethnic neighborhoods. In the rate book under "Ethnic Shelter Packages" are the "Black Package" and "Hispanic Package," which offer saturation of these important commercial areas.

Gannett calls for a 50 percent overage on all printing quantities to allow for replacement because shelters are victims of high jinks and merrymakers who have been known to engage in vandalism. Maintenance crews do seem to fix and replace units regularly and in good speed. But the life expectancy of a shelter poster *is* considerably longer than that of a street poster.

As a city of posters, New York is still not in the same league as, say, Amsterdam, but the level of "street art" has become increasingly more enticing, especially in the fashion genre. The alluring and sometimes sensual posters for retailers like the Gap, Banana Republic, and DKNY (Donna Karan New York) make waiting for the bus a little more tolerable. Reading the often-witty type posters for the *New York Times* classifieds or Daffy's discount retail store helps pass the time. Posters for cultural activities, such as the Liberty Science Center, are eye-catching and instructive for those of the city's denizens looking for diversion.

The bus shelter is a tabula rasa. There are no restrictions (save for certain issues of taste) regarding what can or cannot be shown. Its sponsors are not interested in promoting a high—or, for that matter, low—level of poster design. While the majority of its advertising contents are not worth a second look, the bus shelter in New York and other cities has emerged as a potentially significant medium that allows the continuance of the great tradition of poster design.

Holly Hunt

DESIGNER: RICK VALICENTI

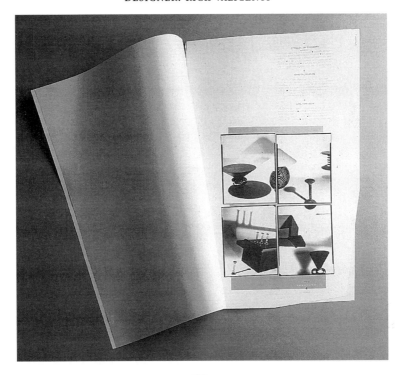

"I am a translator for my clients," explains Rick Valicenti (b. 1951). "They speak through me to an audience that they may or may not know. But in speaking through me, they have to embrace and accept my dialect." This dialect can be traced to a process of problem solving that began in 1981, the year that April Greiman spoke before the Society of Typographic Arts in Chicago. Through her quirky, anticanonical work, Valicenti realized a freedom that he hadn't known existed in graphic design.

In 1975, his first job was drawing key lines at a studio producing recruitment ads, where he became expert with ruling pens (which accounts for the frequent use of hairline boxes in his work). This skill enabled him to get a job designing forms for an Evanston, Illinois, insurance company, which precipitously graduated him into its brochure department. In 1978 he had a cathartic experience at an ICOGRADA (International Council of Graphic Design Associations) congress in Chicago, where he was introduced to some of America's leading designers. "I copped a fever," he says. From that moment he devoured all the annuals, determined to develop his own design voice. On April Fool's Day 1981, after a three-year stint at Bruce Beck's studio in Chicago, Valicenti went solo. Seven years later, tired of doing straight design and being a "good vendor, like a little boy in a clean pressed suit," he decided to alter his method. But how?

Although he's earned two master's degrees in fine arts photography and is an aficionado of letterpress, Valicenti rejected the tedium of commercial studio photography to pursue a method that combined type and photos. Fortuitously, a client offered the opportunity to exercise his newfound freedom.

Holly Hunt wanted a newsletter for distribution at NeoCon (the annual contract furniture conference held in Chicago). "My preconceptions were much different [from] how these pieces ended up," admits Valicenti. "At first I thought I was going to use very straightforward typography because that's what I had been doing all along. But because of the deadline crunch, and since I was working at home in the evenings where there was no drawing table—and thus had no way of ruling and structuring things—I started to hand-draw the pages at actual size." This was a significant departure; instead of character counting, Valicenti was literally scribing the manuscripts. "In the process of reading the manuscript," he continues, "I began to make size and font changes as I drew." Emphasizing certain key words in bold or italic, he added arrows or exclamation points and enlarged the size of words as the cadence of the writing demanded. Pretty soon the page became animated. As Valicenti began to feel more freedom, the look became a spirited typographic mélange in the manner of the Italian futurists, or what Paul Rand calls "rap typography." Owing to the tight layouts, Valicenti says, "I became relaxed, knowing the page would come back from the typesetter exactly the way I drew it." Looks to the contrary, nothing was random. "I set up parameters as I would with any artistic endeavor."

The Holly Hunt newsletter was also unevenly trimmed and bolted with metal clips. Despite Hunt's approval, the newsletter prompted an acrimonious response when published. "Although the content was about taking risks," Valicenti recalls, "when Hunt's managers and merchants saw it, I was sequestered in her office so that everybody could each have their two minutes with Rick to discuss how I had abused their message and products. It was also suggested that I eat the costs for producing an unusable book." Valicenti decided to gamble by offering to absorb the costs if "after two hours they found these books in the NeoCon wastebaskets. Conversely, if people are lured to their showrooms wanting to buy their furniture, well, then, I'm . . . validated." Ultimately he was also vindicated.

Valicenti argues that while he is misbehaving, he is not irresponsibly imposing his approach on clients. "You never impose on anybody who does not want to be imposed upon. I will never send a client to the printer unhappy."

Within a short period Valicenti's rap typography has also become a model for what one critic called "thirstoids," those acolytes who have adopted the surface mannerisms without the originator's zeal and sophistication. Not surprisingly, the imitators have indeed forced Valicenti to pick up his creative pace. "I feel hurried, that I haven't flushed out the experiments yet," he comments, somewhat annoyed. So, without the benefit of reflection, Valicenti is pushed into new realms by those who have misused his methods. "Now I want to see whether the conceptual thrust of a message can be articulated a little differently, whether it's with photographic reinforcement or through scale change, but I am no longer interested in numerous font changes that have become a sort of clumsy, misinterpreted conceit."

While Valicenti has been criticized for taking questionable legibility to intolerable extremes, he argues that his method requires a leap of faith but not of *comprehension*. "I want to feel assured that on some level, if readers will give it more than a passive effort, they'll get it," he says loudly and animatedly to emphasize his point. "In other words, if they sit without their remote control and get up to change the channel, they will discover something else!" Readers will discover a playful use of type and language as well as a variety of graphic subtexts that enhance the primary message. Which leads to the ultimate reason for Valicenti's typographic acrobatics: "I simply want to reenergize the experience of design for the people who come in contact with it," he observes, returning to his normal tone of voice.

D-Toys

DESIGNER: DAVID VOGLER

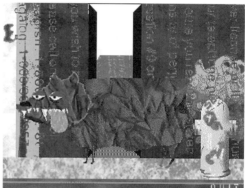

Click on *www.disney.com* or Disney's Daily Blast Web sites and (depending on the speed of your modem) Walt Disney's magical empire instantly pops onto the computer screen, replete with teasers for the panoply of Mickey Mouse products and entertainment designed to capture the hearts of young people and their parents' pocketbooks. The usual fare includes plenty of brand names, lots of animated film stars—including Pocahontas, Aladdin, Jafar, the Hunchback, and Esmerelda—as well as commercials for theme parks, resorts, movies, and television spectaculars. A virtual shopping mall of fun with few real surprises and apparently nothing to make Walt turn over in his cryogenic grave.

Yet hidden surprises do await the child with daring, patience, and an itchy mouse finger. Of course, there's the warm and fuzzy traditional stuff (which, in Disney corporate-speak, are called "assets"). But the intrepid young surfer can also find D-Toys, small applications that can be downloaded and played locally offline—what David Vogler (b. 1962), the former design director of Disney Online, refers to as bits of "edgy spice." "D-toys should be thought of as the digital equivalent of a humble prize in a Cracker Jacks box," Vogler says about these anomalous Disney creations that eschew any and all connections to Mickey, Minnie, Donald, et alia.

Among the Disney Online staff the *D* stands for David because each D-Toy was his brain-child. Even for someone who is a corporate loyalist, excessive contact with cute Disney products resembles overdosing on cotton candy. Vogler, who was previously design director for Nickelodeon special projects (toys and online productions), saw the need for new challenges to keep his creative juices from turning to thick molasses. Given the strict Disney formulas, Vogler understood that resourcefulness and pragmatism were imperative in making any changes. He developed D-Toys to "create a simple, speedy experience that will entertain kids under limited technical conditions," he explains. But it could never have passed muster if he ignored marketing requisites. So D-Toys are also designed to promote Disney Online's Daily Blast subscription Web site: "Each D-Toy has a consistent open and close sequence that promotes the brand and 'advertises' our URL." Unlike most proprietary Disney products girded with impenetrable copyright safeguards, children are encouraged to digitally copy D-Toys, pass them along to friends, and collect them like trading cards.

D-Toys are small-format digital novelties (300k Shockwave files), not games in the sense of scoring or having an objective or purpose. There is no right or wrong way to play with them. They do not require reading instructions and are universally comprehensible, like a Gumby or Etch-a-Sketch toy. Most are interactive, like the D-Toy in which the player types letters or a word on the computer keyboard and with the cursor controls the random screen acrobatics of the letterforms. In another, as the player regulates an on-screen motion bar, a drawing of a child on a bicycle has his lips blown over his face as the bike's speed increases. All are designed without a predetermined Disney style sheet, and include collage, cartoon, and edgy *art brut* renderings, much like the experimental animation on MTV's *Liquid Television*. Vogler himself writes and designs each D-Toy in his spare time and has recruited a support team of Disney artists and programmers to assemble them. Since each one is unique, requiring fresh art and new code, some D-Toys are costly to produce. But others are bargains.

According to Vogler, he was most surprised at being able to sell his superiors on the idea. "I convinced them that D-Toys would capture an 'older' audience that traditionally shuns Disney." But to really succeed he insisted that D-Toys follow his own rigid rules: They cannot use Disney properties; they must employ diverse art styles; they must not be cell animation; they must not require any "back story;" they should be mildly ironic and subversive; they should contain self-deprecating humor or "winks" at Disney; they should appeal to both boys and girls; must be relevant to modern kids' life; they cannot be linear and dependent on an end-result; they must contain hip, ironic, or modern music tracks.

The powers agreed to release one every two weeks, each in currency for a finite period before removal from the site. Over two dozen appeared. But for every one accepted, Vogler admits, "I've got half a dozen that have been 'banned' by Disney as too edgy or progressive." Determining what is suitably un-Disney versus what is totally inappropriate is less clear. As the Disney Company expands into new entertainments (catering to a wide range of audiences from G to R ratings), the standard of what is Disney-acceptable has radically changed, which allowed Vogler a greater chance to play with the content of D-Toys, within limits.

Our Secret Century

PRODUCER: RICK PRELINGER

He calls himself an archivist, but Rick Prelinger is really a treasure hunter who, during the past decade, has uncovered 75,000 of America's least-known treasures. He calls them ephemeral films, but they are really the hidden jewels of the American experience—miles and miles of celluloid showing how the American agenda could, should, or would unfold between the depressed 1930s and booming 1950s. Prelinger has tracked down and saved from extinction these gems of industrial and educational cinema (the kind shown at expositions and schools); further, he has made them available through videotape, laser disc, and CD-ROM. His contribution to American historiography is not simply the preservation of documents but also an astute analysis of their respective importance to the entire culture. He does not trade in quaint nostalgic diversions but examines how American industry, civic groups, and government communicated messages about mores to citizens overtly and covertly.

Prelinger's challenge has been to transcend the often-comic anachronisms endemic to the more mannered and self-conscious of these vintage films. So not all media formats conform to his goal. Producing them on videotape, as he did with *To New Horizons: Ephemeral Films, 1931–45,* and *You Can't Get There from Here: Ephemeral Films, 1946–60* (Voyager Company, 1996), was not an entirely satisfactory solution, since introductory and explanatory material could not be shown with the films, which reduced them to pure entertainment. A book on the subject would have allowed for more explication, but showing stills without actually seeing the motion pictures would have been an ineffective substitute. Moreover, combining print and video would simply be too costly. So Prelinger issued laser discs of these titles as a way to both document and contextualize the material.

Prelinger's second publishing project exclusively on laser disc, *Call It Home: The House That Private Enterprise Built* (Voyager Company, 1995), chronicles the invention and proliferation of suburbia through period films, photographs, advertisements, and texts. Using this multi-access medium to present original material both without interpretation as well as with Prelinger's analyses allows the evidence to be viewed with and without prejudice. By accessing different tracks on the disc the audience chooses whether to read or be read to. The laser disc is the perfect medium if one is wired for it. Unfortunately, there are comparatively few individual owners. So for his next publishing effort Prelinger turned to CD-ROM, which is the most accessible for the largest number of people at present.

Our Secret Century: New Media as Historical Intervention (Voyager Company, 1996–1997) is a collection of twelve CD-ROMs featuring films, textual material, and still images from the Prelinger Archives. These discs investigate different "millennial" themes—"twentieth-century issues about which too little is understood," says Prelinger, who makes what he calls a "historical intervention" by presenting a sampling of original educational, cautionary, industrial, and propaganda films along with comment and critique. These can be seen on CD-ROM in their entirety without any explanation, but they are also complemented by informative production notes, oral and written histories, interviews, and excerpts from supplementary reading.

The title of the series refers to two different kinds of "secrets." One kind, explains Prelinger, includes "hidden histories and issues, like the manipulation of American consciousness through the popular media; the mechanisms by which consumerism is created and sustained; the roots of conformity and control; the landscape as a stage for conflict; and the courses of gender, technology, sexuality, and power." The other "secrets" are simply the films themselves, "evocative documents saved by chance and residing in our archives, but still essentially unavailable to most viewers." The first four discs on the market indicate the breadth of experience and behavior portrayed: *The Rainbow Is Yours* (postwar design and consumerism), *Capitalist Realism* (prewar workers in corporate films), *The Behavior Offensive: Social Guidance Classics* (mostly postwar counseling films on mores and morals), and *Films of Menace and Jeopardy* (unconscious fears and dangers posed as everyday risks at home and on the job from 1936 to 1960).

Ephemeral films from the Depression to the Populuxe era reveal forgotten and/or uncomfortable truths about the recent past while offering evidence of how people were persuaded, conditioned, even brainwashed through fallacy and exaggeration into accepting both benign and potentially dangerous myths about their nation. "The characters, corporations, and institutions in the films," says Prelinger, "tend to be better than life: free-spending consumers, perfect students, overproductive workers, and model children." The process of reviving these films and revealing the motivations behind them not only creates an accessible and interesting base for looking at history but casts light on current social issues.

Through the CD-ROM format Prelinger helps to clarify the historical moment in which the films were produced. Numerous text blocks and QuickTime interviews far exceed the informational capacity of the typical documentary. But even with its great potential for information storage and retrieval, which can render a CD-ROM more than just a novelty, a variety of organizational challenges must be addressed. CD-ROMs require considerable collaboration on the part of writers, editors, producers, designers, and programmers. The process of developing this hybrid between a book and a documentary film forces its developers to look at the material in three dimensions, not simply as one or more linear tracks. Since CD-ROM users are not always encouraged to start at the beginning but, as is the case with a Whitman Sampler, can select any morsel and then devour from there, the job of charting narrative pathways can be difficult, confusion being the primary danger.

Our Secret Century is guided by Prelinger's editorial vision, but its graphic design and navigational logic is the work of Diane Bertolo, a magazine designer and editor of Felix, a journal of computer culture, who has developed the many screens on which the content is presented. Bertolo's design is at once transparent and opaque in accordance with Prelinger's dictate that these discs should have an identity but not be swathed in nostalgic conceit. Therefore, the typography is contemporary, pastiche is rejected, and the only concession to the period is an appropriate use of 1930s and 1940s stills as screen backdrops showing fashions, appliances, and the like. Where obvious design tropes are applied, they are used to take the didactic edge off the subject matter. "I tried to avoid any bells and whistles," Bertolo comments about the often-kitschy components associated with the CD-ROM, which are employed solely to beef up the "multi" part of the media.

With Our Secret Century the table of contents (or main menu) is a good example of how special effects enhance the content, notably the one-inch-square animated icons showing loops of the available films running in syncopation. Click on an icon, and you are transported to a backdrop that frames a small movie screen (which can be enlarged to fill the entire image area or kept small and used as a kinetic illustration juxtaposed next to text blocks). Return to the table of contents, click on either of the two introduction sections, and Boing! a miniature full figure of Prelinger in a Hawaiian shirt against a wall of tinted stills materializes to visually and verbally explain the series and the specific disc. To his right a small sampling of the images zips by on a screen. Click the "find" button, and an even smaller screen pops up, allowing the viewer to fast-forward through the visual portion of the introduction.

Bertolo worked in Photoshop, which allowed both latitude and constraint. Regarding the latter, if corrections are required, the entire makeup must be totally redone (unlike in Quark, where individual elements can be moved or eliminated easily). But she says her biggest problem is more with "type type TYPE!" The 72 dpi (dots per inch) resolution for the CD-ROM limits the range of body type, but she admits trying "a gazillion tests of every available body face" until settling on Palex, a Voyager font based on Palatino. Another concern, which certainly does not arise when designing a book or magazine, is how the user will be viewing the CD-ROM. Since personal computers vary greatly in terms of image resolution, Bertolo has to design for the lowest possible denominator. Working with millions of colors to begin with, she inevitably steps down to the base 250, where she fiddles to the get the imagery right. "At millions or even thousands of colors," she explains, "the pictures look photographic. But if they are not adjusted at 250 colors, images look 'dithered'; it's almost like the difference between magazine and newspaper reproduction."

Our Secret Century is produced using the Oracle Media Objects (OMO) software platform, which allows for greater fidelity and an increased ability to combine full-length film with text components. Herein lies the necessity of having Colin Holgate on the production team. He is an experienced programmer who, with Bertolo and Goldstein, decides which technological advances will increase the accessibility of the CD-ROM. Unlike a book, which is usually charted (or paginated) out precisely before entering the production stage, the CD-ROM is continually being improved as programming bugs are eliminated or by including different navigational functions throughout the design process. This accounts for why *Our Secret Century*'s release was postponed a few times.

Despite this surge of multileveled activity, Prelinger said that producing a book is still much harder. In *Our Secret Century*, "the films take up a lot of space and a big chunk of the content." Hence, what might have been an 80,000-word book on the subject is considerably less in a CD-ROM version. The combination of production notes and other original texts, though not sound bites by any means, are more like extended captions than long historical narratives. But the trade-off is worth it. Although *Our Secret Century* only scratches the surface of Prelinger's huge holdings, each disc provides rare materials that prior to the CD-ROM would have been impossible for a broad audience to appreciate at home.

"We still had breakfast at the hotel in order to keep up appearances, but we found ourselves wilting even before the liftman. I have never liked uniforms—they remind me that there are those who command and those who are commanded—and now I was convinced that everybody in uniform knew that we couldn't pay the bill."

—Graham Greene, *Loser Takes All*

Dressed in black, three-button Mizrahi suits with au courant spiked and dreadlocked coifs, the doormen for New York's Paramount Hotel, selected for their chiseled good looks, evince more attitude than many of the hotel's hippest guests. However, despite this overt embrace of haute couture, the Paramount partakes of a tradition that has dictated the appearance of doormen for over a century. Doormen, the guardians *and* servants of the upper and middle classes, are members of a profession for whom the uniform, whether a designer's suit or a military greatcoat, is more than mere coordinated clothing. Like those worn by a palace guard, the doorman's uniform is a symbol of station, rank, and responsibility.

Aside from the Paramount, doormen's attire for hotels and residences has changed little since the profession began in New York City during the late nineteenth century, when swanky hotels catered to a well-scrubbed clientele and luxury apartment buildings along upper Fifth and Park

Avenues housed the swells of Manhattan. "There is really no reason for change," explains Seralie Busch, spokesperson for I. Buss Uniform Company, the city's oldest family-owned manufacturer, founded by her grandfather in 1892. During the seven decades since I. Buss (originally creators of military as well as police and fire department uniforms) started producing both stock and custom residential doorman attire, changes have been subtle. As Ms. Busch points out: "Uniforms do not conform to prevailing trends in fashion." The style variations reproduced in one of I. Buss's 1930s catalogs do not differ significantly from the current one, except for the illustrations themselves (the former used drawings, the latter uses photography).

The origin of the quotidian "doorman style" is not exactly known. Stuart Busch, president of I. Buss, speculates that it began in the mid-1800s at the leading hotels, perhaps to distinguish doormen from bellhops. Gabriel E. Prio, president of the venerable family business Dornan Inc. (founded in 1924), which originally manufactured chauffeur and butler attire, thinks that uniforms, particularly for private residences, became popular during the early 1930s, possibly because of increased divisions between Depression-era haves and have-nots as well as a desire to signal exclusivity. Scott Markell, regional sales director for Top Hat, Inc., of Hempstead, New York, adds that "there has always been someone at the front door," and these doormen have always worn a uniform of some kind. There is consensus that whenever and however uniforms became standardized, the design and detailing—such as braid, piping, ceremonial shoulder braids, epaulettes, embroidery, and insignia—were inspired by full-dress military costumes from the nineteenth century. The toy-soldier aesthetic prevails today, and most uniform design evokes the seminal models. Seralie Busch cannot trace original designs but she believes—and it is as good a theory as any—that "a lot of uniform companies copied the designs that my grandfather initially showed in his catalogs."

Doormen fall into two groups: commercial (hotel, retail store, and restaurant) and residential (apartment house), each with specific institutional requirements that dictate the nature of their uniforms. Generally, commercial uniforms are more ostentatious. Residential uniforms are conservative. The former demands a military posture, while the latter does not. Commercial uniforms are determined by distinct house styles, and they may vary from season to season within each hotel. A few years ago, the Helmsley Palace's summer uniform had a foreign legionnaire motif, including a khaki short-sleeve, belted jacket and a kepi, the French military round hat with black visor, while its winter uniform included a black-caped, full-length jacket and a top hat. Changes in style may be coordinated to echo interior or exterior renovations of a building, or they might be changed at the whim of an owner. When Leona Helmsley stood at the helm of her real estate empire, she demanded eccentric fashions to distinguish her palace from other hotels.

Residential uniforms adhere to minor variations within a basic range of styles, with customizing done as requested. Among the most popular stock styles from the I. Buss catalog, for example, are the Windsor, a two-button, charcoal gray jacket with silver stripes on the sleeves and lapels with matching trousers; the Gramercy, a three-button, charcoal gray, double-breasted jacket with gold braid on the sleeves and lapels as well as gold-braided trousers; and the Classic, a four-button, single-breasted jacket similar to the Windsor but with gold braid stripes. The Gramercy and Classic include military-style hats with coordinated braid. Changes in residential building uniforms are decided either by co-op boards, the resident manager, or a management group; given their tight budgets, the uniforms rarely diverge from the norms, unless a designer or wannabe designer is on the board. Whim and hubris occasionally dictate change, such as the time the president of the board of a luxury co-op on the Upper West Side decided to dress his doorman in all-year-round, full-dress tailcoats and top hats, a style that overstated the status of the building and was uncomfortable to boot.

While such ostentation may increase the self-esteem of residents, it may also have a deleterious effect on employees. "I don't like wearing uniforms to begin with—especially the same uniform for five days a week, for two or three years—but this is my job and I accept it," asserts a veteran doorman who has served the same Manhattan building (first as porter and then as hall man) for twenty years and prefers that his name not be used. He adds, "But to look foolish is beyond tolerable. I take pride in my work, but I want respect that I can't imagine getting if I looked like a clown." Gabriel E. Piro concurs that "most people don't like to be told what to do or wear and most [residential] doormen don't like wearing uniforms, particularly the military-styled hats." Nonetheless, a uniform is an integral part of the job, and, "if you're a doorman, you have to look the part of a doorman; that's what you get paid for," he concludes.

Playing a role is an apt description. Unlike the guards at Buckingham Palace, doormen are not ceremonial; both service *and* image are integral. In fact, to emphasize this point, Dornan Uniforms calls itself the "Image Maker." For residential buildings the role is a combination of gatekeeper, concierge, bellman, and security guard, each of which demands an official appearance. "Doormen are not police," says Seralie Busch, "but a building with a highly visible doorman is much safer than one without." And so, to a certain extent, doormen are outfitted with security in mind.

With commercial establishments the role playing is even more theatrical, and the doorman's costume has symbolic ramifications. The doormen for Gallagher's Restaurant in New York, for example, are dressed in uniforms of bright red and shiny gold (the restaurant's colors) for increased pedestrian visibility; they are in fact signs as bright as any neon. The Plaza Hotel, among New York's oldest and finest lodgings, has more conservative yet nonetheless distinctive uniforms. According to Scott Markell, who supplies uniforms to the St. Regis, Carlyle, and Four Seasons, in addition to the Plaza, "each hotel wants to advertise their high level of service through the elegant look of their doormen. When you charge $700 a night, you want the customer to feel pampered at every stage." Doormen, therefore, not only open doors but, with that characteristic tip of the hat and knowing smile, are the official greeters of their respective institutions.

Military uniforms signify levels of rank and status; in doorman culture, uniforms indicate certain categories. Searlie Busch asserts that distinctions within the residential ranks are minimal because "all uniforms are more or less uniform." But Scott Markell notes that this is not the case with commercial doormen: "The residential doorman takes less pride in his uniform (durability and mobility is his greatest concern), but the commercial doormen (and particularly the bell captains) are more status conscious." Markell adds that at some hotels certain markings (or hash marks) indicate length of service, and badges are awarded for the quality of performance. But a more important factor in evoking pride is that the better hotels assign their doormen two or more good uniforms per season, while residential doormen usually get only one that must last a few years. "Forget pride," complains one lower Fifth Avenue apartment-house doorman. "This makes dry cleaning almost impossible."

Another form of categorization pertains less to uniforms than to station in the social and professional hierarchies for doormen. Residential doormen belong to Local 32B–32J of the Service Employees International Union (building owners are represented by the Realty Advisory Board on Labor Relations). According to the building services contract, seniority, say, for a thirty-year man, does not translate into any higher base pay (approximately $518.17 a week under the 1991 contract) than that of a comparative neophyte. Only ambition to become a superintendent or a concierge leads to higher pay scales, making Christmas tips a substantial addition to a doorman's annual income. Quality of the uniform to the contrary, being a residential doorman is only a stepping stone (although a very high one, since turnover in the other positions is slow) to a more elevated station. Moreover, according to the Apartment Building Agreement, there are only two service classifications: "handy persons" and "others," which includes doormen, hall men, concierges, and elevator operators. Being a nebulous "other" allows management the flexibility to utilize employees in various capacities. The job descriptions for commercial doormen are not so vague—bellmen carry bags, doormen open doors, and bell captains command the troops. In this area doormen are beholden to their supervisors for the right shift assignments, since at peak hours an ingratiating, hardworking doorman can usually expect an additional $100 a day in tips.

Most doormen (and, gradually, more "doorwomen") have held on to the same jobs for an average of over ten years, with slightly longer average service in the residential area. When a few were asked why they stayed in their jobs, the responses included satisfaction with benefits, nice tenants, and pleasant working conditions, but uniforms were rarely a significant positive factor. "A uniform means authority," says one doorman. "But my only authority is who gets into the building with or without hassle. It's not real authority." And another residential doorman who was snappily attired in a single-breasted maroon jacket with yellow epaulettes and braid comments, "I like wearing a tie and white shirt at work, but I'd just as soon not wear this silly getup." Similar unenthusiastic responses belie the smiling faces of the models shown in the uniform manufacturers' catalogs. In fact, when another doorman is asked whether or not he would rather dress like the doormen at the Paramount Hotel, he states, "I don't need no expensive suit; a blue blazer will do nicely."

MTV Logo

DESIGNERS: FRANK OLINSKY, PAT GORMAN, PATTI ROGOFF

For half a century, the CBS Eye (designed in 1951) was the most-recognized American television trademark. "Bill Golden's mystical Eye . . . never rests and certainly never tires," wrote George Lois in *Adweek* (1982). Yet for the past decade, the logo inspired by a Pennsylvania Dutch hex sign has lost some of its luster, tainted by the network's uninspiring programming and overall network declines in the face of cable TV. Today it is probably less known around the world than the logo for the once-upstart cable network, MTV, with which it shares a certain distinction: Both symbolically underscore the popular culture of their times.

The CBS Eye enjoyed greater audience recognition than either the friendly NBC Peacock (1956) or Paul Rand's geometric ABC (1961), not only because it was the perfect synthesis of symbolic form and content—which it was—and the visual embodiment of television as an all-knowing third eye but also because it represented the "champagne network," which during the 1960s and 1970s produced the best-quality programming of its day. As a commercial mark, it was unsurpassed for formal elegance, and as an aide-memoire, it recalled for the viewer a sense of trust in both the medium and the Columbia Broadcasting System. Therefore, when executives at Warner Amex Satellite Entertainment Company decided in 1980 to launch a twenty-four-hour cable "music channel" (which industry analysts considered real folly at the time), Fred Seibert, the director of communications responsible for commissioning a logo design for the as yet unnamed enterprise, said that the CBS Eye was the standard that they had to beat.

Seibert acknowledged that this challenge was not going to be easy. NBC, for example, went through many unsuccessful logos (including the costly "big *N*," which was the target of ridicule in the national press when it was discovered that the same idea was implemented at a Nebraska public television station for a fraction of the fee) before settling on a combination of graphic elements, including its mnemonic peacock.

During the twentieth century, the trademark business has grown exponentially as multinational corporations have spanned the globe. But Seibert's first instinct was to avoid the companies that churned out expensive identity systems like so many pairs of patent leather shoes. Instead, in 1981 he assigned the mark to a childhood friend, Frank Olinsky; he and his partners Pat Gorman and Patti Rogoff were principals of Manhattan Design, a very small graphics and illustration office tucked behind a tai chi studio in Manhattan's Greenwich Village. Incidentally, they had no previous corporate-identity experience whatsoever. "I went to them because I'd been friends with Frank since I was four years old, and he was talented even then," Seibert recalls. "He introduced me to lots of rock and roll and was always a music freak."

Although the marriage of two Fortune 500 companies, Warner Communications and American Express, gave birth to the music station, few corporate insiders believed that it could possibly have the same potential for success as Warner-AmEx's other cable properties, the Movie Channel and Nickelodeon. At the time of conception, the worldwide scope of Music Television's ultimate influence was as yet unimaginable.

The station was still in the conceptual phase when the young programmer Bob Pittman was named to head the fledgling project. It was his mandate for the logo that ultimately guided the designers. "Pittman told us that [it] could be anything—it could be a barfing dog if we wanted," recalls Pat Gorman (in *Designing with Illustration,* Van Nostrand Reinhold, 1990). "So we knew that he wouldn't be opposed to a pictorial rather than a symbolic or typographic solution. From the beginning we had the idea that it should be something that could be animated, and the very first thing we came up with was a hand holding a musical note." Gorman shot a photograph of Olinsky squeezing a tomato with a pencil sticking out of it; the idea was to represent "fresh-squeezed music." However, this illustrative image did not totally solve the problem. "We were told that the idea was okay, but they needed to have call letters," says Gorman about the stimulus for calling the station MTV. These letters would be the main visual feature, while "Music Television" would be the subtitle. Gorman adds, "We did *MTV* in handwriting with a rainbow pattern, which didn't work at all but nevertheless made us resolve to use illustration in the finish somehow."

The first version of the *M* was initiated by Patti Rogoff, who handled Manhattan Design's production and sales and currently runs the production department at MTV. She recalled walking past a schoolyard, a block from her office, where she noticed a graffiti-scrawled wall. Rogoff says she knew at that moment "this is what the logo had to be." And what it had to be was a three-dimensional letter that evoked street culture. Later, she and Gorman sketched out the basic form. "Frank was out of the office, and I wasn't too keen on [the logo] being exclusively done as letters," Gorman recalls about the marathon session where she and Rogoff drew various interpretations. "[Patti] wanted to have three giant letters, and I was opposed. At the end of the day I modified the *M* and scrawled a little *TV* onto it. When Frank came in and saw the rough logo for the first time, he said it was incredibly ugly—at which time [Patti] rolled it into a ball and threw it into the trash." And in the trash it would have remained had Gorman not retrieved it and convinced Olinsky that it was, in fact, a viable concept. Although skeptical, Olinsky argued that if it was going to be used, a better-looking rendering of the *TV* letters was imperative. "Then came a moment of inspiration," says Gorman. "Frank and I looked at each other—as if we had the same brain for fifteen seconds—and said that the *M* could be like a screen and then the images could be projected on it. The *M* could be an object—it could be a cake or anything we wanted to make it." In other words, the shape of the *M* could be transformed into anything as long as it continued to look like an *M*. With the messenger from the station on his way, Olinsky set about hastily sketching numerous variations.

Back at the station offices, Manhattan Design's brainstorm was viewed with some consternation—MTV executives argued that the *M* was not legible, and suggestions ensued for making it clearer. Gorman and Olinsky had developed the base logo with about "five cool overlays," comments Seibert, to be used for specific shows or segments. They also prepared color models, "because I felt—we all felt—that you had to have a 'baseline' logo." The variations were pinned up on Seibert's wall for weeks because "I couldn't make up my mind." Finally, he decided it would be "very rock and roll to use them all" in animated sequences. The person who actually had the original idea to change and animate the logo as it was ultimately produced is the subject of much dispute, and Seibert acknowledges that many people take credit for the mutation. "As is sometimes the case with corporate crap, it was a notion with multiple and overlapping origins," he concludes.

Nevertheless, just when Seibert thought that the decision on the logo was final, the head of sales lobbied to have it killed because he vehemently objected to sending such a flagrantly unconventional design to potential ad buyers. Seibert recalls, "His boss asked me: 'Do you really think this will last as long as the CBS Eye?' and I answered, 'No.' Why would I think that a rock thing would stand up to the icon of TV logos?" So with uncertainty about whether Manhattan Design's solution was viable, the executives insisted that Seibert approach some "real" designers, including Push Pin Studios and Lou Dorfsman (who, in his presentation, argued that a musical staff, not unlike Manhattan Design's squeeze-ball, was the best solution). But Seibert had faith in the original. "I sandbagged the assignment," he admits, "so they all did terrible work and we were out of time. . . . With a little type variation on the 'Music Television,' the original was approved six weeks before it went on the air."

The televised MTV logo was the perfect embodiment of the raucous rock-and-roll station. Its animated mutability made it as much an anticipated feature of daily programming as the music videos themselves. Manhattan Design was retained to work in a freelance capacity for the station as virtual puppet-masters for the logo, and over time they hired such illustrators and cartoonists as John Van Hammersveld, Mark Marek, Lynda Barry, and Steven Guarnaccia to play with and transform the basic prop. The strength and durability of the logo has been measured in its unique capacity (now copied throughout cabledom) to withstand the intervention of many creative players. "We investigated every possibility and developed an opinion about the rules," Seibert says about the basic philosophy that the front of the logo was a canvas for almost anything that looked good. "They were never written down, but they were the areas [where] we would go and not go."

The most important vehicle for establishing the logo's supremacy was a series of twenty-five animated logos, of ten seconds each, used as promos and bumpers. This included the most recurring and visible spot, the appropriation of the first moon landing, with MTV logos used in place of the American flag. "Additionally," recalls Seibert, "we probably had done three or four hundred promos that were the real heartbeat of the 'newness' of what MTV had to offer the audience."

Nevertheless, during the first two years that MTV was on the air, logo or not, it had not reached management's goal in terms of saturation of the cable market. Most cable operators were very conservative, and, despite the positive audience response in markets where MTV was aired, there was industry-wide resistance to the channel. Warner-AmEx agreed to an advertising campaign, entrusted to David Ogilvy's top-rated advertising agency, Ogilvy and Mather, which handled the high-tariff American Express account. However, the low-billing MTV received attention only commensurate with its budget and eventually an alternative was sought. In March, Seibert hired his "mentor," Dale Pon [who headed Dale Pon Associates, partly owned by Lois Pitts Gershon, the creative agency headed by advertising's wunderkind, George Lois]. "We had already been on the air with the mutating logo for eight months," he says.

Lois proposed that the MTV campaign be based on a takeoff of his well-known 1960s campaign "I Want My Maypo," featuring famous professional athletes begging to be fed their favorite hot cereal. "Lois had a genius for using celebrities in the best and most unusual situations," acknowledges Pon. So trading on generational recognition of the earlier campaign, Lois told Pittman, "Now you're all twenty-five to twenty-six, and we're going to say to the world, 'I want my MTV.'" I explained the commercial, to take the *M* logo [and] always show it with crazy variations (one had a tongue sticking out)." Pon recalls that the MTV executives did not want the crying rock stars, but they did buy into the basic concept, which included the blue-sky wish to have Mick Jagger as spokesperson. "The idea that Jagger would do it at that time seemed impossible," says Pon, who was flabbergasted when he learned that this prince of rock had agreed.

"It is accurate to say that the campaign broke MTV into the mainstream consciousness for the first (but by no means the last) time," Seibert explains, "and was very important in the strategic development of our customer base. But it would be giving it way too much credit to believe it had anything to do with any of our creative development." The commercial announced that if you don't get MTV where you live, pick up the phone, dial your local cable operator, and say, "I want my MTV." It increased the recognition of the brand nationwide, and cable operators were flooded with calls.

As for the logo development, it added dimension to the mutability factor. Under Pon's direction, aided by the technical expertise of Buz Potamkin and Candy Kugel at Buzzco, who developed the process for the background special effects and animated patterns, the logo was emblazoned in the audience's minds. Pon further credits Lois with a significant innovation: "He made the rock stars into the logo. He was the first to do what now seems the most obvious thing—he put Jagger inside the *M*." In the advertising business, wedding the brand to the message is the supreme creative goal; for Lois to inextricably glue Jagger to the MTV call letters meant not only that the front man of "the greatest rock band in the world" was endorsing the product but also that he actually *was* the product.

MTV is a major international brand today—as much an influence as CBS, NBC, and ABC (if not more so). Currently, its logo, like all trademarks for successful businesses, is imbued with myth and girded by rules to protect its mystique. It began as a free-form symbolic expression of rock-and-roll culture (with a sense of the street thrown in) and today still looks similar to the original. Yet it is not as active an attraction as it once was. It still mutates and animates, but that fact is less a function of playing with the form than a reflexive aspect of MTV's corporate-identity culture.

Issues

W hen the late Saul Bass was asked whether the ad for Spike Lee's movie *Clockers* was an homage to his famous graphic identity for Otto Preminger's 1959 courtroom drama, *Anatomy of a Murder,* he bluntly replied: "Homage is just a polite term for stealing from the dead. Well, I'm not dead, and this is plagiarism." The ad for Lee's film adaptation of Richard Price's gritty inner-city novel, featuring a silhouette of a splayed corpse with detached appendages, is so reminiscent of the logo that Bass created over thirty-five years ago that some of his colleagues assumed that he had done this one too. "When a well-known creative person such as me is perceived to have created a knockoff of my own previous work, such a perception is a mortal blow to my reputation," continued Bass.

This appropriation further raises concerns about the rights of artists and designers, the integrity of their work, and the ethics of quoting, sampling, and otherwise stealing existing designs in the guise of reverence and honor, otherwise known as homage.

Clockers has a main title sequence (designed by Balsmeyer and Everett) that owes a spiritual debt to Bass's designs for classic film titles of the fifties and sixties, yet it is as original as Spike Lee's film itself. So was it really necessary to borrow one of the most recognizable graphic icons in film history? It would make sense if Lee's movie was a remake of *Anatomy of a Murder,* but this was not the case. And although the graphic representation was slightly altered, the fundamental difference between Lee's and the original logo was the addition of four bullet holes and a hat, which rendered the derivative more clumsy than Bass's original version. This may be an era of "biting," the street term for appropriation or sampling of high-profile corporate, brand, and film logos, but no one in Spike Lee's organization made any claim that this usurpation was a sociopolitical act in the rave tradition. The *Chicago Tribune* (September 13, 1995) reported that Lee and his designer "have admitted that the *Clockers* art was a conscious nod to Bass's work."

Whether this was merely a nod or a violation of copyright is a question for lawyers. But the threat of legal action by the Preminger estate caused *Clockers* producers to make further changes to the logo by filling in all the spaces between the appendages, resulting in an even *more* inelegant version. Incidentally, this is not the first time that Spike Lee's film advertising has borrowed someone else's image. The poster for the 1991 film *Jungle Fever* bore an uncanny resemblance to a photograph by Ralph Hattersley that was published in a 1963 issue of *Eros*. The photo, showing an extreme close-up of the intertwined hands of a black man and white woman, originally accompanied a taboo-busting photo essay on interracial love. Although the image was consistent with the film's theme, the commissioning of a new version by a different photographer, Todd Grey, stretched the ethical bounds of image appropriation. Although no one owns the rights to intertwined hands per se, this particular photograph was so emblematic of *Eros*'s controversial essay that, although using the original would have made sense, redoing it could be construed as intellectual trespassing. Nevertheless, action was not taken against the *Jungle Fever* appropriation, even though it was run in newspapers and as a huge billboard in Times Square.

Film posters commonly reuse generic mannerisms to signify mystery, thriller, or action themes. But following a common template and stealing another's concepts are distinctly separate ethical issues. A few years back a film comedy called *Moscow on the Hudson* expropriated Saul Steinberg's much-copied *New Yorker* cover of a comic map showing New York City in relation to the rest of the world. Steinberg's lawyers said that the unauthorized, albeit altered version of the map with the title of the film set in the *New Yorker*'s proprietary typeface was infringing on Steinberg's image rights. The producers and ad agency countered that the image was altered enough to make it a unique entity. Yet a judge comparing the two found that they were too similar in form and content and ordered the film company to pay damages. In another case of misappropriation the advertisement for the 1994 film *Boxing Helena* showed a picture of a woman in a box, an exact replica of a photograph by Ruth Bernhard (daughter of Lucian Bernhard) that appeared in her monograph the very same year. In this case, the infringement was contested, but the film's agency never changed its briefly run campaign. Despite protests against creative larceny, the film industry continues to test ethical tolerances, although now some producers and ad agencies do so within the letter of the law.

In autumn of 1995, an advertisement for the much-hyped, NC-17-rated film *Show Girls* featured a curvaceous sliver of woman—her mouth, chin, neck, torso, and leg—that was so elegantly composed, so sensual in its simplicity, and so different from other movie advertising. Yet so curiously familiar because it looked exactly like the cover of the book *The Body: Photographs of the Human Form* by William A. Ewing (Chronicle Books, 1994), featuring a 1992 photograph by Tono Stano—except with a different woman's nose and mouth. It appears that the designer/art director simply traced over the original image, made minor alterations, and had it rephotographed and retouched. Unlike the *Clockers* impingement, however, the producers made no attempt to change this ad. Despite protests from the book publisher, they were not compelled to do so because Stano, who retained exclusive rights to his own photograph, sold the "image rights" to the film company.

Authors routinely sell their rights, allowing producers to adapt their stories to the screen (often by different screenwriters), songwriters sell their tunes and lyrics for such things as advertising jingles, and now Stano has opened the door to the field of image adaptation by allowing the advertising agency to use another photographer to duplicate his unique image with a different model. Since permission for this appropriation was obtained, the original creator profited, but there remains an ethical paradox in "renting" or recycling one's own visual ideas for others to transform.

Even if one concedes that there are very few original ideas left in the world, and so good ones are rare commodities, the practice of buying or renting an existing artwork in order to remake it to fit a particular marketing scheme is a dubious exploitation of original work. Granted, it's nobody's business but the artist's if she decides to sell the essence of an artwork; nevertheless, the broader implications are disturbing. Ultimately, it trivializes the original just as much as an unauthorized adaptation and, moreover, further legitimizes such adaptations while encouraging those in creatively bankrupt segments of the media to pilfer at will. Although there are those who would argue that knockoffs are a fact of life and that it's better for the owner to be paid up front rather than after costly litigation, there are still those who have carefully built their reputations on particular styles or images; for them, selling image rights would be injurious. In the digital era, when imagery is easily pirated and then commodified, complicitous plagiarism is a way of sanctioning practices that should be deemed unethical.

I s speech really free in America? The Bill of
Rights guarantees liberty, but loopholes in our system of law threaten the sanctity of these rights.
As do the pesky bureaucrats who pry open the loopholes—like the midlevel postal official who,
citing vague definitions of obscenity, seized an edition of *Lysistrata* in 1956 . . . or the customs
agent who, citing prurience, banned the film *I am Curious Yellow* from entering this country in
1969. Both resulted in costly court battles in which constitutional protections were ultimately
enforced. Acceptable expression in one state may be unacceptable in the next, owing to local
ordinances based on morality, taste, or what the Supreme Court calls "community standards."
Of course, the idea of censorship is indeed onerous, but unlimited free expression seems to be
frightening, too. Hence society engages in self-regulation as a way to avoid government
interference.

Movie studios and television networks once employed their own censors, who were often
more strict than the law demanded. Indeed this is true in most cases of self-censorship, where an
institution or business is more concerned with the vagaries of morality than the specificity of law.
Hence, much censorship in America comes not from the state but from the private sector. In
magazine publishing today, for example, controversial stories have been hacked and provocative
artwork killed not because they were in bad taste but because some publishers fear an angry
readership more than the ramifications of censorship.

Publishing history is replete with instances of official censorship, whereby some of the world's great literature, such as *Ulysses* (by James Joyce), *Lady Chatterley's Lover* (by D. H. Lawrence), and even *God's Little Acre* (by Erskine Caldwell), have been either indicted or adjudicated as "obscene," "indecent," or "impure." In fact, on more than a few occasions magazines have been subject to official seizure, most commonly on the grounds of sedition or obscenity. In 1917, *The Masses,* a Greenwich Village–based journal of socialist politics and culture, was suppressed under the Espionage Act (which temporarily abrogated the First Amendment) for publishing antiwar commentary. The post office was the instrument of censorship—through revocation of the journal's mailing privileges, severing its lifeline to the public. The case was eventually dismissed by Supreme Court Judge Learned Hand for unlawfully limiting free speech and reasonable opposition, but the magazine could not survive in the interim. *Mother Earth,* a political journal that encouraged draft resistance, was also harassed by the post office. In 1917, the editor of *Mother Earth,* Emma Goldman, was forced to close the journal and start a short-lived alternative newsletter, the *Mother Earth Bulletin,* to keep in touch with her readership. In the bulletin's first issue (October 1917), Goldman wrote: "Under the 'Trading with the Enemy Act' the Postmaster General has become the absolute dictator over the press. Not only is it impossible now for any publication with character to be circulated through the mails, but every other channel, such as express, freight, newsstands, and even distribution has been stopped. As *Mother Earth* will not comply with these regulations and will not appear in an emasculated form, it prefers to take a long-needed rest until the world has regained its sanity." In the guise of "dictator," the postmaster general effectively closed down all the other socialist publications (approximately thirty of them) during the war years. And Goldman, a Russian by birth, suffered a worse fate: She was deported to Moscow shortly after the war, a casualty of patriotic frenzy.

In 1943, *Esquire* magazine, which never set out to bust any taboos, political or otherwise, had its second-class mailing privileges revoked by the postmaster general, who charged that the magazine was not "information of a public character" and so was "non-mailable" because of the sultry renderings of pinup artist Alberto Vargas. If in fact "non-mailable," the magazine would suffer a fatal circulation drop. The case was heard by the Supreme Court in 1946, at which time the postmaster's ad hoc decision was overruled. In his comments, Justice William O. Douglas wrote that the postmaster's action was "a power of censorship abhorrent to our traditions."

Despite these victories over censorship, free speech is continually being challenged. During the Second World War, lawyers began to raise obscenity as a constitutional issue in the courts. Coincidentally, obscenity replaced subversion as the most common reason for censorship of magazines (and other media) after the war. But this is not surprising, since obscenity is often a political issue. The year 1957 was the first time that obscene expression set a landmark precedent in the U.S. Supreme Court. In the case *Roth* v. *United States*—involving two magazines, *American Aphrodite* and *Good Times: A Review of the World of Pleasure,* both accused of violating the postal laws—Justice William Brennan laid down the principle that obscenity was not constitutionally protected because it was "utterly without redeeming social importance." In reviewing the case some years later, Edward De Grazia, a lawyer specializing in the First Amendment, explained that what Justice Brennan meant by "obscenity" was a particular type of material, "which deals with sex in a manner appealing to prurient interest." And what does "prurient" mean? Justice Brennan defined it according to *Webster's New International Dictionary* (unabridged, 1949) as ". . . itching, longing; uneasy with desire or longing; of persons having itching, morbid, or lascivious longings; of desire, curiosity, or propensity, lewd . . ." But Justice Brennan also qualified and, therefore, liberalized the precedent of the *Roth* decision by saying that "sex and obscenity are not synonymous. . . . The portrayal of sex, for example, in art, literature, and scientific works, is not itself sufficient reason to deny material the constitutional protection of freedom of speech and press." This resulted in a number of reversals of state and federal cases in which films and magazines were treated as obscene.

Yet even this liberal attitude did not ensure freedom of all expression. One of the most controversial cases in favor of censorship was *Ginzburg* v. *United States,* in which Ralph Ginzburg, the publisher of *Eros,* a hardcover magazine of erotica—elegantly designed by Herb Lubalin and sold by subscription—and a book called *The Housewife's Handbook on Selective Promiscuity,* a satire on public morality, failed to gain a reversal of his conviction for violating the postal laws. Ginzburg had been convicted of "pandering" through the mails with advertisements that are tame by today's standards. But with the postmarks from Blueballs and Intercourse, Pennsylvania (real Amish towns), he challenged the government's tolerance. In this case, Justice Brennan held that "if the purveyor's [a euphemism for an alleged pornographer] sole emphasis is on the sexually provocative aspects of his publications, a court could accept his evaluation at its face value" and "constitutionally convict." In other words, despite that part of the magazine exhibiting "socially redeemable content," which was true of *Eros,* if the advertising addressed only the lewd and lascivious portions, the advertiser would forfeit constitutional protections to free speech. Justice Brennan argued that *Eros* had been made "available to exploitation by those who would make a business of pandering to the *widespread weakness for titillation* by pornography." As a consequence, Ginzburg is the only publisher in the past fifty years to serve a sentence (eight months) in a federal prison.

From the mid-sixties to early seventies, in the wake of the free speech movement and the throes of the sexual revolution, it was common for alternative magazines and underground newspapers to combine sex and politics despite the clear signal from the courts that limited certain expression. In 1964 *Evergreen Review,* a bimonthly magazine of New Left culture and politics, was seized by the district attorney of Nassau County in New York, who claimed an issue was pornographic. In fact, in addition to newsworthy and critical articles, poetry, cartoons, comics, and satiric illustrations by Seymour Chwast, Ed Sorel, Paul Davis, Robert Grossman, Milton Glaser, and others, nude photographic portfolios were featured regularly. In this case, according to the district attorney's records, "a confidential informant," employed at the bindery serving *Evergreen Review,* "observed black and white photographs in the magazine which showed nude human forms, possibly male and female, but reputed by fellow workers to be two females; and that the forms portrayed various poses and positions indicating sexual relations. My informant further stated having read portions of the printed material . . . [it consisted] of four lettered obscene language." In retaliation Evergreen Review Inc. filed suit to dismiss the complaint and receive injunctive relief and damages based on the unconstitutionality of the act. The court agreed, determining that the seizure was a violation of the Fourteenth Amendment and enjoining the district attorney from further interference with this issue of *Evergreen Review*.

Although American law is predicated on the Constitution and the Bill of Rights, the road to justice is often mined. As long as lawmakers and enforcers continue to chip away at freedom of expression, censorship in all its guises will continue. Justice Potter Stewart once wisely warned: "Censorship reflects society's lack of confidence in itself. It is a hallmark of an authoritarian regime. . . . A book worthless to me may convey something of value to my neighbor. In the free society to which our Constitution has committed us, it is for each to advise himself."

For the first half of the twentieth century, American editorial illustration was such a popular art form that its leading practitioners were held in high esteem as reporters, commentators, and storytellers. However, in the 1950s, photography eroded the impact of narrative art; in the 1990s, Photoshop contributed to reducing editorial illustration to little more than a prettification service used by graphic designers to decorate a page. Showcase annuals still bulge with pages of contemporary paintings and drawings, but many editorial outlets have replaced acute conceptual art with digitally generated work that adds color and texture rather than substance to a publication.

Popular art is, of course, dictated by trend, technology, and the intervention of alternative art forms. Most mass media—from film to television—have been forced to change as the pendulum swings. Likewise, editorial illustration has always been influenced by fashion's ebbs and flows. Throughout the history of illustration, illustrators who could not make the transition from, say, realism to conceptualism, were pushed into increasingly narrower markets until nudged out of the field entirely. Yet, today, change is not a stylistic one (in fact, stylistic diversity is greater now than during any other period). Rather, the change is toward a fundamental belief among many editors and certain art directors that painting and drawing do not offer enough objective value in a media-saturated world concerned with information management and distribution. Relinquishing space to creative illustration is an indulgence that most editorial outlets are unable to afford.

Yet, because magazines are no longer the central information clearinghouses that they once were, this may actually be a propitious time to cede more editorial real estate to certain kinds of narrative illustration. "In a world where magazines can no longer compete with newspapers, and newspapers can no longer compete with CNN, and CNN can no longer compete with the Internet, it's pointless to try to use the magazine as a primary vehicle for information. What magazines can offer is perspective and attitude," argues Art Spiegelman, author of *Maus: A Survivor's Tale*. And what better way to achieve this than through the subjectified lens of the illustrator/commentator?

The most common form of editorial illustration today is the single-image "conceptual illustration," characterized by visual metaphor or graphic symbol that sums up the essence of a text. Sometimes the result is oversimplification, while at other times it is keen interpretation. Regardless, the conventional single image is ultimately a dead end for artists because it limits their ability to contribute to a larger editorial discourse and is little more than a signpost that attracts rather than informs. No matter how well crafted, these images rarely have relevance beyond their immediate utility. So if illustration is perceived as essentially space filler, it is no wonder that editors and designers view conceptual illustration as expendable.

Moreover, two additional forces have impinged upon the integrity of editorial illustration today. A rash of stock art companies are selling bargain-basement generic spots, a practice that invariably undercuts the value of original vision. And, as previously mentioned, Photoshop, one of the most useful digital tools of the computer era, has given the art director and designer the ability to create conceptual-looking or instant art, thus circumventing the creative illustrator altogether.

During the past decade, graphic design has undergone defining shifts in its overall practice. Similarly, illustration is being reevaluated in light of the fact that graphic designers have either usurped or eliminated many of the illustrator's fundamental responsibilities—chief among them, providing alternative and parallel perspectives to a text. The major development back in the 1960s occurred when literal, mannerist illustration (of the Norman Rockwell school) gave way to expressionistic illustration, which provided a commentary on the overall theme of a text rather than merely mimicking it. But in recent years many younger art directors have rejected this kind of illustration as "old school," preferring, instead, to fill pages either with conceptual typographic compositions or layered typo-foto concoctions that give the aura of complexity while simply framing the editorial package.

In response to the increasing decline of substantive editorial illustration, the idea of "authorship" is gaining momentum. For illustrators who choose not to enter the rarefied fine art world (which, ironically, is once again headed toward more narrative art), authorship is a viable alternative to being a slave to text. It is also a way for illustrators to become integral editorial contributors once again.

"The frustration has always been that illustration is based on a manuscript of many words, and the illustrator is given one image to deal with it," says illustrator and painter Marshall Arisman, who, fifteen years ago, launched a unique graduate program at New York's School of

Visual Arts called "The Illustrator as Visual Journalist." (Later the title was changed to "Illustration as Visual Essay.") His goal is to encourage artists to think of the *world* as their texts and develop sequential narratives that would, in effect, illustrate them. The artist is told not only to author stories but also to solve complex formal problems of time and space that are impossible in a single image. The practice, however, is not new.

A century ago, illustrators known in the trade as "specials" routinely reported news events for newspapers and magazines. Later, in the 1950s and 1960s, periodicals such as *Fortune, Holiday, Sports Illustrated,* and *New York* magazine assigned illustrators (included Robert Weaver, Robert Andrew Parker, Alan E. Cober, Julian Allen, and more) to create pictorial essays on a wide range of themes—from exotic travel to eyewitness accounts of military battles. Illustrators were not required to be as objective as writers or even photojournalists but were encouraged to pursue their subjects from personal perspectives and thus intervene with the facts. The artists determined how their stories were reported, while the editor or art director edited the raw material to achieve the most dramatic result on the page.

Sometime during the late 1970s, this approach ceased owing both to reduced budgets and to a shift in emphasis from narrative illustration to information graphics. Nonetheless, at a time when a paucity of editorial space was available for visual essays, when most magazine editors believed that lengthy sequential illustrations squandered space, Arisman's MFA program proffered a return to an equal balance of art and text as a means to add dimension to both commentary and news coverage.

A few years later, another defining event occurred. In 1994 Art Spiegelman's *Maus: A Survivor's Tale,* a comic-strip memoir of his family's struggles during the Holocaust that intersected with his own relationship to their tragedy, won the Pulitzer Prize, the first time a visual book won the prestigious award. Suddenly, the "graphic novel" genre grew (albeit briefly) in popularity, while the visual essay earned more credibility. Around this same time, the *New Yorker,* one of America's least-visual national magazines—yet the outlet for the finest writing— installed at its helm former *Tattler* editor Tina Brown, who, in turn, hired Françoise Mouly, former coeditor (with Spiegelman) and publisher of *RAW,* an alternative comix magazine, as the cover and features art director. (Spiegelman was also hired as a contributing editor.) Mouly persuaded Brown to allocate regular space to visual reportorial essays and assigned such anomalous artists as Gary Panter (comics artist and author of the comic book *Jimbo*) to report on the infamous FBI siege of the Branch Davidian compound in Waco, Texas, and Sue Coe (illustrator, painter, and author of *How to Commit Suicide in South Africa* and *X*) to expose New York's illegal-labor sweat shops (which ironically appeared in the *New Yorker's* annual fashion issue). Since its founding, the *New Yorker* had been known for illustrative covers and gag cartoons, but this was the first time in its history that artists were authors of visual essays.

Nevertheless, the spark to revivify visual journalism was only temporary. Brown soon lost interest, and the experiment petered out (although under a new editor, David Remnick, it seems to be gaining momentum again). Yet the *New Yorker's* attempt was not a failure; it was a first step in a renewed interest in the visual essay as a novel alternative to conventional journalism. The single image will never be replaced, but in the United States a handful of illustrators, cartoonists, and art directors are beginning to push illustration in new directions. This is not to suggest that illustration as visual essay has taken the town completely by storm. Rather, the growth of a few outlets for occasional features, including *Esquire, Texas Monthly, Entertainment Weekly,* and *New York* magazine, is an optimistic sign, as is the fact that *Details,* a men's fashion periodical, now devotes six pages regularly to comic-strip journalism.

Art Spiegelman, currently *Details's* comic-strip editor, insists that "in a world where Photoshop has outed the photograph to be a liar, one can now allow artists to return to their original function as reporters." He also explains that, in addition to opening up greater opportunities for artists, the comic strip as visual essay allows, at least in *Details's* case, an otherwise-trendy lifestyle magazine to address serious content that might be ignored. In addition to articles on cultural events that are typical of the magazine's content—like Kaz's coverage of "Ozzfest," the Ozzie Osborn convention in Akron, Ohio, and Ben Kachtor's report on surfing in Hawaii—Spiegelman has assigned comics artists Joe Sacco to report on the Serbian war-crimes trials in the Hague and Kim Dietch to follow a convicted murderer during his last week on death row at a Virginia prison. Of course, the question arises: In addition to the novelty, what does the comic strip offer of real substance? To this, Spiegelman answers: "When it's completed, there is so much work of compression done by the artist that [the comic strip] gives more information than the same column-inches of prose."

While many editors will dispute the efficacy of turning a death-row inmate into a comic strip, Spiegelman argues that this demands the same quality of editing as the more conventional forms of journalism. "We talk about the assignment before the artist leaves on a story; when he comes back we have a debriefing session, at which point the cartoonist puts something into a readable form. Then the fun begins . . . dealing with the limitations of this form. How do you get something to flow when most data come as unwieldy talking heads and chunks of prose? How do you make it as graphic as possible and still convey as much information at the same time?" While Spiegelman edits "the flow," *Details's* editor Michael Caruso ultimately asks the same questions of any prose writer regarding missing or unexplained aspects of the story, which must be structurally and conceptually integrated. The comic strip requires getting to essences by streamlining the narrative more than a prose article would, but it also offers a visual component that provides even greater access to the story.

The comic strip as essay is an intriguing experiment, but Spiegelman concedes that it is very hard to pull off. There is considerable prejudice among editors toward comic drawings no matter how well they are used. More conventional approaches to graphic journalism are admittedly easier for text editors to accept. So Steven Brodner, a veteran political cartoonist and editorial illustrator whose style is rooted in caricature but is less cartoon-based than most comic-strip artists, has over the past five years covered election campaigns, the presidential impeachment hearings, and the farm foreclosure in the Midwest—and has published a number of visual essays in major magazines. He has proven that an artist's perspective can be fairly consistent with that of members of a conventional press corps, even though the ultimate form is not. "The whole point of any assignment is to find out what is motivating the dynamic of the story and get below the surface," Brodner explains. "I look for people to talk to who will be expected to believe one thing [but] believe another."

A caricaturist by inclination, Brodner prefers to tell people's stories; while his drawing often subtly tweaks a subject's physiognomy, his journalistic visual essays are not satiric. Brodner interviews, records, and photographs his subjects to preserve reality. But after the research is done, he determines the pivotal moments to render. Brief text blocks, quotes by his subjects, are the glue binding his stories, and overall he (literally) paints a very reasoned portrait of an event. He says that his essays are more editorially scrutinized than his illustrations, but the gratification is greater. "You initiate the work and get the credit for having a point of view," he says. "At which point you are not an illustrator, you are an artist." Art is one of those words that makes traditional journalists bristle. So with visual essays the balance between utility and art is critical.

Brad Holland, one of the pioneers of single-image conceptual illustration in the late 1960s, has consistently sought ways of keeping his work relevant to an audience while addressing his own artistic needs. The visual essay has given him a means to both expand his range and resist the rampant trivialization of his original conceptual methods by acolytes who copy the surface but not the substance. In 1985, he started doing satiric visual essays for *Texas Monthly,* including "Sombreros of the Gods," a satiric takeoff on conventional great-men profiles. Later he produced a story on rodeo clowns (the men who distract bulls while fallen riders escape to safety) that has become a model for the visual essay: It not only combines writing and image but also toes that fine line between factual journalism and eyewitness commentary.

Holland's paintings for that story are stylistically eccentric yet totally capture the carnival atmosphere of the event and reveal the complexity of the irascible clowns. For another essay, a prose satire on the problems of being an artist/illustrator entitled "Express Yourself," he chose to explore alternative methods of conveying visual messages. "These drawings attempt to find a completely different way of using art with articles," Holland explains. "I didn't so much illustrate as take the pictures in a different direction. I wanted a drawing style that was more like speech, that was fairly colloquial and would be done off the top of my head." The result was a series of sophisticated doodles of fantastic characters done in gestural masses with colored crayon. The images did not even parallel the text, but, through their peculiarity, they satirized the highfalutin notion of self-expression. For Holland this approach also reveals his dilemma with being a visual essayist: "I don't want to be sent to cover the funeral of Princess Diana," he says. "Rather than what was officially happening, I am interested in why people were going nuts. Watching a breakout of mass hysteria, now that is great for an artist!"

For some illustrators, the visual essay is a means to cover events, for others it is a door to uncover deeper meaning, and for still others its an opportunity to delve into uncharted territory. Concerning the third option, Marshall Arisman and Sue Coe are both obsessed with different aspects of similar protagonists: monkeys. Arisman's recent essay, "Sacred Monkeys," started in 1995 as a series of paintings attempting to show what he describes as the "aura, the inner light that surrounds us all." When he learned that Buddha was reincarnated seven times from a monkey, an "amusement" became an obsessive series of witty and acerbic images that traced the personalities of what he describes as one of the "two sacred animals in the world" (the other is the cat). Although he has been unable to publish the essay in its complete form, he has designed a monkey sculpture garden and written a novel about a monkey titled *Divine Elvis*. "It's a fairy tale on acid," he says. At first, he resisted illustrating his own manuscript until he devised a way to present Elvis, not keyed to passages of the story, as a cathartic character who ages and dies throughout twenty-three images—thus proving that art and text can be supplementary without being symbiotic.

From the metaphysical to the all-too-physical . . . Sue Coe's essay, "Monkey Business," was inspired by a visit to a primate research laboratory at the White Sands, New Mexico, missile base, where hundreds of chimpanzees had been infected with the HIV virus. The primates were in very small steel mesh boxes, although originally they were kept on a moated island until they started to escape. "The vision of the chimps was too terrible for me to draw or think about for a decade, then I started to draw monkeys," she explains. "Nonhuman primates have sophisticated intellectual abilities, feel pain, have empathy and loyalty, but the one gene difference between 'us' and 'them' renders them incapable of speech, so suffering is always mute." Coe had previously spent almost a decade chronicling animal slaughterhouses and abattoirs around the world, the result of which was eventually an exhibition and a book titled *Dead Meat*. This new project was a logical extension of her concern for both animals and humans who are victimized by overarching forces. The pictures are pieces of a large puzzle that Coe intends to build into a total narrative, while at the same time each tells its own tale.

The works of these artists are informed by the past as they address the present. Arisman points out that "the impulse to draw, paint, and tell stories is instilled in us [during] childhood and that doesn't go away." And Coe eloquently reminds us that "visual journalism has always been with us. Grünewald's Isenheim altarpiece, the green decayed flesh of a man being crucified, his limbs, horribly twisted, rotting, not the romantic Christ but a Christ that was painted to hang in a monastery's plague hospice. The patients seeing themselves could identify not with a supernatural being but their own reality. Otto Dix's World War I etchings, the virtuosity of the line etched deep like many bleeding wounds cannot describe war any better. Goya's sketchbook album of the Inquisition, real people seen by him. He risked everything to do that work. And Käthe Kollwitz, watching her doctor-husband minister to the poor and sick, drawing with litho crayon and etching tool, [chronicling] the humanity and misery of Germany between the wars."

Despite the requisite moaning constantly heard about "the sorry state of illustration today," the visual essay is redemptory in many ways. As Coe's pantheon suggests, passionate artists do not cease working because commercial outlets are not available to them. They make art because that is what they must do. Although some illustrators make art because the marketplace rewards them, the truly serious ones—those who have been authors before it became popular—will continue, despite fickle turns in style and fashion, to express themselves through image making. And through such expression they will invariably connect with an audience. In time, more magazine editors will accept the visual essay as an integral component of an editorial mix. "I imagine the future will not be static," adds Coe. "A drawing will link to animation, which will link to a photograph, which will link to sound. The demand for visual imagery will be colossal." And, in the midst of this voracious creation and consumption of imagery, the visual essay offers a unique respite, for, as Coe concludes, "art is about slowing time down, not speeding it up."

N o American illustrator has had a greater impact on popular culture or a more profound influence on generations of American illustrators than Norman Rockwell. He had a gift for reflecting his times through iconic representations of everyday life that became the official art of this nation. From the 1920s through the 1950s, his style was the standard for commercial artists who used realism to illustrate books, magazines, and advertisements. Although none surpassed Rockwell's unerring ability to capture the quintessential human moment, they filled countless pages with representational and romantic paintings that typified the art and craft of illustration. Paradoxically, though, Rockwell's art was both a model for excellence *and* a blueprint for cliché.

What Rockwell chose to portray, how he modeled his characters and applied his paint, derived from an intuitive sense of what would appeal to an audience of average Americans who were unaware of European modernism but who enjoyed pictures that represented their own heroic yet commonplace lives. Because of his success, many commercial illustrators aped Rockwell's manner, which itself owed a debt to Michelangelo and the Renaissance artists whom he had studied; however, most lacked Rockwell's genius for presenting the ordinary through extraordinary composition and gesture. Rockwell liberated American illustration from its reliance on archetypes; he introduced real-life protagonists instead of cardboard heroes. Yet he was the leader of an art form that in lesser hands (and there were many) was an abyss of romanticism and sentimentality. "Rockwell was all about energy," explains Dugald Stermer, chair of the California

College of Arts and Crafts Department of Illustration. "His people were subtly exaggerated, just bordering on caricature to heighten drama and capture the moment. But by comparison, most other illustrators of his day, including those working for the *Saturday Evening Post,* were flat."

Rockwell ran one step ahead of cliché, while his acolytes lagged a furlong behind. "They copied what they thought Norman Rockwell should be, not what he *was*," adds Stermer. Indeed, Rockwell's most popular and populist series of paintings, the "Four Freedoms," were just brush strokes away from mere propaganda of traditional American values. However, by skillfully balancing honest sentiment and uncompromised enthusiasm—by remaining faithful to natural expression and body language—the representations of these virtues were elevated to the level of manifestos of faith, with idealism expressed, as well as being documents of art. "The least well known, but one of his best pictures," comments illustrator Brad Holland, "is *Freedom from Fear,* showing a husband and wife tucking their kids into bed. It is simple and unrhetorical; it is like Vermeer: a genre painting that rises to the level of philosophy."

Similar themes, however, were commonly repeated in banal greeting cards and product advertisements by artists who appropriated the themes, borrowed the mannerisms, but ignored the vision. And while Rockwell is not to blame for the mediocrity that followed in his wake (and not all commercial artists of the day were so bankrupt), nonetheless he became the touchstone for a generational schism, owing in part to fact that his work was misinterpreted by both loyalist and rebel alike. Even today proponents celebrate his work, arguably, for the wrong reasons: "He's more highly regarded for his sentimentality than for his genius with faces," asserts Brad Holland about Rockwell's gift for intense emotional characterization. "He's the American Dickens, and one has to overlook much of what made him popular to realize just how good he was."

Rockwell is the spiritual descendent of some of the great illustrator-storytellers—Winslow Homer, Howard Pyle, and N. C. Wyeth. As such, he is a marker in the evolutionary progression of American illustration. His career took hold in the early 1920s around the same time that photography completely transformed graphic journalism, making reportorial illustration virtually obsolete. But Rockwell steadfastly refused to let illustration descend into triviality. Using the camera as a reference tool, a means of freezing gesture and expression for future reference, his full-color paintings of American life gave bolder dimension to his subjects than many of the black-and-white halftones commonly reproduced in national magazines. While most illustrators, especially those working for the *Saturday Evening Post,* stayed the course, producing reams of quixotic scenes and sight gags, Rockwell maintained a standard of excellence that far transcended a profession more concerned with servicing clients than making lasting art.

Despite his best efforts, by the late 1940s Rockwell was in the vanguard of a waning discipline. Seismic shifts in technology as well as challenges by progressive art idioms conspired to relegate conventional realistic illustration to the status of lesser commercial art. By remaining true to his own idiom, Rockwell unwittingly appeared to oppose the rising tide of abstract and expressionistic methods as they influenced illustrative trends. While he maintained a loyal core audience, the publishing and advertising industries were weaving in and out of stylistic novelty. Rockwell's art was becoming anachronistic.

Rockwell was a hero to many illustrators, but he was also an institution, a symbol of the old order. For the generation of younger, postwar illustrators and graphic designers who embraced the European modern movements—cubism, futurism, dada, and surrealism—he was a relic of antiquity. He was the "Uncle Joe school of illustration," chided Paul Rand, the American modern graphic design pioneer who argued that Rockwell's stubborn insistence on detail and verisimilitude denied the mystery of art. "He was the enemy," asserts Seymour Chwast, cofounder in 1955 of Push Pin Studios, the illustration and design firm that launched the first attack against "turgid postwar narrative illustration." Chwast and other critics cited that formal differences such as realism versus abstraction, detail versus allusion, mannerism versus expressionism, separated the old guard from the new wave. But there also existed philosophical issues distinguishing the urban artist, raised on comics and political cartoons, from the middle American artist, weaned on Rockwell's vision.

As a child in Fremont, Ohio, in the early 1950s, Brad Holland, who became a pioneer of conceptual editorial art in the late 1960s, reveled in Rockwell's *Saturday Evening Post* depictions of an America that he could easily envision as taking place in his own hometown. Chwast, however, had a very different vantage point living in Brooklyn, New York, during the Depression-weary 1930s through the postwar 1940s: "Rockwell not only painted every detail on his canvas, he also presented details of America that really didn't exist: a happy America, a fake America." Similarly another New Yorker, Art Spiegelman, author of *Maus* (a comic-strip autobiography of his parents' lives during the Holocaust), asserts that "Rockwell's paintings were visuals with an agenda; he took the real and turned them into symbols." In his own work Spiegelman continues to subvert these symbols by satiric recasting. He says his influence was the acerbic parodies in late 1950s *MAD* magazines, in which satiric artist Will Elder, who intensely studied Rockwell's technique, "achieved perfect pitch, mastered the innocent surface, and then bit its tail off" in vignettes that looked like the real thing but were instead scabrous commentaries on Rockwell's (and by extension America's) idyllic fantasies. Indeed, Rockwell's legacy can be measured as much by the parodies of his work as by the indelible icons that he created.

As unambiguous as his paintings appeared on the surface, Rockwell's work was interpreted differently by various artists. Holland recalls that, as a child, he liked Rockwell's magazine covers because "they looked like photographs, but in the end, I liked the faces—they weren't pretty necessarily, but they had soul." Conversely, Chwast argues that looking at a Rockwell painting after World War II "was to see America as it could never be again." Meanwhile, Stermer, who published one of Rockwell's paintings when he was art director of *Ramparts* magazine, a 1960s-era left-wing political muckraking journal, points to Rockwell's painting *The Problem We All Live With* (*Look*, 1964), which shows an African-American girl being marched by U.S. marshals into a segregated elementary school. "No other illustrator could have pulled this off the way that he did, when he did," he says about Rockwell's ability to transcend political controversy.

Yet for all Rockwell's complexity, indeed because of it, he was a lightning rod for change. "You wouldn't have needed to make him an enemy if he was a hack," Stermer observes. In fact, Rockwell was such a seminal figure and his work was so ubiquitous, in hindsight, it is axiomatic that he would foster rebellion among certain of his followers. "Since Rockwell was a giant in popularity, I'm sure a lot of people felt that to compete with him they had to level him," asserts Holland. "I could see wanting to *be* Rockwell—to be as original as he had been—*but* not wanting to be *like* him. And that's the challenge posed by every distinctive artist: The essence of tradition is to invite the challenge that redefines it." Hence Rockwell drew respectful fire from the young rebels, but his many imitators earned their contempt.

Seymour Chwast readily admits that "Rockwell" was his catchall term for artists rooted in tried-and-true representational mannerisms that dominated most American commercial art from roughly the mid-1930s until the mid-1950s. Rockwell's influence on the genre was widespread, and those who slavishly followed his surface style were published in all the magazines and illustration yearbooks. The verisimilitude of the kind that Rockwell accomplished so well and that imitators attempted to capture was anathema to the new breed of "expressive" artists who sought to liberate editorial (and possibly advertising) illustration from the stranglehold of academic verities and to reinvest it with idiosyncrasy. Most of all they sought to make illustration that complemented rather than mimicked a text.

Although illustration was traditionally a medium governed more by the rules of accuracy than the vicissitudes of psychology, by the 1950s a new generation of editorial illustrators was unwilling to remain faithful to the prevailing realist aesthetics that were championed by art directors for the leading general magazines, including *Collier's, Saturday Evening Post, Reader's Digest, American Magazine,* and others. Even if the majority of readers preferred Uncle Joe's blemish-free realism, dissent was more vocal, and alternative methods were emerging in some progressive editorial venues.

Shifts in illustrative style throughout the twentieth century were not new, but until the postwar period they had been incremental. The hierarchy of the American publishing and advertising industries was such that style was dictated by "word people." Editors determined the visual content of magazines, with art directors serving as go-betweens who related their editors' compositional, characterizational, and even color preferences to freelance and staff artists. Similarly, copywriters dominated advertising, often providing their own sketches for layouts that illustrators were required to finesse. Word people preferred the status quo and were hesitant to disrupt convention. Commercial illustrators were, hence, routinely treated as appendages— hands in the service of a product or idea— and dutifully followed editorial dictates. Rockwell himself was above the fray; he answered to an art director and editor, but the relationship was of equals. Lesser illustrators' work was closely scrutinized by editorial overseers who demanded accuracy, clarity, and obedience. Independent ideas and concepts were more or less discouraged in favor of precise compositions that rendered most illustrations formal exercises.

During the late 1940s and early 1950s, a school of younger artists, represented by the Charles E. Cooper Studios, a leading New York–based talent agency for advertising art, helped fill advertising and editorial pages with realistic artwork that left little to the imagination or interpretation of the viewer. This was in accordance with the wishes of editors and advertising account executives who feared hidden agendas or ambiguous representations. Even the most accomplished commercial artist was concerned almost exclusively with style—how it looked rather than what it said. Although paintings by the Cooper Studios luminaries Coby Whitmore and Jon Whitcomb were formally looser and less detailed than Rockwell's—and so looked to be more contemporary—they eschewed any semblance of abstraction or allusion that would have given their work additional levels of meaning. At the *Saturday Evening Post,* where Rockwell had sinecure for over four decades, other leading cover and interior illustrators offered approaches that more or less complemented the master. And while Stevan Dohanos and John Fawcett, among them, were not carbon copies of Rockwell (in fact, their focus shifted from New England/Middle America to the Long Island and Connecticut suburbs), the situational comic vignettes of life in white, middle-class America followed the formula that Rockwell had ostensibly originated.

The cult of Rockwell was further promoted by his headlined association with the Famous Artists School of Westport, Connecticut, the East Coast's largest correspondence art school. During the 1950s and 1960s, the majority of faculty members, including leading advertising and editorial illustrators known collectively as the Westport School, were rooted in sentimental, romantic, and heroic representationalism. Together, they dominated a large portion of the illustration market and accepted the major awards from New York's Society of Illustrators, the venerable institution dedicated to the art of illustration. This group, whose advertisements frequently appeared in commercial and trade magazines alike, was the illustration establishment that all wannabes idolized. However, at the same time, the fashion for tightfisted realism was gradually shifting to more casual representation.

In the early 1950s, the American satiric artist Robert Osborn introduced an expressionistic, brush-and-ink drawing style in acerbic graphic commentaries about society and politics. But it was not until the mid-1950s that expressionist editorial illustrators who studied and assimilated the lessons of modern art—including Robert Weaver, Robert Andrew Parker, Tom Allen, and Phil Hayes—broke through the wall of convention, guarded by older agency and editorial art directors. Their painting was more abstract, influenced by such contemporaries as Mark Rothko, Franz Kline, and Willem de Kooning, and their content appeared to be rooted more in personal psychology than in another's text. Whereas Rockwell was controlled, the "neo-expressionists" were free. Whereas Rockwell and his disciples adhered to photographic reference, the younger artists drew from life *and* imagination. They rejected the precisely rendered human form or landscape in favor of filtered recollections. The humanist qualities exemplified in a Rockwell canvas were not, however, forsaken; the younger artists believed that humanism—and a kind of spirituality—could be best expressed by simultaneously looking inward *and* outward. Surface was not an end in itself. A narrative illustration was arguably as much about the composition of abstract elements and the serendipity of accidents as it was concerned with explicit rendering.

It was not that Rockwell's days were numbered by the late 1950s (he continued to have a huge following even after he left the *Saturday Evening Post* in the mid-1960s and moved over to *Look*), but the style that Rockwell had influenced was overtaken by fundamental editorial and design changes throughout publishing and advertising industries. One significant change was the shift from illustration to photography; illustration was no longer required to convey precise details but could evoke ambient moods. In this tidal shift, the responsibility of the illustrator was no longer to mimic a text but, rather, was to imply a message. "Mine was no longer the era of Norman Rockwell, where everything was easy, obvious, and on the surface," replied the late Robert Weaver, the leader of the new illustration of the 1950s, referring to the new content in specialized magazines. "How would Rockwell illustrate the problem of left-handedness?" he asks rhetoricallly, referring to one of his own assignments in *Psychology Today*.

Moreover, monumental, heroic, and romantic illustration was anachronism in a media environment dominated by television. In fact, the "Big Ideas" of advertising's Creative Revolution during the 1960s—sophisticated and witty word-and-image "concepts"—rendered the overly narrative Rockwellian method inappropriate.

Illustration turned the corner in the 1960s, becoming more diverse in both form and content. Although keepers of the traditional flame, including organizations like the Society of Illustrators in New York City (where Rockwell was a member in good standing), continued to propagate the illustrator as painter of narrative tableaux, the so-called new conceptualists—illustrators such as Brad Holland, Alan E. Cober, and Marshall Arisman, who conceived ideas and conveyed them through surrealism, symbolism, expressionism, and dadaist collage and montage—had made important inroads, thanks to their acceptance by a new generation of editorial art directors who were no longer mere go-betweens but who became creative contributors. By this time, Rockwell was respected, indeed he wasn't even being rebelled against, but he was no longer considered a viable factor in the future of illustration. As the late Alan E. Cober once stated about the passing of the torch, "I didn't know I was a young Turk. I just thought it was my turn."

After some initial resistance, the Society of Illustrators recognized new trends and exhibited them along with the more traditional approaches. In the early 1980s a *salon des refusés*, the annual competition/book titled *American Illustration,* was founded to promote alternative methods and encourage illustration that pushed the boundaries. By the late '80s a form of *art brut*, or untutored and naïve mannerisms representing a fervently personal approach to illustration, was accepted and continues to be a viable style.

Although realism and representation have never been entirely rejected, they have evolved away from Rockwell's methods if for no better reason than the fact that the role of illustration today is different from its role when he was working. For one thing, illustration used to be one of the primary visual mechanisms of mass media. Today, however, illustration is subservient to other visual forms in both print and electronic media and at its best provides more cerebral stimulation than documentary supplementation. Illustration is, therefore, more conceptual than the grand painterly narratives of Rockwell's day.

Rockwell's legacy continues to affect millions for whom his paintings distill the real and imagined essence of a bygone age. He launched an epoch that historians refer to as the golden age of American illustration, which serviced the masses through crisp and clean realism, but he also spawned a rebellion that rejected transparency for emotive complexity. Perhaps the best way to appreciate Rockwell is to celebrate his paintings as monuments of American history and accept that they represent a great moment in the continuum of this American popular art.

You don't have to be Jewish

to love Levy's
real Jewish Rye

ew York City was for modern art direction during the mid-1950s through the mid-1960s what Paris was for modern art at the turn of the century, a wellspring of unrivaled invention. Neither Chicago nor Los Angeles had the same critical mass of talent or the business to support it. In New York scores of art directors had commanding positions at ad agencies and magazine publishers, where they not only made an impact on their respective products but also influenced the entire field. Manhattan was, moreover, the birthplace of the "creative," the role that heralded the shift from art service to visual communications. Madison Avenue was Manhattan's Montmartre. Along this traffic-congested boulevard, "creatives" working in glass and stone skyscrapers changed the look and feel of advertising and magazines through an acute conceptual strategy characterized by understatement, self-mockery, and irony. In 1960, adman William Pensyl termed this the "Big Idea."[1] Characterized by clean design and strident copywriting, wed to intelligent illustration and photography, the Big Idea was an expression of the unparalleled creative liberation that was later dubbed the "Creative Revolution"[2] and inaugurated the shift from hard sell to smart sell in advertising and publishing.

One building in particular, 488 Madison Avenue, was the nerve center of this trans-figuration. At the top, one flight of stairs above the reach of the elevators, in a windowed penthouse overlooking "Madvertising" Avenue, was headquartered the Art Directors Club of New York. This professional organization, founded in 1920, attracted an exclusive membership of advertising and magazine art directors who came from blocks around to share—or more likely boast about—their big ideas. They also judged the work for the annual competitions that celebrated and recorded the art directorial achievement setting contemporary standards. Like the bohemian cafés of Paris's Left Bank, the Art Directors Club was the epicenter for the men (and the few women) who became the legends of New York art direction.

Beginning in the late 1940s, some of the most influential media in America were also headquartered at 488 Madison. *Look, Esquire, Apparel Arts, Gentleman's Quarterly,* and *Seventeen* were there, as well as Raymond Loewy's industrial design office and the innovative Weintraub Advertising Agency, where Paul Rand (b. 1914) was art director from 1941 to 1954. By the mid-1950s some of the most significant art directors worked within elevator distance of one another: Allen Hurlburt (1910–1983) at *Look,* Henry Wolf (b. 1925) at *Esquire,* and Art Kane (1926–1995) at *Seventeen.* But 488 was not an island. Across the street, the building that housed the Columbia Broadcasting System (before "Black Rock" was built in 1962) was home to the premier corporate design department in America, where art directors William Golden (1911–1959) and later Lou Dorfsman (b. 1918) produced identity and advertising campaigns that altered the paradigm of corporate and institutional practice. Within a few blocks of this locale worked other equally influential art directors: Alexey Brodovitch (1898–1971) at *Harper's Bazaar;* Helmut Krone (1925–1996), Gene Federico (b. 1918), and Robert Gage (b. 1929) at Doyle Dane Bernbach; George Lois (b. 1932) at Papert Lois Koenig; Leo Lionni (b. 1910) at *Fortune;* Steve Frankfurt (b. 1931) at Young and Rubicam; Cipe Pineles (1910–1992) at *Charm;* Otto Storch (b. 1913) at *McCall's;* and Herb Lubalin (1918–1981) at Sudler & Hennessey, to name a few. Each with a distinctive signature and methodology, they defined the role of the modern art director as manager, editor, and designer all rolled into one.

The job of "art supervisor" dates back to the turn of the century, when its influence on advertising and magazines was comparatively inconsequential. The term "art director" gained currency a short time before the Art Directors Club began monitoring the achievements of New York's advertising and magazine profession in 1920. But, prior to 1950, its competitions focused more on the artists and agencies than on the art directors themselves. The club exhibited a mix from rococo decoration by luminaries like Thomas Maitland Cleland to comic-strip advertisements by anonymous bullpen boardmen at J. Walter Thompson agency. With a few notable exceptions—such as M. F. Agha (1896–1978), who pioneered modern magazine design at *Vanity Fair* and *Vogue*—the art director was a company middleman following copywriters and taking direction from account executives or editors rather than a creative who molded the identity of his or her campaign or publication. The juried Art Directors annuals published between the 1920s and 1940s reveal that art directors slowly gained stature in the late 1930s, but the shift was not fully realized until the postwar years. As a symbol of pending change, however, the name of America's premier commercial art magazine was changed in 1940 from *PM* (Production Manager) to *AD* (Art Director),[3] but it was well over a decade before the Creative Revolution took hold.

The shift began in the late 1930s, when a generation of young modern-inspired artists and designers aggressively sought to change the nature of American practice. Advertising and publishing had virtually ignored the nuances of good design in the modern sense, though they gave lip service to the New Typography through asymmetrical styles and modernistic conceits. "What went before was pretty dull, so it wasn't difficult to make a splash," recalls Gene Federico, who began his agency career in the late 1930s and made his own splash as an advertising art director at Doyle Dane Bernbach in the early 1950s. By 1937, the names Paul Rand, Lester Beall, Will Burtin, William Golden, and Alexey Brodovitch in the Art Directors Club annual were associated with work that rejected the vulgar conventions of commercial practice for subtle and ironic imagery as well as economical type and layout. Their designs bore a visual signature that both framed and distinguished their respective products. They also became representatives of a new genus: the art director/designer, who was responsible for more than supervising layout bullpens, which was the custom at the time. "Clients began to recognize that these guys were not just sign painters," says Lou Dorfsman, who began his own lengthy career designing exposition displays. "They were accepted as artists who understood marketing."

Advertising and magazine publishing were traditionally exclusive professions. At the pinnacle were, respectively, the account executive and editor, who for the most part were Ivy League–educated and belonged to the dominant social and economic class. As molders of popular taste they made advertising and editorial decisions that catered to the biases of their fellows, the leaders of mainstream American business. It was a close-knit gentlemen's club. However, New York was the proverbial melting pot of European immigrants by the turn of the century, and the children of these immigrants comprised the majority in the New York City public schools by the mid-1930s. At that time, in addition to the three Rs, the curriculum emphasized skills that would propel students into viable jobs; commercial art was a fertile profession especially suited to New Yorkers of immigrant backgrounds. So it was in this unique sociocultural environment that the seeds of the Creative Revolution were planted.

Although the advertising and publishing industry's hierarchy was elite, they hired artists who were first-generation Italian- and Jewish-Americans. Secondary schools like Abraham Lincoln High School in Brooklyn as well as the High School of Music and Art and the High School of Industrial Arts, both in Manhattan, offered courses in poster making, illustration, advertising, and typography that combined the teaching of Bauhausian form with mass advertising and publishing techniques. The models for these students were not the fine printer/designers D. B. Updike, Frederic Goudy, or W. A. Dwiggins. Instead, they followed the masters of publicity Lucian Bernhard, A. M. Cassandre, and E. McKnight Kauffer (all of whom were featured in the European design magazines such as *Gebrauchsgraphik* and *Commercial Art*). Many of the graduates continued their education at art schools like Pratt Institute, Parsons School of Design, the Art Students League, and the Cooper Union (and in the late forties and early fifties Alexey Brodovitch taught a class in magazine design at the New School for Social Research); some directly entered the profession, starting in the lower echelons. From this number many eventually advanced into jobs as copywriters and art directors.

The Creative Revolution began when the Jews and Italians assumed influential positions at agencies, influenced in no small measure by the leadership of William Bernbach (1911–1982), the cofounder in 1949 of Doyle Dane Bernbach, who popularized the creative team and encouraged radical changes in fifties advertising. He himself was influenced by Paul Rand when they worked together at the Weintraub Agency in the forties. Raised during the Great Depression, these virtual outsiders were psychologically driven to enter the mainstream but on their own terms. They developed a passion for American popular culture: They devoured the comics and comic books; and many of them dabbled in jazz and other popular music forms as a way to reconcile their ethnic heritages and American lives. Those who chose commercial art sought more financial security—the Depression saw to that—but intuited that there was a potential for creative opportunity as well. So when these children of the melting pot came of age they left their ethnic neighborhoods in Brooklyn, the Bronx, Queens, and the Lower East Side of Manhattan and either by happenstance or design created a beachhead on Madison Avenue.

"Jews became copywriters and Italians became art directors," generalizes Lou Dorfsman in a statement that is disproved by his own career as an art director. But he is right about the influx of brash, ethnic "neighborhood" kids who refused to see the world—or more precisely the marketplace—in the same way that the entrenched aloof media professionals had since the turn of the century. "When the mask of suburban conformism was ripped away and America became aware of its ethnic diversity it meant major changes . . ." writes Lawrence Dobrow in *When Advertising Tried Harder*. "We were itchy, we couldn't stand all that old stuff," recalls Gene Federico about the conventional advertising that he refers to as "different-sized boxes on a page." And so the upheaval was beginning. "Our generation was fresher, wittier, more sarcastic, and therefore more ironic," adds Tony Palladino (b. 1930), the son of Italian immigrants who graduated from the High School Music and Art in the late 1940s and became an advertising and editorial art director/designer by the 1960s. "We had an Old World, European affinity, but a New World, American desire to make change."

In advertising, change was measured by the quality of ideas and the eloquence of execution. As a reaction to the gray-flanneled hucksterism of the past, the new advertising men believed in the avant-garde (i.e., futurist) notion that advertising could change the world. This was a calling, not a job. The art director rose in stature in the fifties in large part due to a personal drive, but even more important was the fact that creative teams, pioneered by Bernbach, wed copywriters and art directors to a common goal. Art directors were required to act aggressively in all creative decisions; art direction was so totally intertwined with writing and design that pinpointing the spot where one left off and the other began was irrelevant. Indicative of this newly realized power was the addition of art directors' names to agency titles; many, like Herb Lubalin, were anointed as vice presidents, and a few, like George Lois and Steven Frankfurt, were presidents.

The anthem of the Big Idea was the phrase "Think Small," a headline written by copywriter Julian Koenig that inspired art director Helmut Krone's 1959 Volkswagen campaign for Doyle Dane Bernbach. "In the beginning, there was Volkswagen," writes adman Jerry Della Femina in his memoir *From Those Wonderful Folks Who Gave You Pearl Harbor* (Simon and Schuster, 1970). "That's the first campaign which everyone can trace back and say, 'This is where the changeover began.'" At a time when advertising, particularly automobile advertising, idolized mythic perfection, this was the first time that an ad rejected pretense and hyperbole in word and picture. It was selling at its most subtle and subversive because the Volkswagen campaign redirected the perceptions of an entire consumer class from the notion that big is beautiful (and American) to small is wonderful (even if it's German). George Lois once noted the irony that not only did this campaign pitch a tiny car in a market of behemoths, but it was a Nazi car, to boot.

In addition to their unrivaled sales appeal, the Volkswagen ads summarized advancements in graphic design dating back to the Bauhaus. Nothing was extraneous, not even a period. And yet it was not cold like the Swiss method. "It was a better use of space, or what we call 'design,'" explains Gene Federico about the shift away from formulaic layout. Although it was not the first ad to be "designed," per se, it was the first design of a national ad to reveal a decidedly American phase of modern thinking rooted in both economy and irony. Because of this campaign, art direction was elevated beyond the board and into the boardroom. Creatives entered the vanguard of the "new advertising," while nuts-and-bolts business matters were left to their Harvard-educated colleagues.

Federico points out that not all clients, in fact comparatively few, had "taken the bait" by the early fifties. But clients and advertising executives saw that the new advertising made quantifiable differences in sales by the late fifties. "It was the beginning of the era of possibilities, a freeing of convention as breakthroughs in one area influenced those in others," says Milton Glaser (b. 1929), who cofounded Push Pin Studios in 1955 and worked with many of the leading art directors of the epoch. "It was a time when doing unconventional things had a tremendous effect, and one person could influence thousands."

The most adventuresome art directors deviated from the norms—broke the rules of type and image, rejected the hegemony of sentimental illustration—and triggered others to do so, resulting in a chain reaction. Soon the followers were doing work on a par with the leaders. And, among the soldiers of the Creative Revolution, the prevailing belief was that utility and effectiveness could be wed to a concern for order and beauty. From the Bauhaus came the idea that it was not important to distinguish between functionality and beauty. From the street developed the idea that the masses could be won over by intelligence. "Good design" became a sort of mantra. "It suggested something to aspire to," continues Glaser.

Magazine art directors aspired to "good design" before their advertising counterparts, but both reached their zenith at around the same time. In magazine publishing the older immigrants led the way. In the late 1920s Turkish-born M. F. Agha, who designed Paris *Vogue* for Condé Nast, was brought to New York, where he transformed *Vanity Fair* (under the editorial leadership of Frank Crowninshield) from a conventionally designed upper-crust magazine into an epitome of urbanity. Agha's introduction of sans serif, lowercase headlines, full-page pictures, and generously undecorated page margins proved that magazine design was more than a printer's afterthought. Agha further laid the groundwork for art direction in the fifties. "The art director has come to play an increasingly important role in the editorial concept of modern magazines," wrote Gardner Cowles, president and editor of *Look* magazine, in the book *Art Directing*

(Hastings House, 1959). "He is no longer just a planner of illustrations and a liaison between the editor and artist. Today's magazine art director plays a major part in the publication structure, from formulation of editorial ideas to the production methods by which the magazine is printed. . . . I'm convinced that in the years ahead the art director will play an even more important role than he does right now."

Magazine art direction was slightly more genteel than advertising, and its pioneers, like Agha, were the aristocrats of commercial art. They set standards in the forties that held sway into the sixties. There were others who prefigured the Creative Revolution in magazines but profoundly influenced it. Alexey Brodovitch, the White Russian designer who worked for Deberny and Peignot in Paris, not only streamlined the look of the venerable *Harper's Bazaar* but transformed fashion magazine content by introducing conceptual photography as an alternative to conventional illustration. Austrian-born Will Burtin modernized the classically elegant *Fortune* by introducing a highly sophisticated approach to information graphics. The Dutch-born, Italian-educated Leo Lionni succeeded Burtin and pushed *Fortune* even further into realms of the classically contemporaneous. In addition to promoting fine artists as visual journalists, he redefined the nature of magazine cover design by inventing the two-tiered image (different illustrations above and below the masthead referring to different themes in the magazine). Austrian-born Cipe Pineles, who assisted Agha at *Vogue* in the late 1930s, helped define an entirely new teenage market through her art direction of *Seventeen* in the late '40s by introducing this group to urbane art and illustration; from 1950 to '58, with *Charm,* she defined a print environment for young working women. Finally, Russian-born Alexander Liberman (b. 1912), the designer of Paris *VU,* followed the lead of Brodovitch by modernizing *Vogue* through fine conceptual photography.

"Today's art director [is an] architect of the printed page," wrote Charles Coiner, art director of N. W. Ayer, in *The 31st Annual of Advertising and Editorial Art.* In the magazine field Brodovitch, Burtin, Lionni, Pineles, and Liberman were among the key architects. Yet they were not brazenly experimental in the avant-garde sense. Their structures were built on firm principles, and with self-assurance and authority they promoted new approaches to type and image, harnessed negative space, and—most important—applied big ideas to editorial design. Some art directors argue that their introduction of photography and fine art to magazines had a critical influence on advertising art direction. And, if conceptual photography is the benchmark of what Gardner Cowles called the "Pictorial Era" of the Creative Revolution, then its roots must be traced to magazines.

By the early to mid-1950s, younger magazine art directors enthusiastically followed their mentors and made further inroads. One of the most progressive of this generation was *Esquire's* art director from 1953 to 1958, Henry Wolf, a young Austrian immigrant who transformed a starchy gentlemen's fashion monthly into a creative environment for photographers and illustrators. He perfected the narrative picture essay, introduced collage as illustration, and designed conceptual covers that stood without headlines. Allen Hurlburt (1910–1983), who was *Look's* art director from 1953 to 1968 and had assisted Paul Rand at Weintraub, epitomized

Gardner Cowles's definition of the editor/designer. *Look* appeared in January 1937, more than a year after *Life* premiered; until Hurlburt began as art director it remained in *Life*'s shadow. "*Life* had great pictures but no design," argues Sam Antupit, *Esquire*'s art director from 1963 to 1969, "*Look* had great photographs and was brilliantly designed." Hurlburt understood dramatic pacing and knew how to integrate expressive typography to complement the pictorial narrative; he designed a magazine of ideas. Other art directors added their own styles and dialects to this unique era: Otto Storch, who took Brodovitch's class at the New School, was art director at *McCall's* from 1953 to 1967 and introduced a retro typographic sensibility that prefigured postmodernism. Bradbury Thompson (1911–1996) brought contemporary classicism to *Mademoiselle* from 1945 to 1959. Art Kane, who later earned fame as a photographer, gave his version of *Seventeen* a typographic and photographic urbanity unknown in today's "teenage" magazines. This was the era when magazine art directors enjoyed continuous runs of many editorial pages that allowed them to establish visual narratives and kinetically pace the stories.

Browse through any Art Directors Club annuals between 1955 and 1965, and the Big Idea in advertising and magazine art direction comes into clear focus. "This was a period when expression of an idea was more enduring than style," says Milton Glaser. Of course, the selected pages and spreads in these annuals are taken out of context, and certain design biases are celebrated over others that may have existed at the time, but the dominant method of advertising and magazine design had much in common. Glaser further notes that New York's art directors formed a comparatively small community and the common language, the ambient art directorial vocabulary, adhered to a basic syntax: classically modern or expressively eclectic typography, conceptual illustration, and both narrative and abstract photography wed to the word. All components were in harmony and evoked a sense of both beauty and meaning.

In addition to common aesthetics, money was the glue that held this epoch of art direction together. According to Jerry Della Femina, advertising art directors commanded upwards of $50,000 a year (the equivalent of three or four times that amount in today's currency). "American advertising was the only game in town," says Lou Dorfsman. "The magazines were flush with ads, and they spared no expense in giving art directors license to send photographers and illustrators around," adds Henry Wolf. Money was indeed available to finance big ideas.

Although magazine art directors deny that advertising influenced editorial design, there was a creative symbiosis between advertising and editorial art direction. Wolf points out that the photographers he used in *Esquire* were often subsequently hired for large ad campaigns. Federico concurs that admen combed *Esquire* and *Look* for visual inspiration. And Sam Antupit adds that he frequently discussed the design of his opening editorial pages with agency art directors before going to press so that their respective layouts would not conflict with each other but had their own integrity.

Art direction further influenced a broader visual culture. "The art director, as we now define his job, has grown steadily away from his early predilection with decorative 'effects,'" according to the Art Directors Club of New York in the introduction to its 1953 annual, "and steadily toward a more scientific approach in the art of communicating ideas. . . . He still fights in the fundamental battle of his trade—good taste versus 'buckeye'—and occasionally writhing in the toils of that effort, he shows signs of schizophrenia when he must decide whether to decorate or communicate." Compared to the mass of visual effluvia, the work celebrated by the Art Directors Club proved to a significant segment of American business that shrill hawking and common-denominator thinking was not necessary to sell wares or present ideas. Advertising and magazine art direction provided vivid examples of how elegance and wit, cut with imagination, could alter mass perceptions, even taste. "The art director has made tangible and practical contributions to the advancement of good taste . . . in this country," notes Walter O'Meara in *The 31st Annual of Advertising and Editorial Art*.

Nevertheless, the influence of the Creative Revolution, like the dream of reason, produced its own share of madness. Or at least mediocrity. By the late sixties, the Big Idea had become a placebo for many advertising and magazine art directors. Although there were still some great big ideas, such as George Lois's acerbic *Esquire* covers in the late sixties, there was also widespread deflation as a result of formulaic solutions. It was impossible to maintain revolutionary fervor over a long period of time. Even the most radical ideas eventually lose stridency and are replaced. When big ideas became predictable, they are no longer big ideas.

"Everything came to an end in the late sixties and seventies," asserts Henry Wolf. "Publishers wanted to make money rather than have beautiful magazines." Or more accurately, print began to run afoul of television. As advertising art directors began turning their attention and ambitions toward commercials, magazine art directors began to feel their own celebrity subside. As the great magazines began to falter, art directors fell from grace or at least farther down the masthead. "I left *Harper's Bazaar* when I could not get thirty consecutive pages in the editorial well," boasts Henry Wolf. This should not be considered nostalgic hyperbole but rather an indication of the devolution of magazines as a prime medium and of the art director as its visual impresario. With the same speed that the Creative Revolution had hit, it ran out of steam. Advertising veered further away from magazine art direction, and magazine art direction on the whole became more service oriented. The golden age of art direction ended and with it went the purity of the Big Idea.

---

1. Although the term may have been used before, it appears in *Print* (May/June 1960) in a quote by adman William Pensyl of Ketchum, MacLeod, Grove, who says, "The big idea serves as the basis for all creative work. . . ." George Lois, the master of this method, used it in the title of his book *What's the Big Idea: How to Win with Outrageous Ideas That Sell* (Doubleday, 1991).

2. Although the original source of this term is unknown, one authoritative reference is in the title of Lawrence Dobrow's *1950s and Madison Avenue: The Creative Revolution in Advertising* (Friendly Press, 1984).

3. The magazine had relinquished its original name to *PM*, a daily newspaper, but the choice of the title *AD* was nevertheless consistent with changes in the profession.

Before the term "graphic design" was coined in 1922 (and commonly used a decade thereafter), New York City was the undisputed commercial-art capital of the United States, owing to the numerous publishing, advertising, and manu-facturing firms with headquarters in the city and its environs. In the early 1900s, New York was home to moderately large commercial-art studios, where, sitting at rows of drafting tables, anonymous layout people created trademarks, signs, brochures, and advertisements. New York had a few major type houses that not only offered commercial typefaces but also produced sophisticated typography.

Yet, despite the influence of these professional studios, most of the layout done in the city was "thrown in" by printers as a loss leader at no extra cost, and the quality of commercial art was erratic at best. In order to set standards, New York's National Arts Club began an annual advertising-art exhibition in 1908, which was open to all. This juried competition, and those following helped to forge a relationship between business and commercial artists, a rather formalized service called "art for commerce."

Gradually, as need developed, individual graphic artists began to advertise a variety of custom services, mostly in trade journals. In the 1927 issue of the *Graphic Arts Yearbook* (an early incarnation of the promotional annuals on the market today) were over four hundred advertisements for an array of New York–based editorial, advertising, and fashion illustrators, letterers, airbrush and mechanical artists. In the same issue were also a few distinctive ads for a new job category called "designer for industry." This unprecedented marriage of craftsperson and artist promised to bring package, poster, and other print design together on one drafting table, practiced by one artist (aided by an assistant or two). During this nascent period of graphic design, concurrent with America's precipitous slide into a devastating economic depression, being a designer for industry implied certain social and civic responsibilities. In truth, however, while a few visionaries collaborated with business to make products better, most designers for industry were glorified layout people who enjoyed varying degrees of success by trading on the increasingly marketable modernistic or art deco styles.

Yet designers for industry were also earnestly attempting to elevate commercial art from a service into a profession. Throughout the late 1920s and 1930s, with the principal exception of publishing, graphic artists in New York were subordinate to advertising agencies—large and small—which hired them on a freelance basis to provide a variety of creative and mechanical services. But, in fact, there was quite a distinction, if not a schism, between a new breed of creative (or artistic) designer and the conventional draftsperson. Organizations like the American Institute of Graphic Arts (founded in New York in 1914) and the Art Directors Club of New York (founded in 1920) encouraged professional excellence and reinforced qualitative distinctions by vigorously promoting the creative over the service aspects of commercial art.

While most trade magazines were either technical or business-oriented, one New York–based magazine from the 1930s, *Advertising Arts,* the bimonthly design supplement to *Advertising and Selling,* was actively promoting commercial artists as invaluable contributors to commerce by featuring articles on their significant developments in package and poster design, window display, direct mail, and other design forms. *Advertising Arts* was also one of the earliest American publications to promote avant-garde European graphic design. This new design had been introduced in Europe over a decade earlier and was beginning to filter into the American mainstream, despite the fear among clients and graphic arts suppliers that the American public would not understand and therefore be unresponsive to progressive advertising techniques. Certain modern tenets such as asymmetrical layout, sans serif typography, and photomontage were eventually adopted by American designers. New York City was otherwise isolated from Bauhaus, de Stijl, and constructivist theory until the mid-thirties; it was not, however, without a homegrown "avant-garde."

Because of the difficult demands placed on industry by the Depression, advertising and design "experts" were called in by business to help regenerate the sluggish economy. Among the most notable for their contributions to everyday product design were Joseph Sinel and Gustav B. Jensen, each proprietors of small graphics and advertising studios catering to the needs of some of America's most prestigious manufacturers.

During the Depression New York was a wellspring for two somewhat intersecting design currents: forced obsolescence and streamlining. The latter was an idea developed by an innovative New York advertising man, Earnest Elmo Calkins, who, in addition to pioneering "creative teams" of advertising copywriters and art directors, claimed that by regularly changing the look of products (usually through stylistic means), one could compel consumers to buy and dispose of these products more frequently, thereby moving the economy out of its doldrums. Streamlining was the dominant style of redesign both in terms of graphics and industrial manufacture—and was applied to the veneers of virtually everything, from pencil sharpeners to ocean liners. Yet the streamline ethic was also developed with the idea of increasing mechanical efficiency through science and engineering. The major proponents of streamlining included two showmen: one-time advertising designer Raymond Loewy and Broadway scenic designer Norman Bel Geddes. Together with Walter Dorwin Teague and Henry Dreyfuss, who also turned from commercial art to industrial design, these men were among the first real design entrepreneurs in America. Each opened spacious New York offices with relatively large staffs, more akin to architectural firms than to commercial art studios.

While New York's industrial designers basked in their respective glories (which peaked with their work for the monumental pavilions and exhibitions at the 1939 New York World's Fair), commercial art was being slowly transformed into graphic design—from service to profession—on a smaller but no less significant stage by a few ardent young New York modernists. They based new approaches on the theories of European design progressives, many of whom had fled the Nazis in the late 1930s.

Yet, before discussing American modernism (or what Philip Meggs, author of *A History of Graphic Design,* calls the "New York School"), it must be acknowledged that during the late 1930s and early 1940s the history of New York graphic design *was* the history of American graphic design. With the notable exceptions of Container Corporation of America and the New Bauhaus, both located in Chicago (and both advancing European ideas of design and advertising), and N. W. Ayer in Philadelphia (America's most progressive national advertising agency), most of the agencies, studios, businesses, journals, and exhibitions promoting American modernism were based in New York or its environs. CBS, the leading corporate purveyor of effective graphic design, was based in midtown Manhattan, as were two of the most influential type/design studios, Huxley House and the Composing Room. The latter sponsored Gallery 303 (the only independent exhibition space in New York devoted to graphic design) and published the small yet content-packed journal *PM* (for "production manager," later renamed *AD* for "art director"), edited by Dr. Robert Leslie and Percy Seitlen.

To appreciate the influence of modernism on the New York design community (and the subsequent reactions to it that fostered other design movements), let's briefly return to some wellsprings from the 1930s. In Brooklyn, students at Abraham Lincoln High School were introduced to European design in art teacher Leon Friend's advanced commercial-art classes. For over three decades, Friend offered the children of immigrant parents to build a career by teaching them graphic and advertising design, illustration, and photography. Many of Friend's graduates became exemplars of American design, including Alex Steinweiss (who designed the first album jacket for Columbia Records and "invented" the container for the 33⅓ rpm record), Gene Federico (a master of modern advertising typography), Bill Taubin (who art directed the "You Don't Have to Be Jewish" campaign for Levy's rye bread), Seymour Chwast (cofounder of Push Pin Studios), and Sheila Levrant de Brettville (chairperson of the Yale University graphic design department). And there were other influential teacher/practitioners, like Howard Trafton at the Art Students' League in Manhattan, who taught Saul Bass, later the pioneer film title designer. At Pratt Institute in Brooklyn, Hershl Leavitt and Tom Benrimo interpreted modernism for a generation of students.

An array of business opportunities and professional support groups made New York an inviting home for a large number of immigrant designers from Central and Eastern Europe. Lucian Bernhard, a German who championed the advertising style known as *Sachplakat,* or the object poster, was among the earliest immigrants in 1922. He set up a one-man studio (with two assistants) and was a prodigious worker, turning out as many as six billboards a month (at twenty-four sheets apiece) for a score of national clients. Also impressive is the list of other accomplished immigrants who established themselves in New York in studios or at magazines and agencies before World War II. Among them were M. F. Agha, Alexey Brodovitch, Cipe Pineles, Will Burtin, Jean Carlu, A. M. Cassandre, Joseph Binder, Ladislav Sutnar, Erik Nitsche, and Leo Lionni. Significant, too, are the native American modernists who adopted New York (and its environs) as their homes, including the midwesterners Lester Beall and Bradbury Thompson. Beall successfully wed Bauhaus ideas with futurist and dada typography, resulting in an unmistakably American vocabulary (dubbed "midwestern modern"), and Thompson enlivened magazine design with playfully rational structures and concepts.

That New York was *the* graphic design city is borne out by its natives who made early contributions to the field. Brooklyn-born Paul Rand had a singular impact on advertising and magazine design with his rational and witty style of modernism that rejected popular sentimental and decorative approaches in layout and typography. Another prominent member of the New York School, William Golden, design director of CBS, was a pioneer of the then-nascent corporate design methodology. After World War II Herb Lubalin, Lou Dorfsman, and Allen Hurlburt also began to make inroads in the areas of advertising and magazine design. It must be noted, however, that with the exception of Cipe Pineles, art director of *Seventeen,* and a few other women, New York design was a male domain until the late 1950s.

The turning point for New York and, thus, for American graphic design in general, marking the transition from the art service to the creative studio, came during the postwar years. Designers were providing not only technical service but also ideas, styles, and identities to business. Among the most significant of the "transitional" studios, Designers 3 and Monogram offered a wide range of eclectic creative services to mass-media clients, among them the publishing and record industries. During this same period corporate America embraced rational modernism (architecture, product, and package design) and invited graphic designers to help mold their communication strategies. In this new era of corporate communications, some veterans felt estranged from—if not ill equipped to cope with—the requisites of big business. Lucian Bernhard, for one, lamented the intrusion of middle-level marketing and communi- cations managers because he believed the quality and effectiveness of his own design suffered when he no longer worked directly with the "men in charge." Yet younger designers not only adapted well to the changes in business but believed that their mission was to change the world through good design. Corporate America was their proving ground. Their job was to organize and systematize, making business messages accessible inside and outside the corporate world.

"Identity" became a watchword of the 1950s. Like little nation/states, American corporations developed "corporate cultures" symbolized by abstract logos and corresponding visual materials. Lippincott and Margulies was the first large identity firm practicing corporate modernism. Later, Unimark, which was headquartered in Chicago but with New York offices headed by Massimo Vignelli, proffered an almost religious adherence to rational design.

The multidisciplinary firm was another key player in the development of New York design. Industrial designers Raymond Loewy, Henry Dreyfuss, Donald Deskey, and Walter Dorwin Teague designed not only machinery but also products and interiors as well as being involved in graphics. George Nelson's firm was concerned with environmental architecture, interiors, and contract furniture, and included a department (headed by Irving Harper and later George Tscherny) that designed promotional materials. This kind of symbiotic relationship proved that there were more opportunities available for the graphic designer than just decorating. In the mid-1950s those graphic designers who were concerned with a big communications picture were serving architects' graphic needs, broadening the realm of graphic design to encompass signage and way-finding.

As design needs changed and paradigms shifted, New York became a hotbed for two conflicting, yet sometimes intersecting, visual sensibilities: modernism and eclecticism. The former is underscored by clean, effective, and often conceptual communications, employing "rational" typography and photography, while the latter is based on historical and vernacular forms. Consistent with the shift in emphasis from decorative to conceptual, design firms (the term "firm" itself suggests a link to business) began to compete with the comparatively smaller design studios.

An early entry into the modern camp, Brownjohn Chermayeff and Geismar, founded in 1957, sought out a broad design base on which to practice. In fact there was not enough available print work to maintain their business, so by necessity the firm became cross disciplinary— including exhibitions and interiors. In 1960, after Brownjohn left the firm, Chermayeff and Geismar designed the groundbreaking abstract logo for Chase Manhattan Bank, a linchpin for them and corporate communications.

Eclecticism was based on revivals of vintage styles and a reapplication of illustration as a design tool. Push Pin Studios was founded in 1954 by Cooper Union classmates Seymour Chwast, Milton Glaser, Reynold Ruffins, and Edward Sorel, masters of this approach. They exhibited a rich historical knowledge cut with a decidedly lighthearted New York vernacular in posters, book jackets, and record covers (all noncorporate communications) as well as through the *Push Pin Monthly*, their promotional magazine. Push Pin's tremendous influence on graphic design can be calculated by the number of derivations appearing in Art Directors Club annuals during the 1960s and by the fact that they were the first graphic design studio to be honored with a retrospective show at the Louvre in Paris.

Yet, despite preferences among designers, New York was not evenly divided into two ideologically segregated camps. The modern and the eclectic sects were numerous. Many designers working under the modern banner would probably reject the idea that they belonged to any "movement" whatsoever. And eclecticism, by definition, is varied and diverse.

In the 1960s and 1970s, as documented through the New York Art Directors Club and AIGA exhibitions and annuals, New York design was varied yet conformed to a "professional" canon. Though standards slowly changed from one year to the next, it can be argued that juries made up of the "old guard" eschewed all but the most undeniably compelling nonmainstream work. Nevertheless, the seeds of design change planted outside the mainstream in the late 1960s blossomed in the mid-'70s when the old guard began to share the stage with newcomers, allowing for the emergence of a "new wave" of typographers and stylists. A few were devoutly modern, others playfully eclectic, and some tirelessly experimental. By this time, New York also shared the stage with other cities that became wellsprings for what is now a national field without regional bias because of shifts in industry and demographics as well as the growing need for graphic design.

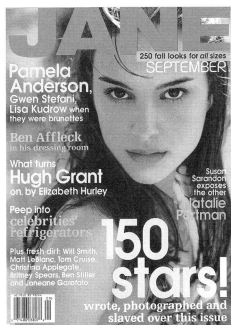

The person or persons who invented magazine coverlines should be dragged out in public, stripped butt naked, and—before undergoing tar-and-feather humiliation—be tattooed all over with the following words in Futura Condensed with shadow and Lightline Gothic ranging in size from twelve to seventy-two points:

Inside:
Special Report:
I Made Magazine Covers Ugly,
Exclusive:
Page 2

Such treatment would be just retribution for the crime perpetrated against magazines by coverlines. Their use today has done more to lower the aesthetic standards of magazine design than any of the other maladies affecting late–twentieth-century periodical publishing.

The coverline, also known as the teaser or refer (short for "referral"), are those headlines on a front cover that announce—or sell—the lead story or entire contents of a particular magazine. With the venerable exception of the *New Yorker* (which prints its coverlines on flaps attached to newsstand copies only, so as not to impinge on the cover art, a practice it borrowed from the late

WigWag magazine), every *commercial* magazine uses them in one form or another. Most are ill conceived.

Okay, not *all* magazine coverlines are grossly handled: *Metropolis,* for one, seamlessly integrates its refers into the overall design; *Atlantic Monthly* tastefully composes the few that it has so as not to interfere with the cover image; and *Rolling Stone,* though laden with an abundance of coverlines, routinely changes typefaces to express the mood of the cover photograph. But these are exceptions to a convention that has turned the most valuable piece of editorial real estate into a waste dump of intrusive typography.

Fashion, lifestyle, and shelter magazines, like *Vogue, Elle, Cosmopolitan, Vanity Fair, Conde Nast Traveler, Mademoiselle, Redbook, McCall's, Brides, Glamour, Jane,* and *Better Homes and Gardens* are among the worst offenders. Headlines crisscross their respective covers like scaffolding in front of a construction site, obstructing any possible effectiveness of the central image. But even worse, when displayed in magazine shops and on newsstand or supermarket racks, their critical mass presents a typographic jumble that negates anything resembling a design standard. Whatever strategic benefit might possibly be gained by having excessive selling copy on the front cover is invariably reduced to almost nil by the fact that most magazines are doing it.

The current practice of squeezing as much hyperbolic verbiage as possible onto a cover started back in the late 1970s and early 1980s, when former Condé Nast design czar, Alexander Liberman (b. 1912), ordered the designers of the fashion and lifestyle magazines under his command to reject haute design in favor of techniques common to sensationalistic tabloids, like the *National Enquirer.* These tropes had already been adopted by the underground press and punk publications. Liberman reasoned that fashion had become too frou-frou and required an injection of grit that could be accomplished through crass graphic design. Concurrently, marketing experts believed that coverlines would increase visibility and attract customers in a highly competitive field. In theory the chaotic approach mirrored changing social attitudes; nevertheless, the shift from the old to a new style—from elegance to controlled sensationalism— marked the first step in a devolution of commercial magazine cover design from pure concept to advertising billboard.

Covers were once designed with emphasis on a strong image. In the 1930s magazines like *Vanity Fair, Vogue,* and *Harper's Bazaar* didn't even use coverlines. When newsstand competition became more intense in the 1950s and 1960s, coverlines were more common, but, as a rule, short headlines introduced a magazine's main theme or lead story, while possibly a few B-heads signaling off-leads were unobtrusively placed in a corner. When that balance between image and text shifted in the 1980s, the aesthetics also changed. Billboards composed of discordant typefaces, dropped out of black boxes or primary color bands, mortised around photographs, and printed in nauseatingly fluorescent colors became the norm. Condé Nast's covers were routinely more cluttered than most, but its competitors sank to the occasion by accordingly junking up their own. Coincidentally, as the overall size of magazines shrank because of higher paper costs, the quantity of coverlines grew. Even magazines that are not part of this genre, such as *Newsweek* and *Time,* have increasingly become more cover-line dependent.

Once the die was cast, coverlines became a widespread "necessary" evil. Certain magazines have tried to be more tasteful than, say, *Vogue* or *Mademoiselle,* but with so many headlines to juggle, even good design intentions are thwarted. On the whole, magazine covers are inferior to much of the advertising inside. Cover images are wallpaper against which headlines are surprinted, dropped out, and otherwise superimposed. As a consequence, the impact of art and photography on the covers of commercial magazines has declined precipitously to the point that startling (or even memorable) covers, like those George Lois conceived and designed for *Esquire* in the 1960s, are rare exceptions to the rule.

Another consequence is that coverlines, and therefore covers themselves, are decided upon by committees in the same way a broadsheet newspaper is planned out. Editors aggressively vie to get teasers for their stories placed on the cover. The designer's role is no longer to solve conceptual visual problems but to arrange or compose type for maximum impact. But even that job is often usurped by editors. A designer for a high-circulation style magazine, who requested anonymity, describes one such cover approval procedure: "The cover subject is decided upon by the editor, usually a portrait of a celebrity who is hot at that moment. After the image is shot and selected, I am given a file of headlines in order of their importance, which I must then somehow lay out so as to highlight sometimes as many as three lead and three off-lead stories while retaining the integrity of the photograph. After I've managed to solve the puzzle, more or less to my satisfaction, the comp is invariably noodled to death with comments like 'This headline is too large; this is not large enough. Why not use a color band here, or drop out the color there?' The bottom line is that the cover has to smack the reader in the eyes at the expense of design standards." Given the challenge involved in trying to orchestrate so many elements, this designer complains that rarely does the process result in good design.

Of course, one can't blame coverlines (or their makers) for all the ills of periodical design. But the way that they have been used—the increasing number of them on magazines—has had a deleterious effect on entire magazine genres as well as the designers that work on them. "And one last thing," adds the designer bitterly. "It is difficult to develop into a really good designer when what is acceptable is so poor to begin with."

People

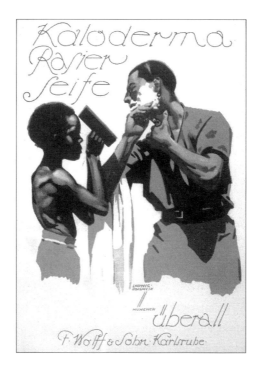

Decades before Germany was carved into East and West, there was a rivalry between North and South, where the graphic arts were as different as the accent of the northern Berliner was from that of the southern Münchener, and just as competitive. Around 1906, *Gebrauchsgraphikers* (commercial artists) in Berlin, led by Lucian Bernhard, spearheaded Germany's revolutionary *Sachplakat,* or object poster, which eliminated superfluous decoration and favored the representation of a single object. Meanwhile, in the Bavarian capital of Munich, Ludwig Hohlwein (1874–1948), a former architect turned *Graphiker,* was in the vanguard of a parallel revolution that rejected such austere simplicity in favor of anecdotal realism. At a time when the poster was the most ubiquitous advertising medium, advertising agents in Berlin and Munich feverishly vied for the nation's leading accounts. But it was the profoundly prolific Hohlwein whose Munich style (or Hohlweinstil) eventually dominated German advertising throughout the late twenties, thirties, and into the forties.

"No one was able to express the fresh, pulsating life which infuses advertising art with such overpowering and captivating force as does Ludwig Hohlwein," wrote an admirer, Walter F. Schubert, in 1926. Although the *Sachplakat* dominated the hoardings, by early 1913 the novelty began to wear thin as third-rate imitations appeared throughout Germany. This is not to say that Hohlwein did not have his share of crass imitators, too, but his brand of heroic realism, which married the influences of German romantic painter Caspar David Friedrich to the

protomodernism of British advertising artist William Nicholson, captured the nation's spirit—
and the consumer's pocketbook.

Poster artists wielded considerable power back then and influenced the buying habits (and
perhaps the thought processes) of a malleable public. Before celebrity testimonials became a
standard feature of hawking and pitch-making, a popular artist served as a virtual spokesperson
for a particular brand or company. The public anticipated the release of that artist's new poster as
if it were a book or play. While today advertising posters and billboards are mostly anonymous
supplements to larger promotional campaigns, when the German poster movements were
rigorous, the poster was the medium that conveyed the strongest message to the largest number
of people. To underestimate its commercial value is to miss a key factor in the consumer
revolution, not just in Germany but throughout industrialized Europe.

Hohlwein, who was born in Wiesbaden on July 26, 1874, entered the limelight after
winning his first graphic arts competition in 1905 with what might today appear to be a prosaic
hunting poster featuring an antler-crowned stag. Being an avid huntsman himself, Hohlwein
adroitly depicted this sacrificial creature given all the majesty of the king of beasts and thus
elicited from the viewer a sense of pride in the ritualistic hunt. Some of his earliest posters were
for hunting and shooting societies, which catered to the Bavarian penchant for blood sports. As a
young architect he designed the interiors of many a hunting lodge, and as a poster artist he
captured the interior life of the hunter. He was also an amazingly skilled though totally self-
taught painter of animals. He could render a horse in all its muscularity because he both studied
and rode horses. For other animals he immersed himself in the details of anatomy.

In 1906 the health food craze that underscores today's lifestyle was prefigured in Germany,
and Hohlwein was commissioned to create posters for "Alcohol Free Restaurants" and to
promote unprocessed foods. His skill at rendering made him the perfect choice for representing
the natural bounty that zealots hoped would convince Germans to embrace nutritional purity
over the heavily advertised packaged foodstuffs on the market. Soon he became the
acknowledged maestro of animal and food illustration.

This specialty was not enough to propel him to the heights of his profession, but it marked
the early stage in a decidedly meteoric rise that made Hohlwein a modern-day court painter. His
patrons were not royalty and aristocracy, although before World War I, the prince regent and the
kaiser made frequent visits to his studio. Rather, they were the kings and princes of business and
industry. Hermann Scherrer, a prestigious Munich tailor for sportsmen, was Hohlwein's first
important client. "Even today the posters that Hohlwein designed for him have lost nothing of
their dash and youthfulness," wrote his friend Walter F. Schubert almost twenty years after the
first one of many appeared around 1909. To promote the shop's merchandise—otherwise
ordinary riding trousers, raincoats, and waistcoats—Hohlwein designed poster vignettes of
sartorially splendid gents that both captured the right pose and made the quotidian iconic. These
pictures were not beyond the ken of the average customer, and even in his more monumental
depictions the figures were as down to earth as his style would allow.

"The form, the face, the expression, the movement, the impression as a whole or in part—

wherever we direct the revealing magnifying glass—we find the same dash, the same arresting, captivating quality, in short the potent canvassing quality," wrote a breathless critic of the day. "These creations . . . have nothing to do with futur-cub- [*sic*] or other isms—they are living, human beings of flesh and blood, living and breathing to their very finger-tips, no matter whether they be Nordic blondes or southern brunettes, man, or woman, drest or undrest [*sic*]."

Hohlwein did not eschew either period or personal style; looking at the posters today, one can easily identify the epoch when they were created. But neither did he resort to graphic tricks or tropes endemic to art moderne, which was au courant at the time. Hohlweinstil defined the period rather than followed it. And while many lesser advertising artists rendered their themes with obvious indifference according to stylistic dictates and templates, Hohlwein was totally absorbed in whatever the subject matter was. His sketchbooks were cornucopias of artistic treasures borrowed from many cultures and different times—"gifts" that he offered his clients and viewers in posters for Sprengel Chocolate, Wolff Cigars, Marco Polo Tea, Artus Steamship Lines, and Wild West Film Co. That he was so convincing in his representations of everything from domestic animals to exotic foreigners was only one reason for his popular acceptance.

Working exclusively from models (often his wife and children), Hohlwein sought the perfect representation. His work lacked the humor found in much Munich cartooning of the time. Instead, German precision was his hallmark. His work was not strictly academic, but his imagination was used for conceptual matters only, not to impose on the figure or form itself. Truth was paramount. Only after making *Vorstudien,* sketches so faithful to nature that not even a photograph could approach the verisimilitude, did he then create the decorative designs and anecdotal compositions he was known for. A 1909 poster for Mayer Sundheimer featuring a bouquet of roses is a case in point: Once he completed the simple flawless sketch from nature, he framed, composed, and highlighted the flowers in such a way that the creation was freed from what one admirer called its "earthly bondage to the widely-effective, ripe, and artistic form of a splendid poster!"

This magic was accomplished at his studio on the Gabelsberger Strasse in Munich where, surrounded by lacquered Buddhas and other artifacts collected from around the world (many of which can be found in his pictures) and under a perpetual cloud of English pipe tobacco smoke, the heavyset, round-cheeked man worked alone on a simple table with his paints and pencils. In contrast to many leading *Gebrauchsgraphikers* of the day, whose assistants and apprentices rendered their work, Hohlwein was perpetually unaided. Every commission was handled personally from start to finish. He took pride in being a loner. Obsession was his religion.

However, not all critics were convinced of the rightness of Hohlwein's method. His technical virtuosity aside, rivals in and out of the *Sachplakat* group argued that he did not always emphasize the object being advertised. That the commodity was not in the center of some pictures caused one such pundits to rail that "Hohlwein advertises himself, not his client." Nevertheless, he mastered both the fatal-dart style of direct promotion and the subtle advertisement that purposefully establishes a mood aimed at a very specific clientele. Hohlwein's art had mass appeal but was never designed to pander to the masses. According to Walter F. Schubert, Hohlweinstil comes out of the culture of good taste: "It seems to me . . . this saturation of the poster with the spirit of the times and society of the day, which serves as a valuable attribute [of Hohlwein's style,] . . . is more important to modern commercial art than all excursions into the heraldic, all coquetting with the antique and all esoteric beating about the bush."

Hohlwein was sought after throughout Europe and the United States. In 1923, a New York exhibition of his posters introduced him to the advertising industry and earned him commissions for Camel and Fatima Cigarettes. In the United States, Hohlwein competed with J. C. Leyen-decker, whose Arrow Shirt Man had become both a successful brand trademark and cultural icon, and with Coles Phillips, whose covers for *Good Housekeeping* and other magazines were equally as influential. Indeed, between Phillips and Hohlwein it is unclear who developed the popular graphic mannerism known as the "fadeaway," where a strong central image literally faded into the background. For that matter the so-called checkerboard device was attributed to Phillips but was repeatedly used in Hohlwein's earlier work. One thing seems clear: Hohlwein pioneered the puddling method, where mineral oil and tempera are mixed, resulting in pleasantly uneven textures. In the American advertising industry, where technique was the deciding factor, Hohlwein's was in demand. But given the competition, he never achieved the same fame as in Germany.

During World War I Hohlwein made posters supporting the "fatherland." These were not typically gruesome depictions of war or venal assaults on the enemy but rather graphic reminders of home-front concerns rendered with characteristic precision. Hohlwein was not a Prussian militarist but he was a Bavarian patriot. When the nationalists of the South opposed the republicans of the North after the war, Hohlwein took a decidedly nationalist stance. For his poster promoting the Stahlhelm (steel helmet) paramilitary (or Freikorps) group of former German soldiers, he was made an honorary member. The poster itself was a masterpiece of persuasion, for he captured the majesty of the profiled, steel-helmeted officer, placing him in a bull's-eye of color that also served as a halo, suggesting a saintly crusader. This marked the first of a long series of works in support of the nationalist cause that evolved into the Nazi movement.

In 1933 Hohlwein wrote a statement in an issue of *Gebrauchsgraphik,* which even in its arch translated version reveals where he stood on the issue of wedding art to—if not politics—patriotism, and by extension the passage indicates the direction his art would take in support of the Nazi regime:

> Today, art, as a cultural factor, is more than ever called upon to take a leading place in building up and conserving cultural values. It must take its place in the front ranks of the legion that Europa has gathered to preserve her individuality against the onslaughts from the East. Art is the best possible disturbing agent for ideas and intellectual tendencies. Commercial art is doubly effective in this sense for it stands in the very forefront, giving form and expression to the daily panorama and forcibly dominating even those who would ordinarily remain impervious to artistic influences. May the best among us realize fully the significance of what is at stake and their own responsibility and may [we] labor creatively and with conviction at the preservation of our cultural civilization and its restoration to perfectly healthy conditions.

Hohlwein's more benign advertising is important to poster history, but his Nazi-era *Plakats* earns the lion's share of attention for its place in propaganda history. At this mature stage in his career he had jettisoned some of the more decorative tendencies in his work for pure painting, which, while decidedly recognizable as Hohlwein's art, was even more traditional in its heroic realism. His figures were given monumental stances and lit to accentuate their grandeur. He did not engage in negative stereotypes, preferring to mythologize rather than demonize. But he did set a standard against which Nazi poster iconography must be judged. It is difficult to say definitively that Hohlwein invented national socialist (or Nazi) realism, but his work was certainly the paradigm.

This southern gentleman was, ironically, known at this time for his depictions of perfect Nordic, Aryan specimens—Hitler youth and bemedaled party members with strong Viking features. Compared to the other Nazi propaganda of the era created by lesser artists, Hohlwein's posters were by far the most virtuosic and perhaps the most effective for the cause in establishing Aryan archetypes. Despite the official removal after the war of all Nazi iconography from all German collections, Hohlwein's posters continue to surface as key examples of the world's most successful, if heinous, propaganda campaign.

Hohlwein became a Nazi party member sometime in 1939 (his NDSAP party number was 294598, which signifies no special distinction or blood orders). He worked directly for the ministry of propaganda and enlightenment in the Nazi régime. But he also completed assignments for other bureaucratic agencies and organizations. In personal papers (obtained by documentarian George Theopholies), Hohlwein notes many jobs where he had tremendous trouble getting paid; indeed he was forced to plead with these clients for his promised fees. It is unclear whether he ever received full recompense, but he continued to do posters for the government and commercial clients who presumably did pay.

In June 1944 his house and studio were directly hit by British bombs, destroying the entire contents of his personal archive. A month later the Brotherhood of Artists in Munich petitioned the Nazis to give Hohlwein temporary housing. As it turned out, the house was located on the grounds of Adolf Hitler's Berchtesgaden estate. Whatever problems Hohlwein had getting paid, he was ultimately honored by the Führer himself (and can be seen standing with him during brief film footage of an event at the main house).

After the war Hohlwein was "denazified," therefore not charged with engaging in felonious Nazi activities and allowed to continue working. Despite the economic devastation that followed the surrender, he continued to make some advertising art until his death from a stroke in 1948. One of his paying accounts was Velveeta, the processed cheese substitute imported to Germany from Belgium. He also earned royalties on images that had been sold to other countries prior to the war and were apparently being reused until the European advertising industry reestablished itself.

Hohlwein was a precisionist, and his images reflect a fealty to craft that even the layperson can (and did) appreciate. He was a model for draftsmen, and close scrutiny of his work evokes the truths of drawing and painting that continue to hold sway. But the best explanation for his success at the time and for the respect granted his virtuosity today is summed up in Hohlwein's own words written in 1925: "I have not changed in my art during all these long years of practice and . . . I have never followed the wild-goose chases of all the short-lived fads and fancies that happened to crop up. I have always been true and faithful to myself, and both inwardly and outwardly I have remained what I was and still am. I have always felt content at heart in the very midst of all this struggle, this wrestling and fearful grind. This feeling is perhaps the best reward for honesty and serious work. Art—and the poster is no exception—is not mere fun and child's play, nor is it a mere passing dance, twirling today and gliding tomorrow."

Leon Friend

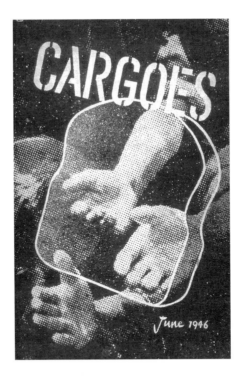

$\mathbf{A}$braham Lincoln High School in Brooklyn, New York, is not as famous as the Bauhaus, Ulm, or Cranbrook—nor is it even especially well known among most New Yorkers, despite the appearance of its old façade in Spike Lee's recent movie *He Got Game*. But for over three decades, between 1930 and 1969, it was a springboard for scores of artists and graphic designers. Lincoln's art department was chaired by Leon Friend, a career art teacher with a special passion for what he called graphic design. Friend's curriculum balanced the fine and applied arts and offered more commercial art courses than most major art schools. He introduced leading contemporary designers to his students and inspired many of them, in turn, to become designers, art directors, illustrators, typographers, and photographers. His program remains a paradigm of mentoring and career development. "For most of us with limited economic resources," asserts Martin Solomon (class of 1948), design director and typographer, "the career choice was to drive a cab. Thanks to Mr. Friend, we could earn a living and be challenged by working with type and image."

Current budgets have been severely slashed for art education at most inner-city public schools because art classes are considered unnecessary today in teaching the three *R*s. But the Abraham Lincoln curriculum encouraged creativity and critical thinking even during the Great Depression, when public funds were even more excruciatingly tight. Mr. Friend, as he was always formally addressed, encouraged individual vision and collaborative activity to low-income Depression-era kids (and later middle-income postwar kids) while giving special emphasis to community service.

He may not have been as well known as design professors László Moholy-Nagy, Gyorgy Kepes, Paul Rand, or Bradbury Thompson. Yet Friend, who was born in Warsaw in 1902 and lived his early years as the son of a shopkeeper in Schenectady, New York, accomplished in a high school setting what many colleges and universities fail to do even today: place the applied arts in a historical as well as practical context. From freshman year his students were taught typography, layout, and airbrush techniques while other schools were teaching basket weaving. The title of his class was "Graphic Design," but this term was defined broadly. His students drew and painted images from imagination and experience, designed posters that invited people to do and know things, and composed pages that presented stories, poems, and images they had written and drawn. They used charcoal, paint, pencils, ink, Zipatone, brushes, and X-acto knives. For Friend, graphic design was an inclusive and expressive activity. "We were taught honesty (in design and application), clarity (of thought and presentation), and fidelity (of concept and rendition)," writes a former student, Edwin Orans, in a twenty-fifth anniversary testimonial booklet.

Friend's curriculum was more than a departure from the standard, cookie-cutter pedagogy; it challenged the common assertion that art education was merely ethereal. His history classes broadened the knowledge of those who took them; his studio classes forced teenagers to solve professional problems; and his guest lecture classes (featuring László Moholy-Nagy, Lucian Bernhard, Joseph Binder, Lynd Ward, Chaim Gross, and Moses Soyer) offered his students a rare introduction to the masters of commercial and fine art. Friend's midterm and final exams required that each student be versed in how culture is defined by the intersecting histories of fine and applied art. What other high school test paper included questions about perspective using E. McKnight Kauffer or A. M. Cassandre posters as visual examples? "The tests show to what extent we, as high school students, were required to comprehend the history of all art and its relationship to industrial, architectural, and graphic design," states Gene Federico (class of 1936), cofounder of Lord Geller Federico, who says Friend inspired him to become an advertising designer.

High school art teachers may be dedicated, but Friend was passionate. "He was a charismatic father figure who gave me an appreciation of typography and design and equated success in these areas with achieving nirvana," says Seymour Chwast (class of 1948), cofounder of Push Pin Studios, who says Friend opened his eyes to design. Although Friend kept his personal life far removed from the classroom (to this day, few alumni know much about his background), he gave his entire professional life to his students. In return, however, he required their devotion, not to him, but to their futures. Needless to say, Friend was not just a catalytic presence but a teacher who (to paraphrase Albert Einstein) awakened joy in creative expression and knowledge. "Coincident with the discipline of learning and the practicing of what was learned was the daily contact over a four-year period with Leon Friend, the man," recalls Alex Steinweiss (class of 1934), the first designer of record albums in the late 1930s. "This in itself was a source of inspiration and psychological strength that went far in developing in the students the rudiments of a lifestyle."

Friend wanted his students—protégés, actually—to have every opportunity to succeed in the real world, and so he founded a quasi-professional extracurricular club called the Art Squad, which for its members was more important than any varsity football, basketball, or baseball team. Participation in this daily program (seven days a week) was limited to thirty students per year representing all the grades. Located in Lincoln's Room 353, Friend gave the Art Squad autonomy under the tutelage of an elected student leader who served for an eighteen-month term. Membership was by invitation and sponsorship of another student; it required a portfolio review by the membership committee. Members worked for a common cause and developed personal strengths. According to Friend, "Each of the 30 talented members is selected for practically life membership by a vote of his peers. . . . For his Squad work [the student] obtains neither marks nor school credit but personal satisfaction in a job well done." Gene Federico recalls: "To be accepted as a member was an honor and privilege." Alex Steinweiss, like scores of others, continued to be an alumnus "lifetime" member for decades after he graduated, which meant donating time and work to the group. Responsibilities for student members included designing and printing posters for school events, maintaining the school's bulletin boards (Chwast remembers designing a poster admonishing students to comb their hair), as well as doing illustration and layout for *Cargoes,* the Abraham Lincoln literary magazine.

The Squad was neither a gaggle of hall monitors nor junior varsity swabs but a dedicated group of young people judged by professional standards. Friend, who had a Charlie Chaplin build, would always arrive in his office at 6 A.M. ("wearing the same gray suit every day," notes Chwast) and expected all squadders to do the same. Steinweiss concurs: "The members of this group usually arrived at school well before classes in the early morning and left for home well after classes were over, often in the early evening." The work ethic was infectious, and the result was remarkable. "Your work wasn't compared with high school work, it was compared with *Harper's Bazaar,*" writes former *New York Post* reporter and former art squadder Jerry Tallmer.

New York City was once a fairly large client for posters, and Friend encouraged students to enter work into citywide public-service poster competitions as well as others for the World's Fair, the American Cancer Society, the Rapid Transit System, and the Department of Sanitation, which offered monetary awards. Sheila de Bretteville (class of 1959), chair of the graduate design program at Yale University, recalls that she won a poster competition designed to encourage people to get regular medical attention. And experiences like hers both gave students confidence *and* separated the wheat from the chaff in a practical manner. Life was Friend's laboratory. De Bretteville says, "He had a rather complete vision of how to mainstream students by introducing them to graphic design, the arts, the community around them, the city, and the history of the design arts profession as he understood it to be. He was eager for us to enter the profession and succeed professionally. The wide range of images available to us through his classes and his personal library [included] Käthe Kollwitz's prints of war's destruction, Cassandre's posters of the delight of drinking Dubonnet, [and] Savignac's utopian [depiction of the] thrill of locomotives. They were presented without differences, as if . . . equal, making it possible for each of us to choose whatever and whichever subject matter [was] attractive to us." Friend's method was so successful that, according to Alex Steinweiss, "many who weren't fortunate enough to win scholarships [to art school] went directly into the art job market upon the basis of their high school training and carved out important careers as art directors, designers, and photographers."

Steinweiss, Federico, Chwast, Solomon, and de Bretteville were only a few of the illustrious alumni. Throughout the years, Friend's classes were a who's who of diverse talents, including William Taubin (art director of the "You Don't Have to Be Jewish" ad campaign for Levy's rye bread), Irving Penn (the photographer who began as a graphic designer), Jay Meisel (photographer), and Richard Wilde (chair of graphic design and advertising at the School of Visual Arts), and other prominent professionals. While not everyone in the Art Squad continued on into a career involving design or the fine arts, the ratio of those who did was significantly higher than at other schools—and directly proportionate to the attention Friend gave to his students.

Although Friend, who was never a designer himself, was inspired by the Bauhaus, he never imposed any specific doctrine on his students other than the requirement to do good work. He was, in fact, so reticent about passing on constricting dogma that he rarely referred to his own book, *Graphic Design* (coauthored with Joseph Hefter in 1936), which was used as a textbook in other schools. Although the book's content is today dated and some of the chapters were a bit parochial at the time of publication, Friend was one of the first American educators to introduce progressive European design ideas. Many alumni say that they did not even know about the book until long after they were graduated, which is odd because in it he gives a very astute explanation of what he wanted students to learn: "The essential factors in successful graphic expression are a knowledge of *tradition* of the craft (though not a slavish nor an academic one), a consideration of the *purpose* for which the design is intended, *imagination,* and a control of the requisite skill which will leave the artist free for self expression."

Because Friend entered the teaching profession at a time when graphic design was a potential means to escape the economic hardship of the Depression, he was by necessity an exponent of practical pedagogy or what one alumnus called "the achievement method." By allowing his students a chance to develop at their own pace and discover their own strengths and weaknesses, Friend made an indelible contribution to many lives. "The impact of his personality on the young in his awakening of immature minds to constructive problems and his skilled guidance of thought patterns are reflected in the exciting careers of his protégés," writes Edwin Orans. In 1969, his former students mounted a commemorative exhibition of their professional work at New York's Architectural League in his honor. Friend was so esteemed that the description of his legacy was placed into the *Congressional Record* by Senator Jacob Javits. In view of the number of alumni who participated in the exhibit and those around today who say they are proud to be "apostles of the creed of Leon Friend," he was indeed the quintessential mentor.

From 1948 to 1955, Elaine Lustig Cohen was married to the charismatic modern design pioneer Alvin Lustig. After his death in 1955 she emerged as a prolific graphic and signage designer in her own right. But this story begins with Cohen's seven-year marriage to Lustig. What she learned from him and how it was translated are crucial to understanding her own modernist practice. How she was employed by former Lustig clients underscores her role as a designer. That is, did they want her to continue "a Lustig style," or was she allowed to develop her own personality? Although she managed his office in Los Angeles and New York and continued to run his business for a short time after his death before founding her own, Cohen's work had its own vigor and identity.

Alvin Lustig wed principles of modern painting and sculpture to commercial art, and during the forties and early fifties he helped define American modernism. As founder of Yale's graphic design department he also exerted great influence on the profession. But in 1950 chronic diabetes began to erode his vision; by 1954 he was virtually blind. Although his impaired condition did not prevent him from directing his wife and assistants in every meticulous detail of the work he could no longer see, his illness forced Elaine Lustig into an accelerated rate of professional maturity. She had learned how to do pasteups and spec type, and she rendered a few of Lustig's last book jackets (while he specced color by referring to the color of a chair or sofa in their apartment). But as a designer she was a total novice.

Lustig died in 1955 and left not only a legacy but many unfinished commissions that clients assumed would be completed by his widow. Little did they know that when Lustig was alive she had not designed at all. "As a rule," Cohen says, "no one in the Lustig office designed except Alvin himself." So his wife and assistants, which included a former student, Ivan Chermayeff, did the dirty work while Lustig—dressed in a crisp white shirt and tie—sat at his immaculate marble desk with only a tracing pad on which he made thumbnail sketches. Yet despite Cohen's inexperience, she had learned enough through "osmosis" to take on the challenges: "With all the pressures of our lives I didn't realize it, but by the time of Alvin's death I really was ready to work on my own."

When twenty-year-old Elaine Firstenberg met Alvin Lustig, twelve years her senior, in 1948 at the opening of a new Los Angeles art museum, she had already been smitten by modern art and wanted to paint like Stuart Davis. When she was fifteen, she accidentally wandered into the Museum of Non-Objective Painting in Manhattan, where Peggy Guggenheim's collection of Kandinsky paintings were exhibited in an installation designed by Kiesler. The modern sensibility touched such a chord that she later enrolled in the art department of Sophie Newcomb College at Tulane University, which was founded on the principles of the Chicago Bauhaus. In those days women were not encouraged to study art as an end in itself, and so Cohen was compelled to take art education courses in preparation for a career as teacher. After graduation, she taught in an LA public school for a year before romance changed her life.

Firstenberg married Lustig after a whirlwind courtship and took a job in his office that she describes as "the office slave." Lustig presumed that she would work in some capacity but hadn't intended to teach her graphic design. "Teaching me was not even an issue," she recalls. "It was, after all, a different time." But he did encourage her to help him with interior design projects by researching and selecting materials for later use. On her own she also made collages for unpublished children's books and sketches of fantasy furniture. She was a talented though untutored draftsperson, who eventually learned how to make working drawings by watching others in the office. Nevertheless, she languished, bereft of the hands-on experience that even her previous teaching post offered.

At the time, California suffered from a weak economy and hardly enough industry to support a healthy design profession. So an invitation from Joseph Albers for Lustig to establish a design program at Yale was a good reason for the couple to move to New York in 1950. Around this time Lustig began to suffer the early symptoms of his illness. Cohen was the only one who knew about the irreversible prognosis, which for a year she kept secret—even from Lustig. "I walked around with a hole in my stomach," she recalls. When she admitted to him that he was going blind, he stubbornly continued to practice business as usual, relying more on his wife than ever before.

When the end came, Cohen was thrust into the vortex of a design business. Only a few weeks after the funeral, architect Philip Johnson, who had earlier engaged Lustig to design the signage for the new Seagram's Building in New York, called Cohen to ask when she would have the first stage of the project—an alphabet—ready for presentation. In the face of this rude awakening, she completed the commission from scratch. Her success forged a beneficial relationship with Johnson. Soon she closed down Lustig's business and began working from home. "I knew that with an office I'd be working only to keep my employees occupied, and didn't want that kind of headache," she explains. Around the same time Arthur Cohen—the publisher of Meridian Books, Lustig's client, the couple's best friend, and later Elaine's husband—called her to say that his new list of thirty book jackets and covers was due. So began another trial by fire.

In addition to hundreds of jackets and covers, Cohen designed lobby signs and catalogs for the Museum of Modern Art in New York, the Museum of Primitive Art, the Museum of Modern Art in Rio, and Lincoln Center (in concert with Chermayeff and Geismar on signage that was never adopted). She was hired by the famed New York architects Harrison and Abramovitz to design graphics for the 1964 World's Fair. Most of her commissions came through architects, whose own designs were complemented by what she called somewhat anonymous work. With her good friend Richard Meier, who had not yet earned his major architectural commissions, she designed various building interiors, including the graphics and interior motif for Sono, an Indian government–sponsored crafts store on Fifth Avenue, which in its day was distinguished for its modern grace and simplicity. In 1963 she began a relationship with the Jewish Museum in New York, designing catalogs, invitations, bags, and exhibition installations.

Her work was resolutely modern. Ornament was eschewed in favor of functional typography. Pure geometry was preferred over amorphous shapes and forms. While not as devoutly utopian as Lustig, Cohen once said that she was "brainwashed" into wanting to design everything. So, in her capacity as a one-person studio, she maintained an exhausting schedule. She quickly developed a visual personality that was at once distinct from like-minded practitioners, such as Paul Rand, Rudy de Harak, and Chermeyeff and Geismar, yet consistent with the same modern art principles.

Cohen's early book jackets, such as Constantine Stanislavski's *My Life in Art* and Rager Fry's *Vision and Design* are evocative of Alvin Lustig's late work, notably in her script signature, which she eliminated after 1957. Her adaptation of simple graphic elements and economical typography were also borrowed from Lustig. Yet, as she developed more confidence in her own vision, she began to experiment more with concepts.

Her knowledge of forgotten twentieth-century avant-garde typography—which she began studying while married to Lustig and passionately continued during her years with Arthur Cohen—inspired a synthesis of classic modern and contemporary sensibilities in her work. *The Writings of Martin Buber* and Buber's *For the Sake of Heaven* both derive from examples of the 1920s New Typography: the former influenced by, yet not imitative of, Schwitters and El Lissitzky; the latter, a synthesis of John Heartfield's jacket collages and Mark Rothko's abstraction. By the early 1960s her jackets and covers suggested a very eclectic vision.

Cohen retained some of Lustig's working habits but not his palette, his type preferences, or his personal marks. Like Lustig, she made scores of tiny idea sketches in order to define a total solution. But unlike Lustig, who in his later years completely intellectualized his work, never, *ever* dirtying his hands with mechanicals, she enjoyed what the hand could do and reveled in the meditative pleasure of doing pasteups, where she fiddled with details. Indeed her work, though rooted in rationalism, depended on the accidents that the hand forced. Design for Cohen was not unlike painting or collage; in fact, it was a game. Playfulness was evident in her interior book work through extended title-page treatments, unconventional at the time, in which a book developed cinematically, building up speed with type that stretched over a number of pages until finally beginning the text. Her fondness for kinetic solutions set her apart from others who practiced the more conventional bookmaking approaches. In the tightly budgeted bookmaking field, using extra pages to establish a book's visual persona was indeed a luxury.

By the time Cohen was totally comfortable with who she was as a designer, she had also reached a dead end. As the sole proprietor of a home/office, she was confined to virtually the same client base that she began with—museums, publishers, and architectural signage. "It had backfired on me that I didn't have an office," she says. "Working alone, I couldn't do large projects." In fact, to get the FAA account in the early sixties, she asked friends to sit at desks in her office and look busy during the client pitch. She had no desire to repeat that kind of folly. So, in 1969, after over a decade of independent practice, she informed her clients that she was turning her attention to painting.

The way Cohen saw it, moving forward as a designer would have forced her to focus on commerce rather than the art of her practice. And unlike Lustig, who believed that design and art were one and the same, Cohen saw design and painting as separate but equal. Her return to painting and collage was not a repudiation of what she had done but another passion in a life of artistic passions.

Before the "new wave" hit America in the early 1970s, some Japanese graphic designers were already playing with many of the quirky visual forms and discordant relationships that typified the Western postmodern aesthetic. Before the Swiss grid was torn apart, Japanese typography was already entering an anarchic multileveled phase. In fact, contrary to the prevailing myth that Japanese graphic design is essentially derivative of Western culture, some of the most progressive contemporary graphic experiments were conducted in Japan prior to their introduction here. A few key Japanese designers can lay claim to these accomplishments, but none more so than Hirano Kôga, who since 1965 has defined the alternative graphic design movement through his posters and book jackets, which both disrupted and eventually influenced the status quo.

In 1964, when sixties countercultures began to emerge in Europe and the United States, Kôga helped found and became the poster, program, and scenic designer for one of Japan's burgeoning underground theater companies, the June Theater, which in 1968 changed its name to the Black Tent Theater. The "theater of outside theaters," as Kôga describes this radical alternative to the traditional, commercial production companies, barnstormed throughout Japan, playing to audiences under a big black tent. The repertoire included politically and socially confrontational Japanese themes as well as adaptations of Brecht and other political Western drama, farce, and musicals. The posters he created during his tenure between 1968 and 1982, when he passed the torch to a younger generation, were stylistically varied. But, today, as a body, they could easily be mistaken as having been influenced by the Dutch, English, or American hothouse approaches that employ multiple transparencies and layer upon layer of typographic material.

Kôga's design for the Black Tent Theater was not so much ahead of its time as it was a unique and distinctive reflection of the Japanese alternative art scene of the late sixties and seventies. Unlike much commercial Japanese design of the period, Kôga's was essentially void of American influence. But in the postmodern sense, he nevertheless liberally borrowed from diverse sources also tapped into by Americans. Most notable was German dada, which he idiosyncratically translated into a Japanese graphic idiom when he jarringly combined the two traditional methods of Japanese writing—horizontal and vertical—which required that the viewer/reader have different vantage points on the same page. Through radically contorted, hand-drawn Japanese characters, he created word images that spoke volumes. And, in a protopunk, ad hoc manner, he jaggedly cut and pasted (or, rather, *threw*) photographs and drawings onto layouts that looked as if they had been designed only minutes before going to press. But looks can be deceiving. No matter how immediate they appeared, Kôga painstakingly achieved his results.

Kôga says his method was not "desk work," which is his way of comparing the clean, staid board work of other Japanese "corporate" designers to the kind of action-design created for the moment. Yet not every poster was slap-and-paste. During the period of the Black Tent Theater, which overlapped with various other projects, he did not adhere to a single style. Some of his most exquisite posters were homages to the nineteenth-century Japanese woodblock tradition; his signature typographic twists brought the colorful retro illustrations up to date. On occasion he also marshaled the strength of a powerful black-and-white photograph, to which he added subversively tame typography, underscoring the force of an image.

Kôga was fluent in many forms of graphic expression before joining the alternative movement. His styles owed much to the same influences that had an impact on left-wing Japanese graphic designers of the late 1920s and early 1930s, such as German expressionism, the Russian avant-garde, George Grosz, and Vladimir Mayakovsky. He was born in 1938 in Seoul, Korea, where his father worked during the Japanese occupation, and after the war moved to Tokyo in 1945. As a teenager, Kôga aspired to be an architect; however, when he was nineteen years old, he entered the design department of Musashino Art University to study graphic design. One of his earliest student posters, a proposal for an advertisement for a book titled *Jump before Seeing* by Kenzaburo Oe, was awarded the grand prix by Nissenbi, the Association of Japanese Advertising Designers and Artists. In the rigidly hierarchical Japanese business system, this prize was the key to a professional career. In 1961, he was hired by the prestigious advertising division of Takashimaya Department Store, where he spent two years designing newspaper ads.

"Designers in those days were considered unimportant," he is quoted in a 1985 interview. "[Clients] were suspicious of the word 'design.'" After two years of stultifyingly proscribed work he quit to go freelance. His left-wing political interests led him in 1964 to help found the June Theater group. Later that same year he also earned his first commission to design a book—*The Wesker Trilogy*, for Shobunkan (Shobun-sha) Publishing Company. Since then he has designed

262

for them literally thousands of jackets and covers, which today provide a vivid evolutionary picture of both his career and visual persona.

Kôga entered the field at a time when Japanese industry began seriously competing in the world market, and so design emerged as a highly respected, indeed commercially necessary profession. Nevertheless, he cautiously notes that he remained rebellious despite the fact that the mid-sixties had become a "golden time" for Japanese designers. "Still a newcomer in a designers' world, I told myself not to fall [into the trap] of people's admiration," he relates. "I wanted to avoid becoming popular . . . so I could do things my own way . . . and not be in a situation where I was always thinking about meeting expectations." Yet, while he unconventionally toyed with the Japanese language in ways that other designers had not previously done, he insists he was not a reformer. "I accepted the Japanese typesetting systems as they were." Moreover, regarding his book work, he believed—and still believes—that the writing was more important than the graphic design. "It is crucial that the book is to be read," he says.

Kohei Sugirua, a Japanese design scholar, comments that through his book work Kôga is responsible for introducing the European style to Japanese graphic design. A great many of his book jackets do indeed echo certain contemporary French methods of typographical punning and some German grid structures. But the European influence is not something new to Japanese design. In the 1920s European layout and imagery were introduced to Japan through various trade magazines and a twenty-six-volume encyclopedia, titled *Commercial Art,* showing how to apply these graphic styles to everything from trademarks to window displays. Kôga has simply extended this legacy. But he also states, "I've never consciously tried to do my work in a European style. Nevertheless I think the European taste was within me before I became a designer." While some of his book jackets are for Japanese reprints of European and American titles from which he may borrow an illustration or other elements of the original foreign design, his work is rarely a verbatim translation. "Turning western idioms into something Japanese is not part of his approach," writes James Fraser in a 1993 catalog accompanying an exhibition of Kôga's work at Fairleigh Dickinson University Library. "Yes, there are influences, but more in that subtlety in which a master draws the viewer's eyes into the unfamiliar by giving an illusion of the familiar."

Despite his rebellious nature, Kôga prefers the book-jacket medium for the limitations that are imposed. "I have to be given some restrictions for my work—in colors, size, etc.," he admits. "[Then] I can come up with more interesting ideas by trying to be as eccentric as possible within the restriction." He points to his "yellow series" of books for Shobun-sha as a good example of how constraints are conducive to great work. Each of the two-color jackets in this series are printed in bright yellow with a hard-to-read bold black *kakimoji* (handwritten character) on the front. While a seemingly abstract design, the characters reveal a message when more than five different books are shown together. Kôga is amused at the thought that some people will understand, while others will miss it entirely.

He also prefers book publishing because he does not want to be an "outsider"—at least in terms of the editorial process. "An ideal system for book designers," he reports, "is one where they are the exclusive designer for the publishing company [not a freelance agent]. I say this because I myself cannot be merely a designer. I have to be working in the group of people who know the plan." As an intimate member of this group—the one who gives the visual identity to the project by extrapolating his own visual identity—Kôga insists that "I try not to reflect any personal matters in my work." He says that within this group comprised of an editor and associates everyone must have an ideal image of how the book is supposed to look. The editor, however, is in charge of "coordinating" people so that everyone in the group shares the same ideal image. Sometimes, of course, this is impossible, and so Kôga draws his image from the images of everyone, and "from there I create my own design." Mari Hyodo, a scholar and translator, says that this seemingly contradictory procedure stems "from the typical mentality of Japanese groupism where public and private affairs cannot be completely separated."

Where Kôga's subjectivity and objectivity totally splits is in the realm of letterforms. "Designing a character is almost like awakening the original soul in it," he says about his deep passion for what he calls the power of letters. Kôga recognizes in kanji, the Chinese-derived characters that comprise one of the principal Japanese forms of writing, a visually unequaled tool. "As a rule, each Chinese character is a picture," he continues. "People from cultures using the Roman alphabet often say that a Chinese character is like a well-composed abstract painting. That may well be true [for them], but for us, these characters give an all too concrete picture. . . . One would be amazed by its descriptive and symbolic impact but also experience a moment of bliss in which shape and meaning coincide and reveal themselves simultaneously." This articulation of a design philosophy goes to the heart of what Kôga hopes will happen when he does his job well: "One would no longer need to wonder which came first, the shape or the meaning. It becomes a composition demanding that the reader receive it with all five senses."

But this statement should not be misconstrued as the search for the perfectly harmonious letterform. Although he calls dreadful typesetting "frightening," within his own qualitative standards Kôga can make understated or overstated typographic choices. "I don't like to make characters look too soft or beautiful but rather have a character that will force people to think and wonder when they look at it." He is fond of *maru-gochi*, round gothic type common on store signs. "I like it, but I'm scared at the same time. Why? Because [it represents] all of these dreadful things, like the label on eye lotion or signs for the Shibashi Station. Nevertheless I use it a lot because *I am* threatened."

His work for other alternative political and cultural manifestations, such as *Takarajimi* (Treasure Island), a magazine now credited with influencing contemporary Japanese youth culture, and the *Water Buffalo News* ("Water Buffalo" implying the toil of Asian people, and this periodical attempting to build unity among working-class people throughout the world) are examples of how Kôga reclaims gothic letterforms from crass commercial use and imbues them with symbolism—indeed, makes them hip. Type used on posters for the Water Buffalo Band performances often reflect the content of a particular thematic show. A particularly rough, hand-drawn headline on a Caravan Band concert poster echoes the proto–*Bevis and Butthead* style of the comic drawing of the featured band.

Recently, Kôga has turned his attention almost exclusively to typography, creating letterforms and compositions that push the Japanese character into new areas of expression. With the exception of a few curious homages, such as *William Morris Kenkyu* (Studies on William Morris, 1991), a comp for a book about the English master in which he readdresses the Morris aesthetic in a uniquely Japanese interpretation, few of his current works bear any resemblance to European models. Over the past decade, as Japanese graphic design generally has found its own unique persona, Kôga has led the way in developing a typographic vocabulary and design language that belongs exclusively to him and Japan.

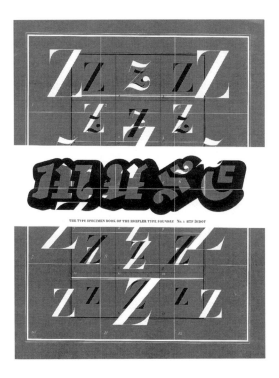

Jonathan Hoefler (b. 1970) is a family man. That is to say, he is interested in the way that type families "evolve in ways that are unconventional." One of his more unprecedented projects is a curiously dysfunctional type family called Fetish, a postmodern joke on type design that he admits is "also kind of a commentary on some of the things that I find curious and questionable about contemporary typography." Fetish 338, Hoefler's first design in a series of typographic musings, collects many of the eccentricities that he says have come to be associated with classicism: "It is overly flowered and ornamented, and rococo and baroque at the same time." A send-up of such typefaces, it nonetheless has pedagogical value in that it forces users to address the nature of typographic eccentricity.

He developed another in this series, Fetish 976, as a parody of those very functional faces used for specific tasks, like telephone directories. "Fetish 976 is designed in a way that aestheticizes the function," explains Hoefler. "It contains many aspects of use, like ink traps to allow for reproduction in small sizes on bad paper printed on web-offset presses. But rather than using these things functionally, the theme of the typeface is to actually *be* an ink trap." These attributes are used in completely unnecessary ways that appear to be technical and functional but are in fact technically and functionally ridiculous. Incidentally, the numerals in the Fetish series titles are also parody. "They come from the fact that every art director I know has a favorite typeface that has a pedigree attached to it. It's always Caslon 540 or Garamond 3. The 976 prefix comes from toll-free calls," he adds.

Unconventional faces, like the Fetish family, reflect Hoefler's developing type philosophy, and to further express his ideas he publishes *Muse,* a catalog cum magazine that both exhibits type and offers commentaries on type culture. In fact, an essay in the first issue of *Muse* critiques the bugaboo word "experimental," which he believes is flagrantly bandied about with regard to type design. Preferring the measured word "speculative," he insists that, "Unfortunately, experimental has become so married to 'unusual,' that it becomes a way of foreclosing the whole discussion on new type. I read an article about one of the faces submitted to Neville Brody's *Fuse* in which the designer said that it could not be evaluated in traditional terms because it is an *experimental* design. To me that is a cop-out. It's either a work of design or it's a work of fine art. . . . But to make no distinction between typefaces that can be used for conveying words and those that can't, muddies the field."

His own speculative typefaces are the means to answer self-imposed questions about type form and function, yet when working on commissions for types for magazines and newspapers, he routinely analyzes whether the world, in fact, needs a new face. Hoefler lists two criteria for designing a typeface: "First, I don't want to design any faces I can't imagine using myself; second, the concerns of readers are paramount, and the art directors I work for are there to safeguard those concerns."

However, readability is only one aspect of what makes a successful type. Hoefler worked on a series of faces called Knockout (a face in different weights: Flyweight, Bantamweight, Featherweight, Lightweight, Welterweight, Middleweight, Cruiserweight, and Sumo), which began as an update of his Champion Gothic, one of the first type families he designed for *Sports Illustrated.* The challenge with this project was to make a face that is functional "in a very bulletproof way, so that a designer can pick one of the faces and use it safely in small sizes for, say, a chart without much difficulty," he confides. "Yet also imbue it with enough character that it becomes interesting in display sizes. There are things about the style of this letter that resonate with me in some way, that I hope come through, both in the very sober applications and their very avantgarde applications."

Hoefler creates revivals, but the results are rarely nostalgic. "There is something about a Hoefler design, call it his personality, that may be rooted in the wood-type era but is totally contemporary," says Janet Froelich, art director of the *New York Times Magazine,* referring to his update of the *Times's* antique version of Cheltenham, which suggests tradition but is not a slave to the original design. "I think it is his attention to detail that stands out," adds John Korpics, art director of *Entertainment Weekly,* who as art director at *Gentlemen's Quarterly* commissioned Hoefler to design Mazarin. "We wanted a strong, masculine face, but not a thick slab serif. Jonathan instinctively knew exactly what characteristics needed to be drawn from both history and the present to accomplish the task." And, although the family of faces commissioned for *Rolling Stone* are slab serifs designed along nineteenth-century lines, they're not explicit revivals. "The type looks like something from Stephenson Blake [the venerable English type foundry] *and* from Herb Lubalin [the late master of phototype]," says Hoefler. "It's got a very specific style to it. But that family of designs includes, in addition to the four Victorian styles, the Egyptian, the

Gothic, the Latin, and the Grecian, a set of italics for all of them, two of which, the Latin Italic and the Grecian Italic, never existed historically—they're mythical."

Hoefler spends inordinate time solving technical problems that leave other designers impatient. His proprietary typeface for Apple Computer, for example, was a challenge "because it had more to do with satisfying engineers rather than art directors, who bring a very different set of notions to the table," says Hoefler. "They're not as interested in the style of letters as in the way in which they're used, the way in which they're encoded, and that was a good challenge for me." In 1991 Hoefler met an engineer who explained that Apple was working on a new technology for type, which ultimately came to be called TrueType GX, which was an attempt to automate a lot of the aspects of typography that are tedious—ligature insertion, smart quotes, things like that. Since Hoefler Text had a broad-enough character set and was steeped in classical typography as opposed to digital typography (it also had small caps and swatches and ligatures and old figures), it seemed a good candidate for inclusion in this project.

Hoefler grapples often with the question of how much can or should a classic (sacrosanct?) typeface be improved upon. His observation: "If someone said, 'You can never improve upon Garamond,' I want to know what they mean. Do they mean the metal punches made by Claude Garamond in the 1930s, or do they mean the Garamond Revival they know from phototype, or do they mean any of the sixty Garamond revivals made digitally? What is that essence of Garamondness that is so ideal, so platonic, and so untouchable? There really isn't one. There are aspects of every typeface that are exemplary and worthy of study, worthy of emulation in fact. But there is no perfection. There is no thing that is insurmountable."

INTERSTATE

TRAFFIC VIOLATIONS
BOLD
Trooper did not take kindly to my interpretive driving style
LIGHT CONDENSED

SPEEDING
BOLD CONDENSED
Rush hour drivers become ever more frantic
REGULAR CONDENSED

CONSTRUCTION AHEAD
BLACK

TORN UP & PLOWED UNDER
BOLD COMPRESSED
Work crews play catch with gobs of hot asphalt
BOLD

Eastbound
LIGHT COMPRESSED
Full of honking and shouting
LIGHT

DECREPIT MUFFLERS
BLACK CONDENSED
Visiting the drive-thru psychotherapist
REGULAR
APPARENTLY I SUFFER FROM AN OEDIPAL STICK SHIFT
BLACK

HIGH-OCTANE PRESCRIPTION
REGULAR COMPRESSED

Familiarity is the foundation of legibility, lending this sanserif a strong edge as one of the most legible faces.

Why are new typefaces designed when there are more than enough to provide today's graphic designers and typographers with material for any need? As early as 1918, in an essay entitled "Art in Type Design" *(The Monotype Recorder)*, Frederic W. Goudy offered an answer: "Our admiration for the work of masters should not lead to the absolute idolatry which would prevent new essays in the field of type design. On the other hand the fine old types should suggest a continued train of perceptions and ideas which the designer may employ that will aid him to create new expressions of beauty and utility . . . lifting up and driving on and preventing unwholesome stagnation. . . ." Type designers must find expressive means and alternative styles that conform to and even define the time in which type is made and used. Although Goudy criticized what he called "the insatiable demand for novelty in printing," he advocated a reexamination of the classics and the invention of unique forms to satisfy new aesthetic and commercial requirements. Of course he could not have predicted that decades after his death a strain of type design in the computer age would become like snapshot photography in the hands of any amateur with access to a scanner and software. But, given the abuse of typographic standards in his own day, this is inconsequential. Goudy knew that only a professional could create typefaces of distinction, whatever tools were available.

Today, there are more ersatz fontographers than in Goudy's day, but only a few are truly skilled to succeed at what he called the "art of type design." For a designer to be so considered, he or she must balance the history of type—understanding its paradigms and standards—with contemporary aesthetics and taste, while also exploring the experimental side. Today, there are a handful of true type masters who have upheld tradition while pushing boundaries, and one such is Tobias Frere-Jones (b. 1971). He has designed a score of commercial typefaces and a sizable number of experimental ones, as well as a variety of custom types for magazines and other graphic designers.

His best-known faces—Dolores, Garage Gothic, Interstate, and Cafeteria—are functional families as well as what he calls "essays" on the subject of type itself. Each font is a story about the nature of letterforms that spans the time from the Trajan inscriptions (second century A.D.) to the era of digitization. Although some fonts are intuitively derived, all his "retail" and "in progress" experimental work is highly disciplined in its adherence to, or challenge of, the fundamental principles of type design. Principles of structure, balance, and proportion that he learned from history have continued to underscore his practice in the digital environment.

In 1986, when he was sixteen years old, Frere-Jones designed his first alphabet, which won the "Best of Age" category in the Type Shop of New York's "Alphabet Design Contest." In an *U&lc* article called "Kid Stuff?" featuring his face, Marion Muller wrote that the award was given "because his 'professionalism' in researching, designing, and rendering his alphabet gives evidence of a promising future in graphics." Yet this hand-drawn, art deco–inspired face was so flawlessly rendered that the judges suspected it might have been done by a designer masquerading as a sixteen-year-old and actually tried to disqualify the entry. In truth, this was not just his first complete alphabet but the first time he'd ever attempted to design letterforms at all. On his own he discovered old lettering manuals from which he taught himself to follow a proportioning system based loosely on the Roman letterforms of the Trajan column.

By the end of his sophomore year in high school, Frere-Jones became obsessed with the concept of drawing letters. "Somewhere between high school and deciding where to go to college, drawing typefaces took over all the other disciplines," he recalls. In 1988, he enrolled in Rhode Island School of Design's graphic design program, believing that he would come out four years later as a bona fide type designer. As it happened, though, type design was not something that anyone there could really teach him. Students were taught how to spec and use type, but the curriculum stopped suddenly when it came to drawing faces. Undaunted, Frere-Jones sought out his own models. He relished Inge Druckery's class, the only one that came close to type design instruction, where students were required to spend weeks drawing Roman inscriptional letterforms without using measuring instruments. He also took on independent study, where he gave himself the problem of drawing a serif typeface based on Nicolas Jenson's 1470 Roman. Using cumbersome Ikarus software, the first to make digitizing type possible, he took an entire semester to create a Roman lowercase and a few caps.

Frere-Jones was in the local bar doodling on a napkin when he remembered that his brother, a rock musician, needed a typeface for his band's posters that would somehow reflect the character of the group. He started to draw one as a Christmas gift for him. "I purged myself of all the nitpicking stuff I had been doing for the past semester," he recalls. Then he created a jerky-looking collection of cartoony letters, featuring the strangest serifs and contoured shapes—with a touch of the fifties, a pinch of the sixties, and a tad of the nineties. Dolores, named after the band, became Frere-Jones's second complete alphabet. More important, it was the first commercial face in his portfolio.

After Frere-Jones began an internship at the Font Bureau in Boston he started working on other faces. One, a proposed adaptation of the letterforms used on parking garage receipts, became his touchstone. "All I had were bits of stuff I had found on discarded tickets in the gutter," he mused about the unrefined, blurry letters reminiscent of an overexposed Typositor setting. Much to his surprise, David Berlow of the Font Bureau was excited by the idea of developing a real typeface from the vernacular and commissioned what was called Garage Gothic.

In 1992, Frere-Jones was hired by the Font Bureau and began work on Nobel, based on the work of S. H. de Roos. He discovered this obscure face, a cross between Kabel and Futura, on a trip to Holland and took a liking to it because it was more "human" than Futura. He began tracking down information about the face before attempting his own version, but "I couldn't find anything," he said, "and only a few people in Holland even knew what it was." Finally, a Dutch friend coincidentally sent him a specimen catalog that contained every Nobel character ever made. While analyzing the specimens, he says, he found various flaws. "Looking back at it, what I really found was the seam between two drawing sessions. De Roos clearly drew the first four styles—Roman, Condensed, Bold, Bold Condensed—but the italics and the light were, I think, drawn by later and less sensitive hands."

The Nobel revival highlights an important distinction between influence and plagiarism as well as between revivalism and originality. Nobel is definitely the continuation of work by another designer who, in this case, was unable to make the adjustments necessary to revitalize the face in the digital environment. In this sense, certain original ideas must be included. "Even if I'm scanning in Nobel and drawing over it," Frere-Jones said about the process, "every point of it is a decision I must interpret. I've never come across any artwork that can be copied and left alone. Everything has to be interpreted, owing to ink squeeze on the proof or some kind of distortion in the reproduction process." Frere-Jones further asserts that when it comes to interpreting historical faces, understanding the original idea is as paramount as separating the form from the technical restraints of the time. In the end, he explains, "a series of guesses and hypotheses must be kept under tight reins or the connection between the historical model and the new face is confused."

Starting with a historical model does not, however, always result in a revival. A face Frere-Jones worked on called Archipelago (which has reappeared as Shell Sans, a custom face for Shell Oil) bears a resemblance to Hermann Zapf's Optima, which began as a revival of Robert Hunter Middleton's Stellar. While in the process of analyzing the forms, Frere-Jones began to see things that "I did not quite agree with," and after a couple of weeks of work on them all the characters were different. "I liked the ingredients but not the recipe," said Frere-Jones, comparing typeface design to soup-making. "You have a basic stock . . . a geometric sans serif stock with certain spices added to it and cooked just so. Nobel, for example, was Futura soup cooked in dirty pots and pans." When there is a direct lineage, he says where a face comes from. Archipelago, however, includes so many different influences that it would be difficult to pinpoint all its original ownership.

One of his most commercially successful typefaces is not a revival but, like Garage Gothic, is derived from the environment, or what he referred to as "blue collar" functional typography. Interstate is based on the alphabets used on U.S. Federal Highway Administration signs. The face was designed using the original sign manual sketches and kerning tables published by the government, which after a year of cajoling they sent to Frere-Jones. The original government letterforms were designed in the early 1960s by Travis Brooks; Frere-Jones conjectures that he was given an assortment of sans serifs, and, as Morris Fuller Benton did when he created Franklin Gothic, was told to come up with a single unifying design. Frere-Jones says that he was attracted to the familiar "material," what he calls the structures and proportions, and to some of the details, like the inexplicably short tail in the lowercase *g*. The government instructions were simplified so that convicted felons could follow them, and therefore the letters and recommended spacing were rather gawky. Frere-Jones cleaned up the forms, built in better spacing, and added punctuation—"Have you ever seen a question mark or semicolon on a highway sign?" he asks—and developed twelve versions, including a light-line set that he calls Kate Moss Four and Kate Moss Ten.

Many of his faces begin as discussions about legibility and perception. The experimental face Chainletter began as an argument between Frere-Jones and a RISD grad student about the impossibility of having a system of measuring the illegibility of a typeface. The student insisted that if one draws a grid of pixels and superimposes the character in question on that grid and then turns the pixels on, it would be most legible on one end and least at the other. Frere-Jones countered that this system cannot measure context, and talmudically insisted that a letter read in context does not necessarily read out of context. "At the time I didn't know how, but someday I knew I would draw a typeface that proved him wrong," he recalls. A few years later he received a flyer about a needle exchange program that was set in Times Roman caps and photocopied so many times that many of letters were entirely eroded. In context there were enough letters to clarify the message, but with the individual eroded forms out of that context, one would be hard-pressed to call an amorphous blob a *B* or a broken twig an *M*.

Theoretical exercises such as the decaying Chainletter, the prickly Vitriol, the architectonic Reitveld (designed with Chris Vermaas), and the artless Demand might easily be criticized for lacking any functional attributes, but even Frere-Jones's most absurd concoctions are building blocks toward understanding his craft and medium. Vitriol, which began with his degree project, was an experiment with a feedback loop in an attempt to find an automatic means to create sharply distorted letters. Reitveld, which expropriates the archetypical de Stijl furniture, began as a game on a napkin in which Frere-Jones and Chris Vermaas would take turns drawing the most ridiculous-looking *A* they could think of. Vermaas drew the Reitveld chair as an *A*, and they decided to explore how easily it would be to make an entire alphabet using this form. While some letters admittedly "need a bit of help," says Frere-Jones, the exercise proved that anything could be alphabetized. In another test of type tolerance, Demand began a technical test based on methods that Dutch type designer Erik van Blokland devised for crunching outlines for certain fonts. In an old ATF type specimen book, Frere-Jones had come across the face called Jumbo Typewriter, which had an anonymous, brutal quality to it, and wanted to get the same effect with his own monospace (equal width between all letters) typeface. Demand embodied technological discovery and the urge to make a brutal face. While some of this experimental material may remain just that, Frere-Jones admits "there are days when this seems ridiculous to put on the market. And other days when I think people will enjoy it, if for only a few weeks."

When Marion Muller wrote in the 1987 issue of *U&lc,* "There seems to be hope of a Toby Frere-Jones in our future," she could not have guessed that the sixteen-year-old would so transcend the flux of that early digital era and reside in the nexus of contemporary type design. But Frere-Jones knew right from the start that type design was not a dying art, as the antidigitarians were predicting; rather, it could offer a source of creative pleasure, intellectual stimulation, and public service unlike any other art form could. He is convinced that it is in type's nature to continually evolve, and so when asked the question "Why does the world really need any more typefaces?" he answers: "The day we stop needing new type will be the same day that we stop needing new stories and new songs."

Bibliography

Abbe, Dorothy. *Dwiggins: Stencilled Ornament and Illustration.* Trustees of the Boston Public Library, Boston. 1980.

Bierut, Michael, Hefland, Jessica, Heller, Steven, and Poynor, Rick. *Looking Closer 3: Critical Writings on Graphic Design.* Allworth Press, New York. 1999.

Cheney, Sheldon. *New World Architecture.* Tudor Publishing Co., New York. 1930

Coe, Sue. *Dead Meat.* Four Walls Eight Windows, New York. 1995.

Coe, Sue. *X.* Raw Books, New York. 1986.

Coe, Sue and Metz, Holly. *How To Commit Suicide in South Africa.* Raw Books, New York. 1993

Dair, Carl. *Design With Type.* University of Toronto Press, Toronto. 1967.

Davies, Karen. *At Home in Manhattan: Moderne Decorative Arts, 1925 to the Depression.* Yale University Art Gallery, New Haven. 1985.

Della Femina, Jerry. *From Those Wonderful Folks Who Gave You Pearl Harbor.* Simon and Shuster, New York. 1970.

Dobrow, Lawrence. *1950s and Madison Avenue: The Creative Revolution in Advertising.* Friendly Press, New York. 1984.

Dobrow, Lawrence. *When Advertising Tried Harder.* Friendly Press, New York, 1984.

Eason, Ron and Rookledge, Sarah. *Rookledge's International Directory of Type Designers.* The Sarabande Press, New York. 1994

Elliot, David, ed. *Alexander Rodchenko.* Museum of Modern Art, Oxford. 1979.

Ettenberg, Eugene M. *Type for Books and Advertising.* D. Van Nostrand, Inc., New York. 1947.

Ewen, Stuart. *All Consuming Images: The Politics of Style in Contemporary Culture* (Revised Edition). Basic Books, New York. 1999.

Friedl, Friedrich, Ott Nicolaus, Stein, Bernard, ed.. *Typo: Wann Wer, Wie.* Könemann Verlagsgesellechaft, Köln. 1998.

Goulden, Joseph C. *The Best Years.* Antheneum, New York, 1976.

Hawkins, Artthur. *Art Directing.* Hastings House, New York. 1959.

Heller, Steven and Chwast Seymour. *Graphic Style: From Victorian to Post-Modern.* Harry N. Abrams, New York. 1988.

Heller, Steven and Fink, Anne. *Faces on the Edge: Type in the Digital Age.* Van Nostrand Rhinehold, New York. 1997.

Heller, Steven and Pettit, Elinor. *Design Dialogues.* Allworth Press, New York. 1998.

Heller, Steven and Pomeroy, Karen. *Design Literacy: Understanding Graphic Design.* Allworth Press, New York. 1997.

Hine, Thomas. *The Total Package, the Evolution and Scret Meanings of Boxes, Bottles, Cans, and Tubes.* Little Brown, New York. 1995.

Hollis, Richard. *Graphic Design: A Concise History.* Thames and Hudson, London. 1994.

Hyland, William G. *The Cold War: Fifty Years of Conflict.* Random House, New York, 1990.

Jaspert, Pincus W., Berry, W. Turner. Johnson, A. F. eds. The Encyclopedia of Type Faces. Blandford Press, Dorset. 1983.

Kern- Foxworth, Marilyn, preface. *Michael Ray Charles: An American Artist.* The Art Museum of the University of Houston, Houston, Texas. 1997

Kinross, Robin. *Modern Typography: An Essay in Critical History.* Hyphen Press, London. 1992.

Lee, Marshall. *Books For Our Times*, Oxford University Press, New York, 1952.

Lionni, Leo. *Between Worlds.* Alfred Knopf, New York. 1997.

Lionni, Leo. *Little Blue and Little Yellow.* Random House, New York. 1959.

Lois, George. *What's the Big Idea: How to Win With Outrageous Ideas That Sell.* Doubleday, New York. 1991.

Lorant, Stefan. *Seig Heil: An Illustrated History of Germany from Bismark to Hitler.* W. W. Norton, New York, 1974.

McGrew, Mac. *American Metal Typefaces of the Twentieth Century* (Preliminary Edition). The Myriade Press, Inc., New Rochelle, New York. 1986.

Meggs, Philip. *A History of Graphic Design* (third edition). John Wiley & Sons, New York. 1998.

Meggs, Philip and Carter, Rob. *Typographic Specimens: The Great Typefaces.* Van Nostrand Rhinehold, New York. 1993.

Mott, Frank Luther. *A History of American Magazines. Vols I–V.* Harvard University Press, Cambridge, Massachusetts, 1957–1968

Paley, Vivan Gussin. *The Girl With The Brown Crayon.* Harvard University Press, Cambridge. 1997.

Poynor, Rick, and Clibborn, Edward. *Typography Now: The Next Wave.* Booth Clibborn Editions, London. 1991.

Reed, Walt and Roger. *The Illustrator in America: 1880–1980.* The Society of Illustrators/Madison Square Press, New York. 1984

Rosner, Charles. *The Growth of the Book Jacket*, Harvard University Press, Cambridge, Massachusetts, 1954.

Shaw, Paul and Bain, Peter. *Blackletter: Type and Naitonal Identity.* Princeton Architectural Press, New York. 1998.

Spencer, Herbert. *Pioneers of Modern Typography.* Hastings House, New York. 1969.

Spiegleman, Art. *Maus: A Survivor's Tale.* Pantheon Books, New York. 1986 and 1991.

Steinbeck, John. *The Grapes of Wrath.* Modern Library, New York, 1939.

Stripling, Robert E. and Considine, Bob. *The Red Plot Against America.* Bell Publishing, Pennsylvania, 1949.

Sutnar, Ladislav. Visual Design in Action. Hastings House Publishers, New York. 1961.

Tanikawa, Syuntaro. *Grandma.* Balloon-Sha, Tokyo. 1997.

Tschicold, Jan. *The New Typography* (Reprint). University of California Press, Berkeley and Los Angeles. 1995.

Warde, Beatrice. *The Crystal Goblet.* World Publishing Company, Cleveland and New York. 1956.

Webster, Nesta. *World Revolution: The Plot Against Civilization.* The Fabian Press, Boston, 1925.

Whitney, R. M. *Reds in America.* Beckworth Press, New York, 1924.

Index

Books from Allworth Press

Design Literacy: Understanding Graphic Design
by Steven Heller and Karen Pomeroy (softcover, 6¾ × 10, 288 pages, $19.95)

Design Culture: An Anthology of Writing from the AIGA Journal of Graphic Design
edited by Steven Heller and Marie Finamore (softcover, 6¾ × 10, 320 pages, $19.95)

Looking Closer: Critical Writings on Graphic Design *edited by Michael Bierut,
William Drenttel, Steven Heller, and DK Holland* (softcover, 6¾ × 10, 256 pages, $18.95)

Looking Closer 2: Critical Writings on Graphic Design *edited by Michael Bierut,
William Drenttel, Steven Heller, and DK Holland* (softcover, 6¾ × 10, 288 pages, $18.95)

Looking Closer 3: Classic Writings on Graphic Design *edited by Michael Bierut, Jessica
Helfand, Steven Heller, and Rick Poynor* (softcover, 6¾ × 10, 304 pages, $18.95)

Design Dialogues *by Steven Heller and Elinor Pettit* (softcover, 6¾ × 10, 272 pages, $18.95)

The Swastika: Symbol Beyond Redemption? *by Steven Heller*
(hardcover, 6½ × 9½, 256 pages, $21.95)

Sex Appeal: The Art of Allure in Graphic and Advertising Design
by Steven Heller (softcover, 6¾ × 10, 288 pages, $18.95)

AIGA Professional Practices in Graphic Design
The American Institute of Graphic Arts, edited by Tad Crawford
(softcover, 6¾ × 10, 320 pages, $24.95)

Business and Legal Forms for Graphic Designers *by Tad Crawford and Eva Doman Bruck*
(softcover, 8½ × 11, 240 pages (includes CD-ROM), $24.95)

Careers by Design: A Headhunters Secrets for Success and Survival in Graphic Design,
Revised Edition *by Roz Goldfarb* (softcover, 6¾ × 10, 224 pages, $18.95)